Praise for Jessica Warner's *Craze*

"[Warner's] prose is both lively and accessible, and she keeps the narrative moving along." —*The Washington Post Book World*

"One of this year's most entertaining and timely books; it should be required reading for politicians and law enforcement officials." —Portland *Oregonian*

"Fascinating . . . [*Craze*] is a crisp, detailed review of the history of the place and period." —Baltimore *Sun*

"Warner evokes a vivid picture of eighteenth-century London, complete with its public hangings and slums that seemed to overflow with gin." —*The Seattle Times*

"Warner writes with great flair. [She] is especially good at bringing to light the role of women in the gin craze." —*Austin American-Statesman*

"[Warner] anchors her arguments in precise, scholarly data. . . . Added to this, she writes like an angel, which makes her as cheerily compelling as a nice G&T at the end of a long, hard day." —London *Daily Telegraph*

"[An] affecting and at times amusing history of an addiction epidemic from an earlier age." —*Forbes*

"Warner shines a bright light on a murky corner of history. She is a master of the telling detail, both in laying out the scope of the epidemic and in pointing out the absurdities of those who sought to curtail it." —Toronto *Globe and Mail*

"A colourful social history of urban eighteenth-century England . . . a compact and tart summary of the gutter-dwelling characters and events that brought the spirit to the fetid alleys of London, Bristol and Norwich." —*Toronto Star*

"Smart, gripping analysis . . . persuasive and compelling." —London *Guardian*

"This well-illustrated, well-referenced book will reward readers and, importantly, teach politicians a valuable how-not-to lesson. In all, a short book to enjoy over a long drink." —*ForeWord Magazine*

"Social history at its gimlet- d review)

ABOUT THE AUTHOR

JESSICA WARNER was born and raised in Washington, D.C. A graduate of Princeton and Yale Universities, she is a professor of history at the University of Toronto and a research scientist at the Centre for Addiction and Mental Health, where she has taught extensively on the history of alcohol and other drugs. She may be reached through her website at www.MotherGin.com.

Craze

Craze

Gin *AND* Debauchery *IN AN* Age of Reason

Consisting of a Tragicomedy *in three acts
in which* High *and* Low *are brought together,
much to their* Mutual Discomfort.

Complete with Stories, *some witty and some not,*

conducive to meditation on

Recent Events.

JESSICA WARNER

 RANDOM HOUSE TRADE PAPERBACKS: NEW YORK

2003 Random House Trade Paperback Edition

This work was originally published by Four Walls Eight Windows in 2002. This edition published by arrangement with Four Walls Eight Windows.

LIBRARY OF CONGRESS CATALOGING-IN-PUBLICATION DATA:
Warner, Jessica.
　Craze: gin and debauchery in an age of reason: consisting of a tragicomedy in three acts in which high and low are brought together, much to their mutual discomfort . . . / Jessica Warner.
　　p.　cm.
Originally published: New York: Four Walls Eight Windows, 2002.
Includes index.
ISBN: 0-8129-6899-9
　1. Alcoholism—England—History—18th century.　2. Gin—England—History—18th century.　3. Liquor laws—England—History—18th century.　I. Title.

HV5449.E5W37 2003
363.4'1'094209033—dc21　2003046929

Random House website address: www.atrandom.com

PRINTED IN THE UNITED STATES OF AMERICA

987654321

To the men in my life,
but above all,
to
JOHN W. F.
and
REESE W.

CONTENTS

PREFACE AND ACKNOWLEDGEMENTS

Containing as Many DISCLAIMERS as
EXPRESSIONS OF GRATITUDE, along with
Divers ENCOURAGEMENTS to the READER

> *Just as he [Tom Jones] arrived at Mr Allworthy's outward gate, he met*
> *the constable and company with Molly in their possession, whom they*
> *were conducting to that house where the inferior sort of people may learn*
> *one good lesson, viz. respect and deference to their superiors; since it must*
> *show them the wide distinction Fortune intends between those persons*
> *who are to be corrected for their faults, and those who are not....*
>
> HENRY FIELDING, *The History of Tom Jones*, 1749

THIS BOOK IS a parable about drugs, about why some people take them and why other people worry when they do. It is set in eighteenth-century London, which was at the time the largest city in Europe. London was home to a vast population of impoverished and unruly immigrants; their behavior, not surprisingly, was a source of constant worry to the people who governed them and sometimes even employed them. That, by itself, was nothing new. But with the introduction of cheap gin in the late seventeenth and early eighteenth centuries, their behavior took a decided turn for the worse, and polite people worried as they never had before.

For thirty-one years, from 1720 to 1751, cheap gin reigned supreme in the slums and alleys of the capital, giving rise to what has since come to be known as the "gin craze." Gin was the original urban drug. Cheap, potent, and readily available, it met the needs of an urban population, numbing countless thousands to the fatigue, hunger, and cold that were the lot of London's working poor. Most of the people who drank gin lived in Westminster (which at the time was not nearly as fashionable as it is now) and East London; the men who made laws for them naturally made their homes elsewhere, primarily in the fashionable squares and crescents that were springing up all over West London. The contrast between the two ways of life could not have been more extreme: one was orderly; the other most emphatically was not.

At its heart the debate over gin was a debate over the nature of cities and the different sorts of people who inhabited them. That debate is of course a very old one, but in the eighteenth century London started to look—and act—very much like a modern city. This shocked and frightened a good many people. It was here, in London, that the sheer density of the population, in combination with the constant influx of new workers from elsewhere in the British Isles, helped create a social nexus comparable to the sorts of complex urban environments that have given rise to more recent drug scares. The same factors helped foster in London new patterns of consumption, of which gin is but one example; they also encouraged individuals to abandon traditional modes of behavior. This was especially true in Westminster and East London, where official controls were notoriously lax, and where gin was, by the same token, openly sold and freely drunk.

The narrative, however, gallops ahead of the facts. Acknowledgements have been promised, and promises must be kept. The research itself was funded by a grant from the National Institutes of Health in Washington, DC. There it was championed by the redoubtable Dr. Jan Howard, without whom the project would almost certainly never have gotten off the ground. Once the project got off the ground it would not have proceeded much further had I not importuned John Beattie on innumerable occasions.

John is a professor possessed of vast knowledge and infinite patience; the one I have exploited, the other I have taxed. In London I continued in what was by now an established pattern of finding kind and knowledgeable people and shamelessly exploiting them. These included, most notably, Dr. Ruth Paley, then of the Public Record Office, and Harriet Jones and Louise Falcini, both of the London Metropolitan Archives. Such happiness, however, was not destined to last, for my next stop was the new British Library. There I encountered a staff that was impervious to exploitation in any form; indeed, such was their fondness for reading *The New York Review of Books* that many could scarce find the time or energy to help readers humbler than themselves.

Sadder but wiser, I returned to Toronto. By now I had become quite adept at finding smart people and putting them to work on my behalf. It was at this juncture that I enlisted several research associates possessed of skills far more impressive than my own. They assisted me in analyzing the statistical data that I had collected while in London, coauthoring the scholarly articles that are in fact the foundation for this book. Smart and long-suffering, they are Minghao Her, Frank Ivis, and Carol Birchmore-Timney. Carol then kindly read and commented on several of the chapters that appear in this book, as did the good doctors Helen Ross and Griffith Edwards. And finally, historians, like the hordes of tourists who descend on England each year, rarely tread on virgin ground. My own work, such as it is, simply would not have been possible without the groundbreaking work of Peter Clark, author of *The English Alehouse* and "The 'Mother Gin' Controversy in the Early Eighteenth Century." Professor Clark kindly guided me through the sources that he had found and consulted, selflessly sharing his insights and knowledge with me. I am entirely in his debt.

Some High and Some Low

MARY BRYAN, hawker of gin and other cheap spirits, and an unwitting pawn in a turf war between two justices of the peace. She appears among the gin-sellers operating in the East London parish of Whitechapel in January of 1736, at which time she lived on Gridiron Alley, just off Whitechapel High Street. Her supplier is none other than justice Clifford William Phillips. In October of the following year she is convicted of violating the Gin Act of 1736, having been rounded up by Edward Parker and his crew. In January of 1738, Bryan is again convicted of selling gin without a license; this time Phillips will help appeal her conviction.

CAROLINE OF ANSBACH (1683–1737), wife of George II and queen of England from 1727 to 1737. Frightened by "bestialities and indecencies" witnessed in Westminster, she becomes "an hearty enemy to distilled and spirituous liquors," much to the embarrassment of her old friend and ally, Sir Robert Walpole. Her inner circle, moreover, includes some of the leading crusaders against gin, among them the physician John Freind, Sir Joseph Jekyll, and an ambitious young cleric named Isaac Maddox.

PHILLIP DORMER STANHOPE (1694–1773), better known as Lord Chesterfield, author of *Letters to his Son* and *Letters to his Godson*. Having been passed over for high office he becomes a leading member of the opposition to Sir Robert Walpole, savaging him both in the House of Lords and in various opposition newspapers. Among the latter are

Common Sense, whose contributors include the young Henry Fielding. In 1743, having once again been passed over for high office, Chesterfield unleashes "the united powers of reason, wit, and ridicule" in opposing the gin act then making its way through the House of Lords. There his allies include Isaac Maddox, a rising young star in the Church of England.

DANIEL DEFOE (1660–1731), literary genius and quite possibly the greatest hack of all time. His father, William Foe, was a member of the Butchers' Company of London, and while Defoe will travel widely, both in England and on the Continent, he is first and foremost a Londoner. True to his calling as a hack, he writes both for and against the great issues of his day. Gin is no exception. In 1726, he writes a pamphlet on behalf of London's Company of Distillers, under the title of *A Brief Case of the Distillers, and of the Distilling Trade in England, Shewing how Far it Is the Interest of England to Encourage the Said Trade*. Two years later, in *Augusta Triumphans: or, the Way to Make London the Most Flourishing City in the Universe*, he blames gin for almost all of the city's many problems, warning that "in less than an Age, we may expect a fine Spindle-shank'd Generation."

HENRY FIELDING (1707–1754), author, justice of the peace, and the man who gave London its first police force. His circle of friends includes William Hogarth, in whose honor he writes *A Dissertation on Mr. Hogarth's Six Prints Lately Publish'd, viz. Gin-Lane, Beer-Street, and the Four Stages of Cruelty*. Fielding's early career is marked by hardship and failure, in large part because he is unrelenting in his criticism of Sir Robert Walpole; in 1745, with Walpole now dead and the Stuart Pretender marching on London, Fielding redeems his reputation by writing and publishing on behalf of the government. As a reward he is appointed a justice of the peace for Westminster; one year later, in 1749, he is appointed the chief magistrate for both Westminster and Middlesex, in which capacity he organizes the famous Bow Street Runners. In the same year he publishes *Tom Jones*. He draws on both his literary talents and on his experience as a magistrate when writing *An Enquiry into the Causes of the Late Increase of Robbers*; among the causes he identifies is gin, whose "dreadful effects" he has "the Misfortune every Day to see, and to smell too."

LETITIA HEATHCOTE, an informer briefly residing in the Westminster parish of Soho. Her lover is Thomas Loach, with whom she will testify on several occasions against the people who foolishly sell them gin. One of these is Catherine Croft, who along with her husband Thomas runs a prosperous public house in Westminster. In the ensuing trial several of the witnesses brought by the Crofts tear "the said Heathcote's Cloaths" and threaten to murder her. When Thomas Croft later attempts to find the pair he is informed "that they were gone away . . . and had robbed their Lodgings of several things."

SIR JOSEPH JEKYLL (circa 1662–1738), member of Parliament from 1697, and Master of the Rolls since 1717. Cause of death: "mortification of the bowels." With the help of the queen and Thomas Wilson, he pushes the Gin Act of 1736 through Parliament, much to the annoyance of Sir Robert Walpole. In addition to gin, he also wishes to suppress state lotteries and stage plays. The last of the great Puritans, Jekyll is the butt of many jokes and much satire, including these two lines by Pope:

> . . . *Jekyll or some odd old whig,*
> *Who never changed his principle or wig.*

ISAAC MADDOX (1697–1759), bishop of the Welsh diocese of St. Asaph from 1734 to 1743, bishop of Worcester from 1743, staunch supporter of the Societies for the Reformation of Manners, and early advocate of inoculations against smallpox. A Georgian success story, Maddox was born in the London parish of St. Botolph, Aldersgate, only to be orphaned at an early age and sent to a charity school to acquire the rudiments of an education. He is briefly apprenticed to a pastry chef, but showing more aptitude for books than for baking, he chooses instead to make a career in the Church of England. There he rises quickly, becoming a curate at St. Bride's, Fleet Street, in 1723, and a clerk of the closet to Queen Caroline in 1729. Five years later, in 1734, he is elected bishop of St. Asaph. In 1743 he is elected bishop of Worcester, at which time he joins other members of the House of Lords in opposing repeal of the Gin Act of 1736; in January of 1751, he again speaks out against gin, this time to an audience that includes the mayor and aldermen of the City of London.

THOMAS PELHAM-HOLLES (1693–1768), duke of Newcastle-upon-Tyne and of Newcastle-under-Lyme, secretary of state for the southern department from 1724 to 1754, and prime minster from 1754 to 1756 and again from 1757 to 1762. In his capacity both as secretary of state and as keeper of the rolls for the county of Middlesex, he will take an occasional interest in enforcing the various gin acts that are passed between 1729 and 1751. In 1736, just as the gin act passed earlier that year is about to take effect, he skips town, leaving Walpole and the queen to face down the London mob.

EDWARD PARKER, exciseman and quite possibly the most hated man in London from March of 1737 until his death in December of 1738. He is one of several excisemen employed by the commissioners of excise "in detecting... Retailers of Spirituous Liquors." During his brief reign of terror he organizes and directs gangs of informers in Westminster and East London, securing, by one count, upwards of 1,500 prosecutions under the Gin Act of 1736. Upon his death Parker is "interred in a private Manner...for fear the Mob should tear his Corpse to pieces." A month later, the justices of Westminster discover that Parker and their clerk have been pocketing part of the fines paid by gin-sellers.

WILLIAM CLIFFORD PHILLIPS, a justice of the peace in East London, a commissioner of the sewers, and a lieutenant colonel under Lord Cornwallis. A distiller himself, he supplies Mary Bryan with small amounts of gin to hawk about the streets. His business activities endear him neither to his fellow justices nor to the excisemen who scour the streets of London in search of gin-sellers. In 1737, matters come to a head when Edward Parker and his crew round up Mary Bryan and drag her before a rival justice of the peace. By the time it is all over, in 1743, Phillips has been kicked off the commission of the peace, notwithstanding his complaint that "being left out of a Commission when once in leaves an Odium upon the person as if guilty of malepractice."

SIR ROBERT WALPOLE (1676–1745), *de facto* prime minister of Great Britain, 1721 to 1742. He is, by his own confession, "no saint, no Spartan, no reformer." Mindful of the landowners who dominate both houses of Parliament and who make much of their money by selling grain to distillers in the capital, Walpole is cool to any legislation that threatens the British distillery.

WILLIAM OF ORANGE (1650–1702), Protestant, Dutch prince, and king of England, Scotland, and Ireland from 1689 to 1702. His lifelong feud with Louis XIV of France will embroil him and his adoptive country in a series of increasingly costly wars on the Continent, each time forcing the Crown to look for new sources of revenue. One of these will be a homely beverage known as gin.

THOMAS WILSON (1663–1755), bishop of Sodor and Man, member of the Society for Promoting Christian Knowledge, and author of *Distilled Spirituous Liquors the Bane of the Nation*. Despite its off-putting title, Wilson's little book is a surprise best-seller, going through two editions in the early months of 1736. Wilson himself wears sensible shoes and prides himself on his austerity. Because he presides over one of the poorest dioceses in Great Britain, Wilson is always short of money, his much-vaunted austerity notwithstanding. On three separate occasions he will approach his patron, Sir Joseph Jekyll, in hopes of securing an additional prebend; each time Wilson will come away empty-handed.

INTRODUCTION

Your well fed squires and wealthy grandees,
Pamper'd and proud with plenty and ease;
Who night waste in debauch and riot,
And sleep till dinner time at quiet;
But little dream, of what the poor
In need of stand, and what they endure.
No wander, if such swear and damn,
At mention of a low-pric'd dram.

ELIAS BOCKETT, 1730

ONE SATURDAY, in March of 1736, William Bird left his house in Kensington in the care of Jane Andrews, his maid. Once Bird was out of sight she, too, left the house and went to a gin shop she often visited. There she met "a Drummer of the Guards of her Acquaintance," a chimneysweep, and an individual described only as "a Woman Traveller." Andrews invited all three back to her employer's house, where they continued to drink from ten in the morning until four in the afternoon. It was at this point that Andrews "proposed to the Company... that they, and she, should go to Bed together," upon which all four "stript, and ... went into one Bed." Wishing privacy, Andrews had taken the understandable precaution of closing both the doors and windows of the house; even so, it was not long before "a Mob, hearing of this Affair, surrounded the Door, and disturbed the happy Pairs...."

I

Of all the things that money could buy in eighteenth-century England, privacy was the most elusive. Nowhere was this more true than in the nation's towns and cities. There men and women lived and worked cheek by jowl, constant and invidious witnesses to each other's small triumphs and large failings. They are conspicuous in Hogarth's street scenes, just as they are conspicuous by their absence in Gainsborough's and Reynolds' enormous portraits of lone aristocrats. Even aristocrats, with their vast retinues of servants and inescapable social obligations, were never quite alone; nor, given the tenor of the times, would they have sought out solitude, for once out of the limelight they risked the worst of all possible fates in eighteenth-century society, that of being ignored.

While the absence of privacy cut across class lines, it especially affected the urban poor, exposing their squalid lives and petty vices to the scrutiny of their neighbors and the censure of their social superiors. This state of affairs was by no means new, but in the early eighteenth century an old vice, drunkenness, suddenly acquired new prominence, thanks to the introduction of gin and other cheap distilled spirits to the mass market. Distilled spirits had been widely available in England since the late sixteenth century, but until the early eighteenth century only the rich could afford to drink them in large quantities. For their part the poor had used them only occasionally, sometimes as a treat, and more often as a type of medicine or cure-all. In the early eighteenth century, however, distilled spirits suddenly became both cheap and widely available, and when this happened they very quickly emerged as the drug of choice among the nation's urban poor.

Cheap, widely available, and several times stronger than the traditional alcoholic beverages of the English working classes, gin was the first modern drug. Its enormous popularity gave rise to what has since come to be known as the gin craze, which is generally viewed as having started in 1720 and ended in 1751. In 1700, the average adult drank slightly more than a third of a gallon of cheap spirits over the course of a year; by 1720 that amount had nearly doubled; and by 1729, the year when the first act restricting sales of gin was passed, the number had nearly doubled again, to slightly more than 1.3 gallons per capita. The figures include only the population fifteen years of age or older, although there were as yet no formal restrictions on minors' access to alcohol. In 1743 annual consumption peaked at 2.2 gallons per capita, after which the craze at long last started to abate. By 1752, the year after the passage of the final gin act, annual per capita consumption had fallen by nearly one half, to 1.2 gallons, only to drop by half again by 1757. From this point on annual consumption remained fairly constant for the next two decades, at about 0.6 gallons per capita.

Unlike beer and ale, which had for centuries been the traditional beverages of the poor, gin's effects were instantaneous, leaving "a Man...no time to recollect or think, whether he has had enough or not. The Smallness of the Quantity deceives him, so that his Reason is gone before he is aware." Time and time again men and women who might ordinarily have drunk a pint or two of beer drank a pint or two of gin instead, often with disastrous consequences. A man described as a "Plush Weaver" drank a quart of gin in less than half an hour. The following morning he drank another "Pint at a Draught"; by day's end he was reportedly "raving mad." A week later a laborer by the name of George Wade went to a public house in Westminster, "drank a Pint of Gin off at a Draught, and expired in a few Minutes." A group of men in Newington Green "persuaded a poor Labourer, in a Frolick, as they call'd it, to drink three or four Pints of Gin giving him a

Shilling for each Pint, which he had no sooner done, but he fell down, and died immediately." A man and his pregnant wife died in very similar circumstances, having shared nearly two bottles between them.

The dates, 1720 to 1751, are arbitrary at best. Consumption had been rising steadily before 1720, and it was actually higher in 1717 than it would be in 1720. The year 1751 is equally arbitrary. Demand had in fact peaked back in 1743, and while the Gin Act of 1751 doubtless had a salutary effect on consumption, it was not until 1757, when a succession of crop failures forced the government to ban the use of domestic grains in distilling, that consumption actually dropped below the levels reached in the early 1720s. The dates do, however, have the advantage of corresponding to how contemporaries perceived events: few people worried publicly about gin before 1720, and just as few people worried publicly about it after 1751.

That, in turn, points to the central theme of this book, namely, why people worry at some times and not at others. In the case of the gin craze, concerns over drunkenness bore very little correspondence to actual consumption, begging the question of whether a reforming elite was reacting to gin *per se* or rather to larger and more intractable threats to their society and way of life. This is the same critical question that confronts us in our own responses to drugs and the people who use them.

In the case of gin, consumption peaked in the early 1740s, while complaints—and the laws enacted in response to them—peaked much earlier, in the 1730s. Parliament, in other words, paid attention to gin only when it actually had the time to take on issues that it might otherwise safely ignore. And so four of the eight gin acts were passed in the otherwise uneventful 1730s, compared to just two in the turbulent 1740s. These last two, moreover, were designed not to impose sobriety on the working poor, but simply to raise new funds for fighting the War of Austrian Succession (1740–1748). The real pattern behind the gin acts was very simple: people worried about gin when very little else seemed to be happening—and when the government was flush. And so people worried about gin and passed laws against it in times of peace, and conveniently forgot about it in times of war. Or, rather, they did not so much forget about gin as choose to treat it as just another source of revenue. Two centuries later, in 1933, another legislature would also find itself short of funds; soon after this realization, it put an end to Prohibition by passing the Twenty-first Amendment.

Analogies, however, can be a tricky business, especially when they are drawn between two very different societies. Three hundred years ago, when gin was just starting to become popular in England, there was no police force in the modern sense of the word. In principle, justices of the peace worked for free, as did the male citizens who were forced to volunteer their time as constables, in which capacity they reluctantly dragged suspects, many of whom were their friends and neighbors, before justices who were themselves often members of the same community. In most cases, moreover, the burden of prosecuting offenders fell on their victims, many of whom were naturally reluctant to spend what little time and money they had in court. The costs could be staggering. In or around 1738, for example, William Goudge spent £24—a small fortune by contemporary standards—in prosecuting three informers for perjury; this did not include the £10 that he had already paid upon wrongful conviction under the Gin Act of 1736.

Nor, for that matter, did Parliament play a particularly active role in shaping social policy. It has been estimated that of the some fifteen thousand bills considered by Parliament between 1690 and 1790, only about one thousand were in some way concerned with social policy, and of these, only half ever became law. These were, from the perspective of the crusaders against gin, daunting odds, forcing them to come up with new and increasingly sophisticated ways of getting Parliament to pay attention to them and their message of moral reform.

Political parties, moreover, were poorly delineated. In principle there were the Whigs who supported the Hanoverian succession, and the Tories who did not, but in reality the differences between the two parties could be exceedingly subtle. Over the course of the 1720s, for example, numerous Tories chose to support Sir Robert Walpole and were duly rewarded with offices in his administration; at the same time, numerous Whigs were to be found in opposition to Walpole, making common cause with the Tories who remained true to their principles.

The real divide was not so much between Whigs and Tories as it was between court and country. The former consisted primarily of officeholders who could be relied on to support the Crown and its ministers as long as they were paid to do so, and the latter consisted primarily of country squires who either out of principle or ineptitude had failed to benefit from the spoils of government. It was from the ranks of these country squires that a new Tory party was recruited. The Whigs, by contrast, emerged as the new court party, and with each passing year cemented their hold on power, largely by dispensing patronage and limiting the number of eligible voters wherever possible. In this they were remarkably successful, so much so that by the eighteenth century the entire electorate had been whittled down to about 85,000 men, 15,000 of whom controlled half of all seats in the House of Commons. This compares to a total population of just over five million in 1700, and just under six million in 1750.

Throughout the period of the gin craze, the Whigs remained firmly in power; they were, however, far from monolithic. In the case of gin, some Whigs were prepared to tolerate it; others, men such as Sir Joseph Jekyll, wanted nothing more than to legislate it out of existence.

These are important points. For one thing, they tell us that a drug scare can occur in a society as yet lacking a police force and larger political and bureaucratic structures. The closest thing that eighteenth-century England had to a modern bureaucracy was the Excise Office, and as such its commissioners and officers were destined to play a prominent role in the war on gin. The same points also underscore the extent to which eighteenth-century England was held together not by the state and formal institutions, but rather by the willingness of most of its members to accept a status quo rife with inequalities. England was remarkable for its stability—certainly when compared to the upheavals that were to beset its more autocratic rivals on the continent—but its underlying institutions were in fact entirely fragile. The Stuarts, who had been ousted back in 1688, constituted the biggest and most obvious threat to the nation's stability. In 1745 they very nearly succeeded in returning to power, reinforcing in everyone's mind just how vulnerable their kingdom and society really were. Given the essential fragility of the nation's political institutions, and given the very real external threats that existed up until 1745, it is hardly surprising that even the slightest threat to the status quo was a source of enormous alarm to the nation's governing class.

Gin was one of those threats, and the men who sought to put the genie back in the bottle wanted nothing more than to return their society to a golden age that was rapidly receding into the past.

This, in turn, raises the thorny question of exactly what to call the people who fought so hard against gin and the people who drank it. They were reformers, but in what sense of the word? For one thing, their agenda was anything but egalitarian. On the contrary, they believed that their society functioned best when each member accepted his or her station in life. For most people this meant accepting a life of drudgery and poverty, leaving a lucky few with a great deal of time and money on their hands. Nobody seriously challenged this vision of society until the very end of the century, and when that challenge came, in the form of the French Revolution, England managed to survive with its institutions and social structures very much intact.

The ideological differences between the people who hated gin and those who merely tolerated it were in fact entirely subtle, and basically boiled down to this: the enemies of gin resented any form of consumerism and conspicuous consumption on the part of the poor, while the people who tolerated gin were prepared to allow the poor a certain degree of latitude in how they might spend their very limited incomes. One group looked back in time to the essentially static economic theories of the sixteenth and seventeenth centuries; the other looked forward in time to the endless possibilities promised by Adam Smith in *The Wealth of Nations*.

Nor did the enemies of gin have much in common with the leaders of the great temperance movements of the nineteenth and early twentieth centuries. For one thing, they never advocated abstinence from all forms of alcohol. Nor could they have. Alcohol—be it beer, gin, wine, port, or rum—was an indispensable staple of life in eighteenth-century England, both in London and in the country. This was as true of the poor as it was of the rich, the only difference being the quality and types of alcohol that each could afford. Thomas Turner, a prosperous shopkeeper in Sussex, was a habitual drunkard, recording in his diary on numerous occasions that he "came home and went to bed drunk." Samuel Johnson was also a notorious drunkard, being unable to drink "wine or any fermented liquor... because he could not do it in moderation."

Because alcohol was ubiquitous in English society and because it was a major source of both taxes and employment, no one, the enemies of gin least of all, had any intention of imposing abstinence on an unwilling nation. Nor were these same men themselves willing to set an example by voluntarily abstaining from strong drink. At most they hoped to set the clock back to the years before gin had supposedly corrupted the morals and work habits of the working poor. Their social vision could, in a moment of extreme political weakness, be imposed from above—but never accepted from below. Its glaring inconsistencies were not wasted on Caleb D'Anvers, a pseudonym used by Nicholas Amhurst when he routinely attacked the Ministry in *The Craftsman*. "The *common People*," he wrote in August of 1736, "are highly obliged to Those, who take so much Care of Them; but why should not some Care be taken of the *great People*, as well as the *little*? For, if we are not misinform'd here, They stand in full as much Need of it."

The enemies of gin were equally inconsistent in their treatment of beer. At the time of the craze—and indeed for the duration of the century—per capita consumption of strong beer remained both high and remarkably constant, at approximately thirty gallons a year. Even so, at no point during the gin craze did anyone implicate beer in their attacks on drunkenness and its associated vices. On the contrary, even the most ardent enemies of gin encouraged workers to drink beer, believing that it would enable them to work all the harder. Even the economist Josiah Tucker, who in his heart of hearts wanted to ban the manufacture of distilled spirits altogether, recommended beer and ale on the assumption that "when laboring People use these Liquors in a *moderate* Degree, they are enabled and supported to Work the better...." It also helped that the industry was well represented in Parliament, with no fewer than ten brewers being elected to the House of Commons between 1720 and 1751.

The idea that distilled spirits should be banned outright started to gain in popularity only in the early 1750s, and even then only among a handful of reformers. Two anonymous letters, one published in *The London Magazine* in March of 1751, the other in *The Gentleman's Magazine* in April of the same year, went so far as to argue that the entire industry should be suppressed. And Josiah Tucker confessed that he would favor abolishing the manufacture of all spirits in England if doing so "would put a stop to the manufacture of those liquors in all Countries." But again, these were the views of a very small minority, and it was not until the early nineteenth century, with the advent of the temperance movement, that it became fashionable to talk about banning distilled spirits altogether. It was an even greater leap to talk about banning all alcoholic beverages and not just spirits, and this did not occur until well into the nineteenth century.

When temperance emerged as one of the major social movements of the nineteenth century, it succeeded in large part because its leaders advocated abstinence for rich and poor alike, thus ensuring that their message would not be rejected out of hand by working men and women. They also succeeded in broadening their appeal by embracing a variety of other progressive causes, including women's suffrage and, in some instances, trade unionism. And it helped that the advocates of temperance came to embrace abstinence from all alcoholic beverages—and not just those consumed by the poor. This was patently not the case in the eighteenth century. On the contrary, the agenda put forward by the enemies of gin was unabashedly elitist, taking its cue from an essentially hierarchical vision of the social order in which rich and poor were governed by two very different sets of rules.

The leaders of the great temperance movements were reformers in the modern sense of the word; the enemies of gin were not. But again, what shall we call them? One possibility would be to do as the sociologists do and call them moral entrepreneurs. Howard Becker coined the phrase back in 1963, using it to describe men (and women) who lead moral enterprises or crusades and sometimes even moral panics. They care passionately about rules, and make it their business to alert the public when they are broken. Seen from this perspective, the gin craze witnessed three separate moral crusades, the first culminating in the passage of the Gin Act of 1729, the second in the passage of the Gin Act of 1736, and the third in the passage of the Gin Act of 1751.

Moral entrepreneur, however, is a somewhat unwieldy term, and it is especially jarring when used in the context of a society that is culturally and linguistically very remote from our own. The better term—and one that fits better with how contemporaries described their world—is *moral reformer*. The two words together convey reform in the backward-looking, Protestant sense of reform. They also convey, if only indirectly, the larger goal of the war on gin: to reform the morals of the working poor.

The efforts of these moral reformers were of course doomed. For one thing, their underlying vision, rooted as it was in the ideals and institutions of a rural past, was altogether too simple for the times. For better or worse their beloved England was changing and its population was on the move, leaving farms and hamlets in search of employment and opportunity in the nation's towns and cities. At the beginning of the century, less than 20 percent of the population lived in towns with 2,500 or more inhabitants; by its end that amount would grow to more than 30 percent, with agriculture employing an ever smaller percentage of the workforce. Further disappointments awaited when moral reformers attempted to impose their vision on the people of London. Unlike the institutions of eighteenth-century government, London was large and complex, and its problems were those of a modern city. Encompassing the old City of London, the fashionable neighborhoods to the west of it, and the slums to its north, south, and east, London was by 1700 the largest city in Europe, with a population of perhaps 575,000; by 1750, that number would grow to 675,000. What had once been distinct towns now formed one vast conurbation, into which more distant and still partly rural parishes were being gradually and inexorably drawn.

Every year the metropolis attracted thousands of new immigrants, without, however, offering them either adequate housing or secure employment. Gin naturally appealed to these people, providing solace to some and part-time employment to others. Young, poor, and bound by only the most tenuous of ties to their employers and the larger community, they were a source of endless worry to their social superiors. Especially worrisome were the Scots and the Irish, who by one tally accounted for perhaps 13 percent of the city's population.

London's immigrants included, as they always have, rich and poor alike, the former being increasingly concentrated in London's fashionable West End, the latter in Westminster, Southwark, and the slums to the north and east of the City of London. Westminster, with its thousands of drinking establishments and its uneasy mix of rich and poor, was ground zero in the ensuing war on gin. It was here that Parliament met and the court and main departments of government conducted most of their business, and it was here that rich and poor existed side by side, much to the annoyance of the well-heeled men and women who had to pass through its teeming streets en route to Whitehall and Parliament. Their annoyance was writ large in the debates surrounding the Gin Act of 1743, at which time Lord Lonsdale was quoted as saying:

> ...whoever shall pass among the Streets, will find Wretches stretched upon the Pavement, insensible and motionless, and only removed by the Charity of Passengers from the Danger of being crushed by Carriages or trampled by Horses, or strangled with Filth in the common Sewers; and others less helpless perhaps, but more dangerous, who have drank too much to fear Punishment, but not enough to hinder them from provoking it, who think themselves in the Elevation of Drunkenness intitled to treat all those with Contempt whom their Dress distinguishes from them, and to resent every Injury which in the Heat of their Imagination they suppose themselves to suffer, with the utmost Rage of Resentment, Violence of Rudeness, and Scurrility of Tongue.

Gin was just as popular in East London as it was in Westminster, but its enormous popularity would almost certainly have attracted rather less attention had it been confined to the slums of East London. After all, no man of influence would willingly step foot in the lanes and alleys of East London, but no man of influence could possibly forgo an appearance in Westminster.

The distaste of polite men and women for gin and its drinkers also reflected a growing divide—both physical and cultural—between rich and poor. Nowhere was this divide more evident than in the practice of charity, with the wealthy few increasingly avoiding direct contact with the poor and instead endowing foundling hospitals, almshouses, and other institutions that were at a safe remove from their own homes. These were the same people who built high fences around their rural estates and purchased new houses in London's fashionable West End. There they lived in tidy rows and crescents, lobbying Parliament to have their streets cleaned, paved, lit, and patrolled. In this they were remarkably successful, and as the century wore on London became a cleaner, neater, and safer city. Gin naturally posed a threat to this blueprint for a new and improved London: it was hawked about the streets; it was sold and drunk in thousands of disreputable gin shops; and its drinkers were widely regarded as public nuisances. Gin belonged to the messy world of open-air markets and shambles, and like them, it was destined to be a victim of gentrification.

The gin craze was first and foremost an urban phenomenon. It occurred in a society whose ideals and institutions were still very much rooted in a rural past, and as such were inadequate to meet the complex challenges posed by a modern city and an increasingly heterogeneous population. Like other and more recent recreational drugs, gin offered a quick escape from the frustrations and monotony of everyday life. And because gin appealed to the urban poor, it threatened a social system whose very existence depended on their willingness to defer to men who were in fact quite powerless to control them. Hence the fear, as expressed by Lord Hervey in 1743, that gin was destroying "all voluntary Submission," putting "an End to Subordination," and raising "every Man to an Equality with his Master, or his Governour." The story of the gin craze is the story of two very different crises. One occurred in the worried minds of the men who governed and employed London's poor, the other in the teeming slums of Westminster and East London. Rarely, if ever, did one reflect the other.

Gin may have adversely affected the mental health of its critics, if only because it caused them no end of worry, but there is simply no getting around the fact that gin often had very real effects on the physical health of its drinkers. Londoners, very simply, drank more liquor in the first half of the eighteenth century than they ever had before. And many, when down on their luck, would appear to have substituted gin for food, thus compounding the former's effects. Thomas Wilson, for example, observed that "Since the drinking of Gin less Milk is sold and the farmers about Islington have decreased their stocks of Corn." Likewise, when the Gin Act of 1736 first took effect, it was widely reported that "Since the Suppression of *Gin*, the coarse Pieces of Beef, &c. has sold much better at the several Markets about Town than before. . . . "

Moreover, when gin was drunk it was often drunk in large quantities, thus greatly increasing the risks associated with each binge. This was in large part due to the fact that gin was still very new to the mass market; as a consequence, there were as yet no norms limiting where and when individuals might drink it. The same effects can be seen in parts of post-colonial Africa: as workers migrate from rural areas to the cities in search of work, they abandon traditional and generally weak alcoholic beverages in favor of stronger European beverages; they do so, however, without the benefit of rules and rituals that might limit the harm that can come from drinking beverages that are both strange and strong.

When gin was consumed in enormous quantities and on an empty stomach, its effects could be fatal. Even by itself, heavy drinking would almost certainly have contributed to an increase in coronary heart disease, just as it has in modern Russia. Thomas Wilson, perhaps the most influential crusader against Mother Gin, claimed as much in 1736. Distilled spirits, he observed, "when...not drunk in such large Quantities as to kill immediately, but are daily used; then, besides many other Diseases, they are apt to breed *Polypuses* or Fleshy Substances in the Heart...." Wilson's friend, the physician Stephen Hales, had made very similar claims in his *Friendly Admonition to the Drinkers of Brandy, and other Distilled Spirituous Liquors*; like Wilson he was simply repeating what was already common knowledge among medical practitioners.

Then there is the issue of size. Eighteenth-century men and women—and especially poor men and women—were a generally puny lot; for this reason they were poorly equipped to metabolize large quantities of alcohol. Once again, the real problem was one of poor nutrition coupled with backbreaking work, the combined effect of which was both to delay and stunt physical development. In the royal dockyard in Portsmouth, for example, it was found that the adolescents employed in the rope yard were too small to do the work of grown men; the problem was sufficiently vexing that the Navy Board intervened in 1744, directing that new hires "be full five feet high and fifteen years old, but if not of that height, then to be sixteen years of age, well set and able lads capable to labour...."

The effects of gin were doubtless further compounded by beer, which both men and women continued to drink in staggering quantities even at the height of the gin craze. The number of barrels brewed in and around London dropped slightly after 1725, remaining stagnant well into the 1760s, but on a national basis per capita consumption remained remarkably constant, hovering at thirty gallons a year for most of the century. The fact that the amount of beer brewed in London declined only slightly at the height of the gin craze suggests that the harms associated with gin were caused not by gin alone but by gin in combination with other alcoholic beverages. Indeed, with the exception of the peak years of 1740 to 1751, the amounts of distilled spirits consumed in England were about equal to those consumed on a per capita basis in North America in the late 1970s and early 1980s. The amounts in question were, in other words, high but hardly heroic. They were, moreover, laughably low when compared to the amounts consumed by Americans in the early years of the republic. But again, these comparisons must be balanced against the fact that the average English adult continued to drink vast quantities of strong beer before, during, and after the gin craze.

This particular pattern, of adding on beverages rather than substituting one for the other, obviously created real problems for many of the people who drank gin, especially when they were already in poor health or were suffering from the effects of a diet that was both poor and erratic. To that extent, then, the reformers were correct when they said, in effect, that London was in the midst of a public health crisis. They neglected to add, however, that poverty itself was very bad for one's health, as were overcrowding and the absence of sanitation in any recognizable form. London was indeed in the midst of a public health crisis, but its root cause was poverty and not gin.

Act I

IN WHICH A New AND Bewitching Liquor
IS INTRODUCED TO AN Unwary Nation

CHAPTER ONE

Strong Waters

Since to drive away cares, or the plague of Dull Thinking,
All men more or less give themselves to good Drinking,
To refresh their tir'd Senses, and chase away Sorrow,
Grief, Pain, and the troublesome thoughts of to morrow:
Yet in the choice of the Liquors Disputes have arisen,
What to one Palate's grateful, to others is Poison...

RICHARD AMES, *The Bacchanalian Sessions*, 1693

ON 27 OCTOBER 1688, William of Orange, stadtholder of the United Provinces of the Netherlands and husband of Mary, daughter of James II of England, was stranded in the small Dutch port of Hellevoetsluys. His old enemy, Louis XIV of France, was once again on the move, and French troops were poised to invade the Netherlands. A few miles away, in the stormy waters of the North Sea, William had at great cost and even greater risk assembled an armada of 225 ships, ostensibly to come to the rescue of his fellow Protestants in England. Winter was fast approaching, and with it the prospect that William would not only have to call off his invasion of England, but also leave his own country vulnerable to being invaded by the French. The following day, however, the storms that had been buffeting the Dutch fleet lifted; two days later William set sail; and four months later, with James II now in ignominious exile in France, William was crowned along with his wife Mary.

A triumphant Parliament had toppled a Catholic and crowned a Protestant. But it had done so at the price of dragging England into an interminable conflict with France. At the time no one could have predicted how long or how costly that conflict would be. Over the next 126 years, from Blenheim to the Plains of Abraham to Waterloo, England would fight a total of six wars against a country much larger than itself, each time adding to the national debt and forcing Parliament to raise ever larger amounts of money for men, ships, and weapons.

One of the ways in which Parliament raised money for the wars of William III and his successors was by taxing a beverage called gin. Aside from its name, this beverage bore little resemblance to what now passes for gin. It was made from the worst possible ingredients, and because of this it was flavored with fruits and other additives in an attempt to mask its harsh and musty taste. Gin was the punch of the poor, and for one generation, from 1720 until the passage of the eighth and final Gin Act in 1751, the taxes paid on this homely beverage helped finance the acquisition of an empire while also lining the pockets of its leaders. The story of gin in England is the story of war, taxes, and the greed of a nation's leaders; it is, above all, a modern morality tale, set, as it was, in what was then Europe's largest city and occurring at a time when men and women of all classes were not only eager to experiment with new tastes and sensations, but also suddenly had the means to do so. And so while distilled beverages had been available in England since at least the end of the Middle Ages, their use became problematic only when England started to become something approaching a consumer society and its manufacturers had achieved significant efficiencies in producing and distributing their goods. Even then, the ensuing crisis was for the most part limited to the nation's largest and most modern city. That city was, of course, London—capital and marketplace to an empire.

That, however, was all in the future. Our story begins several centuries earlier and hundreds of miles away, in the Italian university town of Salerno. It was there, in the early twelfth century, that spirits were first distilled from wine. Like opium, these spirits were originally used as a type of medicine, under the guise of *aqua vitæ*, or water of life. From Italy they made their way across Europe, first in the southern grape-growing regions, and only much later in regions too inclement to produce grapes. These early spirits were commonly known as brandy, or burnt wine, and for several generations they were neither widely drunk nor widely distributed. It was not until the end of the Middle Ages that *aqua vitæ* emerged as a popular alcoholic beverage in its own right. In 1496, for example, the city of Nuremberg restricted sales of brandy because it was already a cause of "serious misconduct and disorder." Over the next several decades a series of other German cities, including Augsburg, also placed restrictions on its sale and use.

Even as distilled spirits entered the mass market, they continued to be widely used as a medicine, and this doubtless added to their appeal while also blinding consumers to their potentially deleterious effects. When, for example, a young woman in Hackney "was taken with a violent Fit of the Cholick" in 1738, her landlady "gave her a Glass of Geneva, which gave her Ease." And when in 1737 a pauper woman was found naked in a ditch outside London, local workers kindly revived her with a glass of gin. Because distilled spirits continued to be used as a medicine, contemporaries were caught off guard when they were first widely sold as a recreational beverage. Abruptly and without warning, men and women were faced with a seemingly insurmountable paradox: the same substance that seemed to revive some was also capable of harming and even killing others.

Because they could not grow grapes, northern Europeans were at a considerable disadvantage when it came to distilling, and it was only over the course of the sixteenth century that they finally mastered the art of distilling spirits from mashed grains. By the second half of the century Poles were already distilling and drinking spirits from grain, albeit in small quantities. At the same time the Scots were producing whiskey in ever-increasing quantities, so much so that in 1555, and then again in 1579, production had to be temporarily banned in order to avert shortages of grain. For the time being, however, these beverages were generally of poor quality, and unlike brandy, were unfit for export. Then, in the mid-seventeenth century, the Dutch invented the beverage that is now known as gin. Credit for the invention goes to Franciscus de la Boe, otherwise known as Dr. Sylvius, of the University of Leyden. The new beverage was originally known as *genever*, and it was made by redistilling pure malt spirits with juniper berries. This process made for a smooth and reasonably palatable beverage that was, in its own way, almost as good as French brandy.

One of the markets for this new and greatly improved beverage was England, which by the end of the sixteenth century was already importing large quantities of French brandy. The Elizabethan satirist Thomas Nashe, writing in 1592, included among his rogues' gallery of drunkards Fol Lang the Fencer, who died "sodainly...drinking *Aqua vitæ*." A sermon dating from 1624 mentions "three young men meeting to drinke strong waters" in

Essex; these they drank in half pints, with the result that "one fell dead in the roome, and the other prevented by company coming in, escaped not without much sickness." By 1635 there were already drinking games to determine who could drink the most *aqua vitæ*. Three women, for example, might share "a bottle of Aquavitæ, or Strong-Waters...till two of them decease...then the surviving Gossip may carry away the Bottle whole (if she breake it not by the way) and that by the way of survivership." "We have strong waters," John Taylor recorded in 1637, adding that they are "stronger much than Wine: One with a quart of water drunke may be."

By 1643, distilled spirits were sufficiently common in England to be included among the luxuries subject to the excise duties newly imposed by Parliament. They were originally taxed at the rate of eightpence per gallon; in 1654, the rate was reduced to just twopence per gallon for spirits manufactured in England, but it was increased by fourpence per gallon on imported spirits. Three years later, an act of Parliament mentioned the existence of "strongwater houses," while according to Defoe the nation "suddenly...began to abound in strong Water-Shops" upon the cessation of hostilities with the Netherlands in 1674. These shops sold crudely flavored spirits, of which a beverage known as aniseed water was the most popular.

By the second half of the seventeenth century, then, there was already a strong demand for distilled spirits in England, with those who could afford them insisting on French brandy or Dutch gin. Both imports owed their popularity to the conspicuous failure of English distillers to produce a drinkable beverage. This failure, in turn, can be attributed to the use of ingredients that were at once inferior and indiscriminate; whether by accident or by design, these ingredients were used as long as grain was both scarce and expensive, that is, from the early days of the industry in the late sixteenth century until well into the seventeenth century. In 1593, a man by the name of Richard Drake was granted a patent to produce distilled spirits. The same patent authorized Drake to correct existing abuses in the trade, including the use of hogwash and brewers' dregs by local distillers. Drake, however, would appear to have failed in his mission, for as late as 1668 members of the London Company of Distillers were still using such unappetizing ingredients as "Afterworts of Wash . . . musty unsavory or unwholesome Tilts or Dregs of Beer or Ale," "unwholesome or adulterated wines," and "unwholesome sugar-waters."

It was not until the early 1720s that English distillers succeeded in producing a halfway drinkable beverage, coinciding with an appreciable drop in the real price of wheat and other grains. They did so by making two simple changes. First, some—but by no means all—started to use marginally better ingredients, primarily in the form of malted corn, molasses, and cider. Sir Joseph Jekyll noted as much in 1736, claiming that thirty or forty years earlier, the industry had used only "the *worst* of our Grain." But again, only some distillers went this route, while the industry as a whole was anxious to avoid even the appearance of using grain that might instead be used for bread. Hence the distillers' insistence in 1736 that they were still using "the worst of grain," or what was commonly known as "Distiller's Grain." This was, to quote one of their hacks, nothing more than "coarse foul damaged Grain" that was unfit for bread.

The second change made by the distillers was as cheap as it was effective, and that was simply to mask the product's awful taste by compounding it with a variety of additives, most of them sweet and fruity. These included aniseed, juniper berries, elderberries, sugar, cherries, raspberries, and other fruits. The mix was then diluted with water, providing the poor with a cheap substitute for the fruit punches enjoyed by the rich. English distillers had, in the words of Defoe, finally "found out a way to hit the palate of the poor, by their new fashioned compound water, called Geneva...."

Like Dutch gin, Geneva, or English gin, went through two stages of production. In the first, malt distillers produced pure spirits, or what were known as low wines. Large-scale enterprises dominated this end of the trade, and in greater London they were represented by the Company of Distillers. Because their operations were large and thus difficult to conceal, they were easily monitored by local excisemen. The ease with which they could be monitored and taxed, along with the fact that many of the men in the trade were politically well-connected, helps to account for why Parliament was often sympathetic to their interests.

In the second stage of production, low wines were delivered to compound distillers. Compound distillers were so-called because they compounded or flavored raw spirits with a variety of additives. It was at this juncture, too, that they diluted the mix with water. Once this was done the finished spirits were sold by a wide variety of individuals, including the compound distillers themselves. Unlike the wholesale distillers, the compound distillers were both numerous and small-scale, making it fairly easy for them to evade both regulation and taxation. By the same token, they were easy targets whenever Parliament chose to rein in the sales of distilled spirits. Relations between compound distillers and members of the London Company of Distillers were ambivalent at best. Compound distillers provided a ready and seemingly inexhaustible market for pure malt spirits, but because they catered primarily to the poor, they ultimately threatened the reputation of the entire industry.

The growing use of additives, along with the occasional use of better grains, was the single most important factor in creating a market for English spirits, the consumption of which climbed steadily from 1720 on. Defoe, writing on behalf of the London Company of Distillers in 1726, observed that "the ordinary people are now so very well satisfied with the malt spirits, and especially with their new compositions, that they do not seek French brandy in such a manner that they formerly did." Over the next several years English distillers continued to improve their product, although it is unclear how many of their innovations were intended for the low-end market. In 1728, *The London Evening-Post* reported that a patent had been issued to "Mr. Stammers, a Distiller," granting him "the sole Use and Benefit, for the Term of Years therein specified, of his new Invention for rendring English Spirits equally as good as French Brandy." An advertisement dating from January of 1736 boasted of "BRANDY, universally confessed as fine as *any Foreign*; and daily more and more used instead of it," adding that it was selling "less than *Half* foreign Price"; at the same time, the advertiser offered "GENEVA, of the Right HOLLAND Sort, (made in *London*) the most different thing in the World from the *English* Geneva."

Despite these modest advances, concerns over their ability to compete with foreign spirits continued to dog English distillers for many more years, and are writ large in the rhetorical skirmishes preceding the enactment of the famous Gin Act of 1736. By 1747, when *The London Tradesman* was first published, the industry was in many ways still struggling, having "arrived at a very great Perfection, though not near so much as it is to be hoped it may." Indeed, it was not until long after the gin craze that English distillers were able to produce gin that could compete with its Dutch namesake, or so we might reasonably infer from a letter circulated by the London Excise Office in 1772. In it an astonished exciseman noted that "the Spirits and Geneva distilled and made at Islington and Maidstone are so near in Colour and Flavour to those imported from Holland that persons not well skilled in the Distillery Business are unable to distinguish one from the other...."

Another significant change, this time in nomenclature, also dates from around 1720. The word *geneva*, itself derived from the Dutch *genever*, was already in use by 1706, but it was not until the early 1720s that it became a byword for spirits distilled from English materials and compounded or rectified with one or more flavorings. An early example appears in the court papers of the Old Bailey, with a prostitute by the name of Martha Dobson calling for "a Pint of hot Ale and Geneva" in 1720. A year later, in 1721, the justices of Middlesex singled out "Persons Retailing Brandy, Geneva and other Distill'd Liquors." Geneva, in turn, very quickly came to be known simply as gin, and over the next several years the new word gained steadily in popularity, so much so that in 1729 the clerk employed by the London Company of Distillers referred to the act then pending in Parliament as "The Bill for laying a Duty upon Compound Waters or Spirits commonly called Gin."

So by the 1720s, English distillers had at long last succeeded in creating a cheap—if barely drinkable—substitute for Dutch gin. It is doubtful, however, that they would have made much progress had they not also been the beneficiaries of a series of protectionist acts passed during the late seventeenth and early eighteenth centuries. These acts, in turn, came about because the Glorious Revolution had placed William of Orange on the throne of England, without, however, giving him the money with which to resume his war with Louis XIV of France. For that he needed Parliament.

Parliament, however, was dominated by large landowners, each of whom had a very simple problem: their estates were producing altogether too much grain. The great landowners were themselves also partly to blame, having consolidated their holdings and introduced new and improved forms of farming. Even worse, the demand for their grain was stagnant, thanks to a prolonged slump in the growth of the English population. The slow growth of the population, in turn, helped keep wages high, leaving the working poor with what might generously be described as disposable income. The combined effect was to drive down the price of grain and other foodstuffs while adding to the cost of the labor employed in harvesting what was for some an unwelcome bounty. These same factors go a long way toward explaining why both the supply of cheap spirits and the demand for them grew by leaps and bounds in the late seventeenth and early eighteenth centuries; by the same token, the domestic distillery had fared poorly for much of the seventeenth century in part because wages were depressed and grain was scarce.

As long as grain was plentiful, landowners were the natural allies of domestic distillers, who were touted as providing a potentially inexhaustible market for surplus grain. Landowners were also their most important allies for the simple reason that they dominated both houses of Parliament. "There is nothing that ever more required the Care of the Legislature, than the preserving and improving the British Distillery," the London Company of Distillers would remind lawmakers in 1735, adding, "It is by the Consumption of Grain that Rents are raised, Tillage kept up, Labour and Industry of the common People rewarded, the Revenue improved...." Even in 1736, in the face of strong pressure to restrict sales of all distilled spirits, the prime minister, Sir Robert Walpole, hesitated, briefly defying the will of a determined and ultimately successful coalition within his own party. Walpole was, according to the Earl of Egmont, "not for totally destroying the distillers since the landed interests were so benefitted from spirituous liquors made by them...."

Even when they finally chose to intervene, landowners were faced with the problem of making good any shortfalls to revenue that might result from clamping down on sales of gin. One option, of course, was to raise the land tax. This option was naturally resisted by landowners, all the more so when restrictions on sales of gin also threatened to reduce the demand for grain. The landowners' options were especially limited in times of war, that is, when the Crown needed additional revenue, and this was one of the reasons why the enemies of gin were successful in Parliament only when the nation happened not to be at war. Even then it took a great deal of skill, cunning, and outright luck to convince landowners to vote against their own financial interests by persuading them that they had even more to lose from a breakdown in social discipline in the capital. The Gin Act of 1751 would mark an important turning point, for by then the population was once again growing, and with it, the price of grain. Under the circumstances landowners could at long last afford to dispense with the distillers, and dispense with them they did.

Returning now to William III, it was only natural that he should want to deprive his old enemy of the resources with which to wage war, and one of the ways to accomplish this was to ban imports of all French liquors, including brandies. At the same time, the Crown, faced with the escalating costs of waging war on the Continent, needed to increase its revenues by increasing taxes on luxuries. These naturally included distilled spirits, which had been taxed at fairly modest rates since 1643. While wary of voting William unlimited amounts of money, the landowners sitting in Parliament nonetheless had a vested interest in finding new markets for their surplus grain, and to this end they were prepared to support legislation designed to protect English distillers from foreign competition.

The first of these acts dates from 1689, and banned imports of all distilled spirits, including French brandies, for the next three years. One year later, in 1690, Parliament raised duties on domestically produced spirits while allowing anyone to manufacture and sell them. This particular clause was intended to increase output by rescinding the metropolitan monopoly enjoyed by the London Company of Distillers since 1638. Then, in 1692, Parliament lifted the ban on imports of distilled spirits; at the same time, however, it raised duties on French spirits, again in an attempt to "encourage our own manufacture of spirits made of corn." Just five years later, in 1697, Parliament again raised duties on all French imports, including brandies, while in 1701 and then again in 1710 it raised duties on domestically produced spirits. In the process the Crown became increasingly dependent on excises on distilled spirits as a source of revenue, so much so that at the height of the gin craze, between 1740 and 1750, they accounted for approximately 10 percent of all public revenues in any given year. During the same decade excises on distilled spirits accounted for approximately 20 percent of all revenues generated from excises. This figure did not include the already substantial excises paid on malt; nor did it include licensing fees paid by publicans.

All told, Parliament nearly doubled excises on domestic spirits between 1690 and 1710. The net effect was to drive up the going price of domestic spirits, from one penny to three halfpence a half cup; this increase, however, had absolutely no effect on consumption. Domestically produced spirits continued to be exploited by a succession of ministries intent on finding new sources of revenue while placating the landowners who dominated Parliament. Parliament taxed these spirits almost as vigorously as it taxed beer in the decades immediately following the Glorious Revolution, more than doubling taxes on spirits in 1690, but barely increasing them in 1710. Taxes on beer and distilled spirits moved more or less in tandem, and by themselves account for neither the solid growth of the British distillery after 1688 nor the relative stagnation of the brewing industry in the first half of the eighteenth century.

Legislation did, however, contribute to the growth of the domestic distillery in two important ways. First, it effectively kept out foreign and more palatable brandies at a time when domestic distillers were still struggling to produce a drinkable beverage. To quote from a pamphlet commissioned by the London Company of Distillers in 1710, "Ever since the Former and Latter War with *France*, and the great Duties laid on Foreign *Brandy*, the Making of *Brandy* from Malted Corn, and other Materials, hath greatly encreased, and been of Service to the Publick, in regard to Her Majesty's Revenue, and the Landed Interest of *Great Britain*."

The second way in which legislation helped distillers was by its relative absence in the industry's early years. That is, Parliament helped distillers by allowing the industry to grow virtually unchecked for more than forty years, from 1688 to 1729. In the absence of regulation the forces of the marketplace, including changing tastes and rising real wages, effectively drove demand. The only significant intervention during this period of time occurred in 1701, when Parliament required all individuals retailing distilled spirits to do as other publicans did and take out a license before two justices of the peace. This modest requirement was repealed just one year later, in 1702, leaving distillers free to open as many outlets as they wished. The offending clause, it was claimed, had proven "a great hindrance to the consumption of English brandies."

The absence of regulation would in all probability have made very little difference in a time of stagnant or declining real wages. This, however, was not the case in the first half of the eighteenth century, that is, in the decades both before and during the gin craze. Moreover, several factors, starting with the relative cheapness of grain, helped keep down the price of gin just as real wages started to rise in the early decades of the eighteenth century. There is also evidence suggesting that distillers deliberately kept prices low in order to increase the volume of their sales. This was, at the very least, a risky strategy, and it probably helps explain why so many distillers went bankrupt in the 1730s. One pundit, writing in 1747, observed that "The several Classes of Distillers, notwithstanding the high Duty, have a Secret of making large Profits: How they can pretend to pay the Revenue, and sell sound Spirits for so small a Price as they do, I own is a Mistery. . . ." Most compound distillers probably kept prices low by adding more water to their product when faced with new taxes or higher prices at the wholesale level. Samuel Johnson, for one, accused them of manipulating the proof of their spirits in order to keep prices down, claiming that it was their "Practice...to give their Spirits thrice the Degree of Strength required, by which Contrivance, though they pay only the Duty of one Pint, they sell their Liquors at the Price of three; because it may be encreased to thrice the Quantity distilled, and yet retain sufficient Strength to promote the Purposes of Wickedness."

The sheer density of outlets selling gin and other alcoholic beverages also contributed to keeping prices low. The author of one letter, dating from September of 1736, claimed that there were at the time as many as 120,000 such establishments in England, or one for every ten households. To the extent that countless families sold beer and other alcoholic beverages out of their houses, this claim may not have been wide of the mark. In some neighborhoods in the capital, such as Holborn, the ratio of gin shops to houses was as low as one to five. These figures become even more impressive when allowance is made for the countless men and women who hawked gin about the streets and along the roads leading into the capital. Stiff competition, in turn, forced publicans to absorb any modest increases in taxes or in the cost of raw materials, rather than passing them along to their customers. The price of beer, for instance, remained remarkably constant for much of the eighteenth century, and it was only when excise duties were raised by 60 percent, from five to eight shillings per barrel, that publicans in London raised the price of a quart of porter from threepence to three and a halfpence. This occurred in 1761, and was the first such increase in living memory. In the case of gin, the going price would appear to have been three halfpence for a quartern, or a half cup. The price amounted to slightly more than a thousandth of the typical maid's annual wages, a figure that gives some idea of just how cheap distilled spirits were at the time. According to Defoe, this price had been in effect since about 1710, and there it remained until the passage of the eighth and final Gin Act in 1751. In 1734, a man named George Douglas offered a publican a halfpence for a quarter of gin, only to be told by his companion, "Damn your Blood . . . What do you bring me here for, if you have got no more Money?" Douglas and his companion then left the establishment only to return a few minutes later with a penny, which, pooled with the halfpence, allowed the pair to buy a quarter of gin. The sources occasionally mention drams sold for as little as a penny apiece, without, however, specifying just how much gin a penny actually bought or whether its contents were greatly diluted.

Putting it all together, the supply side of the equation looked like this: the Crown needed new revenues, and the landowners sitting in Parliament needed new markets for their surplus grain. To this extent the Crown and Parliament were prepared to cooperate in drafting legislation designed to protect domestic distillers from foreign competition, thus greatly aiding an industry that by itself had been unable to corner the domestic market. For their part, consumers now had disposable income to spend on gin, thanks in large part to the relative cheapness of foodstuffs in the first half of the eighteenth century. These same factors helped keep the price of gin down, thus allowing it to enter the mass market.

The demand side of the equation was much trickier, especially since English gin was a truly awful beverage. Nor, for that matter, would gin have made much headway in a culture too hide-bound or too stratified to permit experimentation with new tastes and sensations. It was fortuitous, then, that gin made its debut in England in the early years of the consumer revolution. It was a time when people of all classes had not only the means but also the inclination to acquire new goods and to experiment with new beverages and stimulants, including, most notably, rum, coffee, tea, and chocolate. Defoe observed as much in 1726, noting that "There has been for some Years, and still continues among us, a national Gust or Inclination to drinking stronger and higher pric'd Liquors than formerly; I do not say we drink more, or more to Excess . . . But the Stream of the Nation's Palate runs, I say, for stronger and dearer Liquors."

Like many of his contemporaries, Defoe was not entirely comfortable with this trend. He complained on at least one occa-sion that "Our very Plough-Fellows drink Wine now a-days: Our Farmers, Grasiers, and Butchers, are above Malt-Liquors; and the wholesome Breakfast of Water-gruel and Milk-pottage is chang'd for Coffee and Tea." This complaint, that ordinary people were living above their station, would figure prominently in the ensuing campaign against gin and the people who drank it. Thomas Wilson complained that "even the *meanest* part of *Mankind* . . . Instead of being contented with *Beer* and *Ale* brewed at home of their own Malt . . . must now have *Tea* and *Spirits* at six times the Expence. . . ." In the same year, in 1736, a man writ-ing under the pseudonym of "Blackacre" complained bitterly of farmers whose wives and daughters "wear Silks and Topknots, drink Tea, and lie on Down Beds," while in 1743 Lord Bathurst was quoted as saying that farmers "have of late relaxed their fru-gality, and suffered themselves to be tempted by this infatuating

Liquor, nor is any thing now more common than to find it in those Houses in which Ale, a few Years ago, was the highest Pitch of Luxury to which they aspired...."

At the heart of these complaints was the lurking fear that ostentation on the part of the poor might blur the outward signs of class and privilege. Robert Drew, a conservative cleric, singled out "luxury and profuseness" in a sermon preached before the Societies for the Reformation of Manners in January of 1735. Theirs was an age, he told his horrified audience, in which "Each man is desirous of appearing to be what he is not, by making a figure in life above himself, and mimicking his superiors in unnecessary expenses." The same fears are to be found in a description, dating from 1744, of a maid freshly arrived from the countryside and already demanding more money to spend on the newest fashions:

> Her Neats-Leathern Shoes are now transform'd into Laced-ones; her Yarn Stockings are turn'd into fine White-ones; and her high Wooden Pattens are kick'd away for Leathern Clogs; she must have a Hoop too, as well as her Mistress; and her poor scanty Linsey-Woolsey Petticoat, is chang'd into a good Silk one, four or five yards wide at the least. In short, plain Country *Joan* is now turn'd into a fine *London* Madam, can drink *Tea*, take *Snuff*, and carry herself as high as the best.

Nowhere was this new ethos of consumerism more pronounced than in London, where wages had always been higher than elsewhere in England. High wages helped create an enormous market for products of every possible description, as did the sheer density of the population. London was also the place where social controls were especially lax, leaving consumers of all classes free to experiment with the newest fashions and products. These factors all help account for why the demand for gin was much higher in London than elsewhere in England.

London was and is, of course, unlike any other city in England, and to this extent contemporaries were prepared to tolerate its many vices, including its growing infatuation with gin. They were, however, deeply alarmed by the prospect that gin was gaining in popularity in the provinces, which, unlike London, had always been idealized as unassailable bastions of conservatism and virtue.

As early as 1728, a Jewish shoemaker in Portsmouth stood accused of selling "a distilled liquor called Geneva," while by 1736 it was possible to claim that "this dreadful Mischief" was no longer confined to the capital. On the contrary, "there was not the remotest Town or Village free from it; the Husbandman, the Manufacturer, the Handy-craftsman, the Labourer, all those upon whose Strength and Industry their own Livelihood and the Trade and Business of the Nation depend, were infected with this Vice. . . . " And by 1750 it was possible for one alarmist to claim that "In some villages in England there is now a greater quantity of gin consumed than of ale," although this was, in point of fact, highly unlikely.

Newspapers also mention gin in the provincial centers, including Bristol, Norwich, and Portsmouth. Portsmouth's publicans cried foul after the Gin Act of 1736 took effect, claiming in 1737 that their livelihoods depended on selling gin. Their mood was, however, much improved just one year later, with *The London Evening-Post* reporting that "the Taverns and Publick Houses there are in high Spirits, and are laying in great Stocks of Liquor, and making other Preparations, expecting a deal of Company and a roaring Trade there this Summer, *to visit the Fleet....*"

It was at this time that a local woman by the name of Margaret Hubball was convicted for violating the gin act then in effect. Margaret Hubball was particularly unfortunate, for very few people outside London were ever convicted of selling gin without a license. As a rule, provincial magistrates were loathe to penalize local publicans, especially when the evidence against them was brought by excisemen or paid informers. In one case, several informers "took a Country Journey" to Devonshire, only to have their testimony "dismiss'd, the Justices not taking the Informers for creditable Witnesses." And when several other informers succeeded in entrapping retailers in Hampshire, the justices there reduced the fines to just fivepence each, in the hope that "This ill Success...will put an End to the Progress of such Rascals."

The primary reason why provincial magistrates were reluctant to single out gin-sellers was because gin did not constitute a serious threat in communities outside London. In the words of an editorial published in the *Craftsman*, gin "hath got too much Footing amongst us in the Country; though not to such a Degree as some People seem to imagine, or affect to make others believe." In 1751, for example, the assemblymen of Norwich appointed a committee to draft "a Petition to Parliament to prevent the excessive Drinking of Spirituous Liquors," suggesting that the city was awash in gin. It was a logical supposition: after all, Norwich was at the time the second or third largest city in England, making it an obvious market for distillers. And yet over the lifetime of the Gin Act of 1736, from 1736 to 1743, only a few dozen of Norwich's publicans were convicted for retailing distilled spirits without a license, compared to the thousands who were convicted in the capital. *The Norwich Mercury* lists a total of thirty-three convictions, all but two occurring between July of 1737 and July of 1738, while the minutes of local quarter sessions, both in Norwich and the nearby community of King's Lynn, also show that only a handful of individuals were ever indicted for violating the act. The impression is confirmed by the records kept by the commissioners of excise, who as of March of 1738 had paid more than £1,300 to informers in the capital, compared to just £55 to those daring enough to operate elsewhere in England. Further confirmation can be found in the parliamentary debates surrounding the Gin Act of 1736, at which time it was claimed that London was home to approximately twenty thousand of the nation's forty thousand gin shops. If accurate, this figure means that half of the nation's gin shops catered to just 10 percent of the population.

Aside from publicans and distillers, the people who profited most from the growth of the English distillery were the landowners who supplied them with raw materials. They were for the most part based outside London, and to the extent that their numbers included members of Parliament, these were the men whom the enemies of gin needed to convert to their cause. One way of doing this was to tell them, rightly or wrongly, that their own towns and villages were awash in gin. But most gin was manufactured and sold in London, and to the extent that landowners resided at a safe distance from the capital, they could ignore the drunkenness for which they were in large part responsible.

The problem was that very few large landowners could avoid London altogether. London was where landowners invested their earnings, bought and sold land, found marriage partners, and routinely sued each other; above all, London was where landowners came for the social "season," which could stretch all the way from October to June. Their distaste for what they saw en route to the symmetrical squares and crescents of West London was above all of an esthetic nature. In the gin lanes of Westminster and East London they were confronted with a chaos and squalor that was far removed from the tidy spaciousness of their Palladian villas—and altogether too close to their own orderly townhouses. It is to these gin lanes—and to the men and women who inhabited them—that we now turn.

CHAPTER TWO

A Curious Machine Makes a Brief Appearance

Suppose on search—it should appear
Ten Bunters dy'd in every year
    By drinking to excess;
Should thousands innocent be led
Into despair, and lose their bread
    Such folly to redress?

The Gentleman's Magazine, November, 1736

IN 1738 IT WAS ILLEGAL to sell gin and other distilled spirits without a license. This by itself was nothing new. The practice had been illegal since 1729, but in 1737 Parliament had passed a law that rewarded informers for going after poor people who sold gin as a sideline. When this happened, thousands of small gin-sellers were suddenly put at risk. They responded by inventing a vending machine that was fondly known as "puss and mew." It worked like this: a customer approached the machine and said, "Puss." Behind the machine was concealed a vendor who responded with "Mew." Out came a drawer and into it the customer deposited a few coins. No sooner was this done than the vendor snapped back the drawer, only to push it forward a few moments later, this time with a dram of gin.

These machines were to be found all over London, and for a few months they succeeded in baffling informers and infuriating local justices of the peace. The career of puss and mew, brief and farcical though it was, underscores a basic point, and that is just how difficult it was to drive the people who sold gin out of business. Tough, resourceful, and on occasion devilishly ingenious, they were players in a vast black market; sometimes desperate and always determined, they were willing to take enormous risks while reaping only meager profits.

Most of the people who took these risks did so because they were very poor. They looked and acted very much like the people who drank gin, and unlike established publicans who had licenses to keep and renew, they had no stake in controlling the behavior of their customers. This frightened a good many people, so much so that each of the major gin acts, starting with the Gin Act of 1729, sought to restrict sales of gin to licensed public houses, where, it was hoped, middle-class publicans would uphold middle-class standards of decency and public order. This lofty goal was not fully achieved until the passage of the final Gin Act in 1751. Until that time, the vast majority of the people who sold gin did so without a license, cheerfully risking the prospect of a fine or imprisonment in the local house of correction. For these men and women, selling gin was often the difference between poverty and destitution, providing them with much-needed extra income in the face of employment that was seasonal and erratic even in the best of times. In many ways, they were doing exactly what their social superiors wanted them to do, which was to stay off the dole.

As a rule, gin-sellers thrived wherever local authorities were weak, corrupt, or simply overwhelmed by the numbers and problems of the people in their midst. Nowhere was this more true than in the sprawling suburbs outside the old City of London. It was here that rents were cheap, and it was here, too, that social controls were notoriously lax, thanks in large part to the absence of magistrates willing or qualified to police their own neighborhoods. "I am," confessed one contemporary in his travels through one of these parishes, "very much concerned for the Gentlemen in the Commission of the *Peace* here, who enjoy but a slender Share of that Blessing themselves, they being almost worn out in determining and healing the Breaches as continually happen among these various Species of People."

This vacuum allowed thousands of men and women to sell gin openly and without a license, just as it allowed their friends and neighbors to drink as much as they wanted wherever they wanted. In East London, a high percentage of gin-sellers were to be found in the poorest back streets, that is in its lanes, courtyards, and alleys. Not surprisingly, these were the areas with the lowest property values and hence the lowest rents, making them especially attractive to the thousands of indigent job-seekers who descended on the capital each year. The count made in 1736 shows that at least 164 of the houses or shops selling gin and other cheap spirits were located on lanes, compared to 71 in courtyards and 57 in alleys. These establishments were, moreover, located in some of the capital's most infamous neighborhoods. Cock Lane, for example, was home to at least fifteen retailers, along with any number of streetwalkers; Rosemary Lane, with twenty-one retailers, was equally notorious. In 1728, a grand jury singled out several "disorderly Geneva Shops about Rosemary-Lane and Tower-Hill, that harbour and entertain Thieves and Street-Robbers." Other retailers were to be found clustered around the capital's shambles, with at least seventeen operating off Butcher Row and another seven off Hog Lane.

Three other retailers, all in Whitechapel, operated just outside the local prison, catering to inmates and visitors alike. Two of these establishments were located behind the prison, and the third was located on the road leading up to it. Their activities are not at all surprising, given the fact that both beer and cheap spirits were openly sold and drunk in the capital's workhouses, prisons, and lockups. In 1727, for example, the wardens of the workhouse in Finsbury forbade their inmates from bringing "Geneva or other distilled Liquors . . . into the House," with first-time offenders to "be kept in the dark room for a day on Bread and Water. . . ."

In the case of prisons and other lockups, jailers and their servants profited from sales of both beer and distilled spirits to inmates, so much so that when the practice was finally banned in the 1780s, several jailers in London were compensated in the range of £200 to £350 each. The earliest complaints about gin in prisons date from the 1720s. In 1725, for example, Bernard Mandeville complained that strong waters were "swallow'd in every Part of *Newgate*," the city's chief prison. The practice continued even after the Gin Act of 1736 effectively banned all sales of gin, with *The Daily Journal* reporting that "The Prisoners in the Liberties of the Fleet and King's Bench, thinking they can't be in a worse Condition than they are at present, are resolved to continue selling all Sorts of Drams; where a vast Number of People repair to drink them." By November, just one month after the act had become law, several prisoners in Newgate had followed suit and were selling gin "amongst their fellow prisoners . . . especially after Locking up at Nights, by which very great Disturbances have frequently Ensued." The ringleaders included Benjamin Brooke, "a Debtor in the said prison," and Sarah Greenwood, who sold gin "publickly amongst the prisoners." The servant of at least one warden was also implicated. The following August two excisemen duped a tapster in the King's Bench Prison into selling them a dram of gin, "but not knowing his Name, and endeavouring to find it out, they were discover'd; upon which the Prisoners duck'd and pump'd them...." On the south bank of the Thames, in Southwark, the turnkey at the Marshalsea Prison also sold gin and other liquors to the inmates; this was, according to *Read's Weekly Journal*, "a Perquisite belonging to their Places."

Roads were an ideal venue for selling gin because petty vendors could set up and move small stalls without taking out a license or paying rent. In 1736, there were at least thirty-nine roadside outlets operating in Whitechapel, in addition to twenty-seven more along Mile End Road in Stepney. At least twenty other vendors operated along Kingsland Road, as did several of the people who informed against them after the Gin Act of 1736 took effect. Not surprisingly, these stalls were operated by individuals with little or no capital. One of these was a poor woman who sold "a Cup of Ale and a Dram for the Relief of Travellers, in the Five Fields on the Road to Chelsea"; her story appeared in local newspapers because five men broke into her hut "and stripp'd her of all she had, even her Bedding and Wearing Apparel, leaving her nothing but an old Petticoat to cover her." Another stall, described as "a Moveable Hut or Hovell lately placed and set up and Ever since and unto this time used by some Obscure person or persons," was situated along one of Portsmouth's major highways in or around 1742. Local authorities sought to close it down, alleging that it was patronized by "Rogues, Wastrels, Vagabonds and other disorderly persons of both sexes both by Night and by day...."

And finally, countless men and women simply sold gin out of wheelbarrows, baskets, or even boats. In East London there were at least twenty-two watermen who sold gin as a sideline, presumably on both sides of the Thames. These petty hawkers occupied the lowest rungs of the trade in gin. Licensed publicans resented them because they siphoned away business, and reformers despised them because they were dirty, coarse, and raucous. They were, in the words of one hack:

> ... the very Rubbish of the Creation, the worst of both Sexes, but most of them weather-beaten Fellows, that have misspent their Youth. Here stands an old sloven in a Wig actually putrify'd, squeez'd up in a Corner, recommending a Dram of it to the Goers-by: There another in Rags, as rusty as a Nonjuring Clergyman's Cassock, with several Bottles in a Basket, stirs about with it, where the Throng is the thinnest, and tears his Throat like a Flounder Fellow, with crying his Commodity: And further off you may see the Head of a third, who has ventur'd in the middle of the Current, and minds his Business as he is fluctuating in the irregular Stream: Whilst higher up, an old decrepit Woman sits dreaming within on a Bulk, and over-against her, in a Soldier's Coat, her termagant Daughter sells the Sots Comfort with great Dispatch.

Like the men and women who sold gin out of ramshackle stalls, petty hawkers could pack up and move at a moment's notice, thus thwarting any attempt to license or otherwise regulate them. And because they were mobile they were to be found wherever crowds gathered, whether to watch an execution or gawk when the corpses of notorious felons were put on public display at or near the scene of their crimes. When felons were subjected to this additional indignity their bodies were left to decay, attracting,

with each passing day, hordes of birds, vermin, and curious spectators. In 1736, an enterprising countryman noticed that a bird had
built a nest among the rags clinging to the skull of a malefactor;
seeing a business opportunity, he promptly removed the nest and
sold its occupants "at a good Price, being esteem'd very great
Curiosities by the *Virtuosi*" of his home county. One year later, in
March of 1737, the bodies of Maw the Soldier and Morat the
Black were hung in chains in Shepherd's Bush. There, on the first
day of their being exposed to public view, they attracted thousands
of spectators, catering to whom were stalls selling both ginger-
bread and gin. The combined effect was too much for polite society. *Read's Weekly Journal* reported that "the Black hangs in a very
indecent Manner, he has nothing over his Face, but was quite
exposed, with his Mouth wide open, and his swelled Tongue
hanging out, and looks very frightful; he is hung in his Green
Livery, but without Shoes or Stockings...." Several weeks later
the bodies were still on display at Shepherd's Bush, where according to *The London Evening-Post*, "they look dismally, and begin to
smell, and being so very near the Road will soon be very offensive
to Travellers." Despite the stench, the gin-sellers continued to do
as brisk a business as ever.

Gin-sellers also did well at public hangings. Hogarth
included a gin-seller in *The Idle 'Prentice Executed at Tyburn*, while
Bernard Mandeville, who is best known for *The Fable of the Bees*,
denounced the practice of allowing condemned felons to stop
"three or four, and sometimes half a dozen Times, or more, before
they come to their Journey's End," each time downing a dram of
gin. Sometimes even the hangmen were drunk. On one occasion
in Hereford, the hangman was described as "intoxicated with
Liquor, and supposing there were three order'd for Execution, was

The Idle 'Prentice Executed at Tyburn, *by William Hogarth, 1747. Gin insinuated its way into the many entertainments available to London's poor, perhaps the most popular of which was watching one of their own die a slow and gruesome death by strangulation on the gallows at Tyburn. To the right, the gin-sellers ply their trade; their customers include several women perched in a cart. By courtesy of the Guildhall Library, London.*

going to put one of the Ropes about the Parson's Neck as he stood in the Cart, and was with much Difficulty prevented by the Goaler from so doing."

At the very bottom rung of the black market in gin were thousands of women, most of them single. Almost all of these women were poor, but few would appear to have been destitute, quite possibly because they supplemented their meager incomes by selling gin. One, Elizabeth Bowman, even operated a puss and mew. She was eventually apprehended and convicted under the Gin Act of 1736, spending two months in the house of correction at Tothill Fields in the spring of 1738.

As a rule, the women who sold gin had yet to establish roots in the neighborhoods where they lodged, leaving them free to come and go as they chose. It was for this reason that few people were prepared to come to their rescue when they were caught—as they so often were—selling gin without a license. By way of contrast, when the wife of "a reputable Publican" in Covent Garden was convicted under the Gin Act of 1736, "a Hundred of her Neighbours went, some in Coaches and others on Foot and redeem'd her, and brought her at Night in Triumph to her own House."

There were three reasons why selling gin appealed to so many women: it required little or no capital; it did not require membership in a professional organization; and it was one of the few occupations from which women were not effectively or explicitly excluded. It was, in other words, a means of economic survival.

Their suppliers consisted almost entirely of men, with the London Company of Distillers admitting only four women (compared to 225 men) between 1721 and 1759. One of these suppliers was Clifford Williams Phillips, a justice of the peace who also happened to be a distiller. Phillips sold gin to a hawker by the name of Mary Bryan, and came to her defense when she was charged under the Gin Act of 1736.

The women who hawked gin did so at considerable risk. They were several times more likely than men to be charged and convicted under the Gin Act of 1736. They were also several times more likely to be sent to prison once convicted. Thus of 586 defendants too poor to pay the penalty mandated by the Gin Act of

1736, 428 were women, a ratio roughly consistent with the overall population of the capital's houses of correction.

Most of the women listed in the records, or 949 out of 1,113, were listed without an occupation and without a husband, suggesting that they belonged to the vast population of young single women newly arrived in the capital. For them, hawking gin was one of several ways of making a living in an economy that was both seasonal and subject to sharp fluctuations. "I turn my hand to any thing to get a penny," one was quoted as saying, adding, "Sometimes I sell things in *Leaden-hall market*; and sometimes I do an odd chare at one house and sometimes at another." Hawking, moreover, had the additional advantage of being one of the few occupations dominated by women.

Hawking gin, however, was physically demanding work, in addition to being technically illegal from 1729 on. These two factors may account for why so few older women entered the trade. Only thirty-four of the 1,113 female retailers known to have operated in greater London were widows, hardly an overwhelming number; moreover, it was not uncommon for women in their twenties or even their teens to be widowed. Rose Biquall was married at the time she was committed to the Middlesex house of correction for violating the Gin Act of 1736, but was widowed shortly thereafter, while among the defendants profiled in *A Short History of the Gin Act* was a woman "who had lived twenty Years" in her parish. *The Daily Journal* reported that "one Chapman, an elderly Woman," was sentenced to the house of correction at Tothill Fields for selling gin "on the Footway to Chealsea...." And two female retailers, Elizabeth Judd of Westminster and Mary Blake of Southwark, died while in prison for violating the Gin Act of 1736. They may or may not have been old. In all probability, they simply succumbed, as so many did, to "jail fever," or what is now known as typhus. In 1738 it was noted that the Surrey county jail was exceptionally crowded and "very sickly on account of the great number of prisoners there for selling spirituous liquors." It was at this time that the wife of John Saxby came down with "jail distemper" while incarcerated in the Southwark house of correction; upon her release her husband and mother also contracted the disease, as a result of which all three died.

In addition to the women who hawked gin, there was also a much smaller number of women who sold it out of stalls, cellars, and the like. The counts of retailers, incomplete though they are, show that among the women selling gin there were 117 chandlers, three greengrocers, two fruiterers, two cooks, one pawnbroker, and one tobacconist. At the top of the pyramid were women who were either publicans or distillers in their own right, or who were their *de facto* partners through marriage. This was a small and elite group, and it included Mary Goudge, the wife of a distiller, and Catherine Croft, the wife a prosperous victualler in the Westminster parish of St. George Hanover Square.

Members of this last group were relatively unaffected by the various legislative acts passed against gin and the people who sold it. And when, like Catherine Croft, they were caught selling gin without a license, they had the financial means to stay out of jail. They may even have benefitted from attempts to reduce sales of gin, if only because each of the gin acts effectively sought to drive petty hawkers out of the trade. By the same token, the women who hawked gin stood to lose the most from attempts to clean up the trade, and this, in turn, links the campaign against gin to a larger campaign to regulate the pre-industrial marketplace and drive from it occasional vendors—most of them women—who hawked their goods in public spaces. This is exactly what was accomplished when the most draconian of the gin acts, the Gin Act of 1736, became law. Amendments made to it in June of 1737 and June of 1738 rewarded informers for prosecuting poor as well as prosperous retailers, and it was during this period that prosecutions, primarily of poorer retailers, peaked. The defendants in these actions consisted disproportionately of women, the majority of whom were probably hawkers. Thus while women accounted for slightly less than 20 percent, or 472 out of 2,377, of all known retailers in East London and the City of London, they accounted for nearly 70 percent of the individuals charged under the Gin Act of 1736.

There were occasional protests on the part of the women who suffered so unfairly under the Gin Act of 1736. These protests typically took the form of attacks on informers, with women participating in at least seven of fifty-seven such attacks between 1737 and 1742. But there were also isolated protests against the hardships that the act imposed on petty retailers in general and on women in particular. Hence the "Thing who refused to tell her Christian name" and the "Woman who refused to tell her Name" upon being committed to the Westminster house of correction early in 1739. And then there was Judith Wamsley, who in April of 1738 "was Committed to the Gatehouse for intruding herself in a forceible and Contemptuous manner before" Westminster's justices of the peace, "Insulting them in the Execution of their Office, and threatening the Informers that she wou'd wait their coming out."

Much less is known about the gin shops themselves. Hidden from view and known only to local customers, these shops have all but vanished from the historical record. The few people who bothered to describe them were for the most part their worst enemies, making their descriptions suspect at best. There were doubtless many gin-sellers whose activities were perfectly respectable, examples of which surface from time to time. A man named John Canfield, for example, admitted to drinking until four in the morning with four other men; the group then asked a woman who lived "up one pair of stairs" in the house where they lived to sell them a dram, "but we being in liquor, she would not let us have any." Elizabeth Bailey and Elizabeth Cooper were also refused service after "Attempting by Menaces & Ill Useage" to buy spirits from a woman in Westminster. And then there was the barman who went too far. A woman came into his shop, and demanded gin. This was in 1741, and the barman, probably suspecting that she was an informer, refused her service. This led to a row, and "in his Rage he threw a Can of Boiling Liquor over her, which scalded her in so miserable a Manner, that though she was immediately carry'd to St. Bartholomew's Hospital, where all possible Care was taken of her, she died . . . in Extremity of Torment."

To the extent that most gin shops consisted of nothing more than a spare room, they were probably no better—and no worse— than the other run-down dwellings frequented or inhabited by the working poor. The gin shops were squalid, but so, too, was much of London itself; their clientele was unseemly and on occasion poorly behaved, but so, too, were most of the people who lived and worked in the capital. To hate one was to hate the other, which is to say that the campaign to shut down the gin shops was rooted in a larger distaste for the squalor and squabbles of the poor.

This raises an important question: to what extent should we believe what we read about the gin shops, especially when the sources are hopelessly skewed in favor of their enemies? Obviously, the gin shops provided their customers, many of them recent immigrants to the city, with a place and a reason to congregate, and this by itself frightened a good many people. Their critics pointed to the corrupting influence of plebeian sociability, seeing in each such gathering potential partnerships in crime or debauchery. In October of 1736, an editorial claimed that "The Places where these Liquors were sold, became by these Means not only the Receptacles, but also the Nurseries of Thieves and Murtherers; here they were initiated in the Mysteries of Villainy, they joined in Confederacies, and laid the Scheme of their future Enterprizes...." The same themes are to be found in a pamphlet published by Henry Fielding in 1751. "Gin-shops," he wrote, "are undoubtedly the Nurseries of all manner of Vice and Wickedness. There it is that old Practitioners in Roguery assemble, where meeting with young idle Fellows, who elope from their Parents, Friends or Masters, they instruct them in all the Arts and Tricks of their own Profession, which is, of robbing on the Highway, picking Pockets, forging Hands, breaking open Houses, Clipping and Coining, and all other Crimes...."

These claims were not entirely groundless. In 1743, for example, James Newbold was indicted for keeping a disorderly house in the London parish of St. Brides, where, it was alleged, "He sold Gin, and entertained all Sorts of bad Company"; it was also claimed that at least two convicted robbers had frequented his house. At the same time, however, thousands of perfectly ordinary men and women somehow managed to frequent gin shops without becoming violent and dangerous felons. The gin shops were, after all, among the very few public spaces where the poor were actually welcomed, and most of their customers were generally law-abiding as long as they were employed, resorting to petty larceny only when unemployed or otherwise unable to make ends meet.

Because they were first and foremost places where ordinary people gathered, the gin shops, along with public houses in general, also functioned as places where prostitutes and their customers might meet and conduct their business. This, in turn, further tarnished the image of the gin shops, if only in the eyes of men who found their pleasures and partners elsewhere. Not surprisingly, prostitutes often enjoyed a symbiotic relationship with the proprietors of London's gin shops: the one brought business, in the form of johns who were cajoled into buying dram after dram of gin before going to bed; the other refrained from asking embarrassing questions when asked for the use of a room.

We know something about these women because so many of them ended up on trial at the Old Bailey, where they were invariably charged with robbing their befuddled customers. In 1742, for example, Joseph Reeves remembered that a woman by the name of Elizabeth Howard had asked him "some Questions, and then we agreed to go in and drink." Once inside she "call'd for a Quartern of Gin, and after that, for a Pint of Hot, and then we went into another Room, where *we stood pretty close together.* . . ." Howard took advantage of the moment to pick Reeves' pockets, upon which she "whipp'd out of the House." In June of 1743, Daniel Flannigal had high hopes of spending the night with two women. The evening started innocently enough, with the two women calling for gin. Flannigal later recalled that he "gave them Two-pence half-penny for it, they said it was not enough, so I gave them another Half-penny...." This, too, was not enough, and it was at this point that one of the women insisted on "a Present of something else," which in this case happened to include Flannigal's shoe buckles. James Powell "happen'd to light on" Clare Dickinson at "about one in the Morning," whereupon she asked him for a dram of gin. Powell himself drank three drams, only to discover that his purse and watch were both missing. Richard Summer lost his watch under very similar circumstances; in his own words, a woman by the name of Elizabeth Allen "ask'd me to make her drink; so she pick't me up, and carry'd me to a House, and we went up Stairs: I staid an Hour with her, drinking Gin...." She was, he added, "a Stranger to me, but yet I would go and drink with her...." John Godday told a jury that he "met with a Woman, who stopp'd me, and asked me to give her a *Drink*, and she carry'd me into a Room up one Pair of Stairs in *Salisbury-Court*...." Another woman then entered the room and picked his pocket. Charles Dickerson claimed that Elizabeth Jarvis accosted him "between 10 and 11 at Night" and "asked me to give her a Dram"; he then followed Jarvis into a room, upon which "she called for a Quartern of *Raspberry*." A few minutes later Jarvis and two other women assaulted Dickerson and stripped him of his clothes. And from *The Weekly Register* there is the story of "a poor Countryman, who came but the Day before out of *Gloucestershire*," only to be "robb'd of all the Money in his Pocket, by two Whores, who pick'd him up date the same Night in the Street, and carried him" to "a disorderly Brandy-shop."

It is also true that people often quarreled and squabbled when they drank gin. *The Grub-Street Journal*, for example, reported that "two women being very drunk with gin, one struck the other in the face with her patten, and beat off her nose." In another incident, reported in *Read's Weekly Journal*, "two Women at a Ginshop in Golden Lane having Words, one took a Bottle off the Compter and struck the other over the Temples with such Violence, that the Woman is since dead...." Gin also played a role in the death of Elizabeth Lewis. According to one witness, Lewis was "pretty much in Liquor" just before Susannah Carter threw a knife at her. Carter, who was subsequently convicted of manslaughter, also claimed that Lewis was drunk at the time. "I got up between three and four o'Clock that Morning," she told the court, "when she came in drunk; I got some Gin for her, and she would have had me have got some Tobacco; and as I would not do that, she abused, and aggravated me very much...."

Reformers looked at incidents like these and concluded that gin made people violent. They were right by half. Gin almost certainly reduced inhibitions, removing, as Fielding put it, "all Sense of Fear and Shame." One truism, however, must be balanced against another: fights can only occur where people happen to meet. In eighteenth-century London, poor people were most likely to meet other poor people in gin shops. And it was in these shops, whether because they were drunk or because they knew each other too little or too well, that men and women were most apt to bicker and squabble.

The reformers were on firmer ground when they criticized the keepers of gin shops for encouraging their customers to pawn goods—whether their own or someone else's—for gin. When a woman by the name of Jane Grew wanted a pint of gin she stripped an infant of its clothes and pawned them at a chandler's shop in Ram Alley in Spitalfields. When Samuel Heep stole four pounds of candles he "sold them to one *Stambridge* in *Porridge-Pot-Alley*, for a Quartern of Gin and 4 Pence in Money." And when John Purder of Marylebone was indicted for assaulting Emanuel Slater he claimed in his defense that two bricklayers had asked him to pawn the victim's coat, using the proceeds to buy thirty drams of gin; they are then supposed to have pawned the tools of their trade, presumably to buy still more gin.

What did the gin shops look like? This is not an easy question to answer. For one thing, their critics rarely bothered to describe them, quite possibly because few—if any—had ever stepped foot in one. The evidence, such as it is, suggests that most of the so-called "gin shops" consisted of nothing more than an unremarkable room or two behind a storefront or residence, prompting the exasperated justices of the Tower Hamlets to complain "that every separate Room in some Houses is become a place for vending *Distilled Liquors....*" Indictments from the height of the gin craze point in the same direction, mentioning in most instances a house or shop with one or more separate rooms for drinkers. In August of 1738, for example, Margaret Tyson was indicted for selling gin "in the Room of a house" in Hammersmith, while Elizabeth Armstrong was likewise indicted for selling gin "in the Room of a House" in the parish of Saint Giles-in-the-Fields; and two months later, in October of 1738, Mary Tidcomb was caught selling gin "in the Room of a house" in the parish of Saint Martin-

Vintry. In another incident, also dating from 1738, an informer by the name of Elizabeth Cull duped an unwary publican into selling her gin in a room behind his shop. And when Martha Hopkins wanted a glass of liquor, a night watchman directed her to a nearby house; the door was open and Hopkins "went in—into the lower Room,—a publick Room, and drank a little Gin there."

Many—and possibly most—of the shops that sold gin also sold a variety of other goods. Chandlers' shops accounted for slightly more than one-tenth of all establishments selling gin in East London between 1735 and 1736, compared to slightly more than 13 percent in the City of London in 1751. These shops seem to have catered primarily to women, affording countless "servant maids an opportunity of tippling...." According to Henry Fielding, their clientele consisted primarily of "Females, Servant-Maids, and the Wives of middling Sort of People who live there-abouts, who perhaps will visit the same Shop ten Times in a Day, under Pretence of some sleeveless Errant, on purpose to repeat their cordial Draught...." Eliza Haywood also took the chandlers' shops to task for serving gin to women, warning that if maids "fall once into a Chandler's-Shop-Acquaintance, give Ear to the Tittle-tattle of the Neighbourhood, and furnish their Quota of Intelligence, they must take their Glass of course."

Newspaper accounts and court records provide additional evidence. Susan Strafford, who stood accused of receiving goods stolen from Charles Sims, frequented a chandler's shop "in an Alley in *Chancery-Lane*" and "sometimes drank a Dram there...." Lydia Clapp, a notorious informer, entered a chandler's shop in West Smithfield with the intention of buying a dram of gin. And in 1743 *The Westminster Journal* reported that "two well-dress'd Women with Capuchins on went into a Chandler's Shop near St

James's Square, and one of them pretending to be ill, begg'd the Woman of the Shop to let her have a Dram...."

Young men also frequented the chandlers' shops, attracted, no doubt, by the prospect of procuring both women and gin. According to various reports dating from the 1720s and '30s, it was "too common a practice among chandlers and others, where servants are continually going on one occasion or another, to tempt and press them to drink and even give them drams...." Thomas Wilson, author of *Distilled Spirituous Liquors the Bane of the Nation*, similarly warned that "Masters will every Day have greater Reason to complain of bad and dishonest Servants, especially whilst that scandalous Custom prevails amongst Chandlers and other lower Trades, of giving Drams, making them incapable of doing their Business...."

Because so many of the rooms where gin was sold were hidden, their proprietors could operate without a license as long as they escaped the notice of the local justices of the peace. The justices of East London admitted as much in 1736, conceding that they had no way of counting the "many who sell privately in *Garrets, Cellars, back Rooms*, and other Places not publickly exposed to View...." And when the Gin Act of 1736 took effect, Thomas Croft, a publican in Westminster, simply ceased to sell gin out of his front room, and instead sold it discretely out of a back room to trusted customers.

For their part, customers had no difficulties in finding the many hidden places where gin was sold. On the contrary, the gin shops were by all accounts frequently packed, a function, perhaps, of just how small they were. Martha Hopkins, for one, remembered being surrounded by "a great many People drinking Gin," while according to a Swiss aristocrat visiting London in 1726, "These taverns are almost always full of men and women, and even sometimes of children...."

The man who wrote these words was César de Saussure. He was doubtless astonished by the presence of so many women in London's gin shops. Paris had its taverns, but they catered primarily to men. In London, by contrast, women were among the gin shops' best customers, drinking side by side with men. When, for example, two old acquaintances, one male, the other female, ran into each other in 1742, their first thought was to go drink a dram of gin together. Both, however, were down on their luck, and so they "agreed to toss up Heads or Tails, who should treat...." And when Robert Stafford met Elizabeth Jerron in 1720, he offered to treat her to a pint or two of wine. No sooner had she accepted his offer than he shoved her "headlong into a Brandy-Shop," where after several drinks they were joined by another woman. It was at this point that Stafford "let down his Breeches, pull'd up his Shirt, and bid them see what he had got."

Stafford's display notwithstanding, it was the behavior of the women who drank gin that most offended polite society, if only because so many of them seemed to prefer drinking gin to producing and raising the nation's next generation of soldiers, sailors, and laborers. And because thousands of women both sold and drank gin, the beverage very quickly took on a feminine folk identity under the guise of Mother Gin or Madam Geneva. John Barleycorn, it seemed, now had a feminine rival. And with her ascent came a great deal of talk, most of it unflattering and much of it untrue.

CHAPTER THREE

The Ladies Succumb

Fierce as Armenian tigers *Shrews that bawl,*
Subjoin'd *in love,* GIN taught *to Catterwal:*
GIN taught *'em to revive the* Bacchian *rite,*
To dance stark-naked the Black Joke *and* White;
T'alarm at mid-night Guards that sleeping stand ...

Mother Gin, a Tragi-comical Eclogue, 1737

IN THE SUMMER OF 1742, several women, some of them prostitutes and some of them thieves, spent the night in a tiny lockup in Westminster. The crowding was unbearable, and one of the inmates, Phillis Wells, died during the night, presumably of asphyxiation. Shortly after this incident William Bird, the keeper of the lockup, was charged with her death. According to Ann Norton, who was called on to testify against him, "I heard them cry out for Air and Water; and they cried out Fire and Murder, and that there was a Woman in Labour. I head them cry they would give a Shilling for a Quart of Water, and five Shillings for a Gallon." Bird, she added, had done nothing in response to their pleas, saying to no one in particular, "Damn the Bitches, they want Gin."

In accusing the women in his custody of causing a commotion in order to drink gin, Bird was appealing to an association that was already well established in the minds of his contemporaries. That association linked women and gin, casting them as its particular devotees. Gin was commonly known as "the ladies' delight," and took as its folk symbol Madam Geneva, otherwise known as Mother Gin. And, as everyone knew, Mother Gin was "held in the highest Esteem by those of her own Sex, even of the first Quality, being admitted into their most *private Apartments*, ever *at hand* to administer Relief under the many Disappointments and Afflictions, so unfortunately incident to that tender Part of Creation."

Nowhere was this more true than in London. It was here that women emerged, for the first time in history, as heroic drinkers in their own right, drinking vast quantities of cheap gin, sometimes on their own, sometimes with other women, and sometimes with men whom they had just met. Their reign of intemperance was destined to be short-lived, falling as it did between the death rattle of puritanism and the advent of the great temperance movements of the nineteenth century. It also happened to coincide with a period of relative prosperity and enormous mobility, with thousands of young women descending on the capital every year in search of jobs and husbands. Neither, of course, lived up to expectations, and the few jobs that were open to women tended to be poorly paid.

The flip side was that working women were largely left to their own devices, and when they happened to have a moment of leisure and a little change in their pockets many of them chose to spend both in London's gin shops. Wittingly or not, they mocked middle-class notions of femininity: they worked; they got drunk when they could; and when they had children they often neglected them, if only because they had neither the time nor the resources to devote to their care.

Not all women, however, were equally free to drink gin wherever and whenever they wanted. Rural women almost certainly had a harder time getting hold of gin than did their sisters in London. In London itself, it was really only young single women who were more or less free to drink as they chose, a function, no doubt, of the fact that relatively few people were invested in supervising their movements and activities.

Once a woman married and became rooted in her community and neighborhood, the rules started to change. She could still drink gin, but she was subject to censure if her drinking was deemed excessive or conspicuous. It was perhaps for this reason that "good Wives" discretely "furnish'd their little Fire-side Cupboards, with a needful Bottle for a cherishing Cup"—or so Defoe would have us believe. Even so, married women managed to drink enough gin to worry the justices of Middlesex, who on at least two occasions complained of children who roamed the streets "whilst the husband and perhaps his wife also are drinking and spending their money in geneva shops...." Their habits were also singled out in a letter published in *The Grub-Street Journal* in 1737. Its author proposed a ban on sales of all distilled spirits "to either women or children," arguing that this was the only way to help the "many husbands...who see their wives and children ruined, without knowing how to prevent it."

The underlying morality is not hard to spot: wives who became too fond of gin ran the risk of ruining both themselves and their reputations, in addition to neglecting their husbands and families. This theme appears as early as 1722 in Defoe's *History and Remarkable Life of the Truly Honourable Col. Jacque.* In it the hero,

Colonel Jack, marries a woman who dies as a result of drinking to excess. She had, in Defoe's words, progressed "from a Sup to a Dram, from a Dram to a Glass, and so on to Two, till at last, she took in short, to what we call drinking." The same theme can also be found in a series of lurid stories variously appearing in London's newspapers and in the ever-popular installments of the *Sessions Papers of the Old Bailey*. In 1735 *Read's Weekly Journal* ran the story of a wife who "came home so much intoxicated with Geneva, that she fell on the Fire, and was burnt in so miserable a Manner, that she immediately died, and her Bowels came out." The following year *The Grub-Street Journal* ran the story of a journeyman turner who upon "going home ... found his wife excessive drunk with Geneva, upon which he put her to bed but lay himself upon the floor till 4 in the morning. . . . " He then tried to rouse her, only to find that she was already dead. In 1739, Thomas Bridge, charged with having stabbed his wife to death, claimed that she had been drinking gin for the better part of a day; he also claimed that she had insisted on drinking yet another dram before going to bed, leaving a disgruntled Bridge to fix a sandwich for himself and their young child. A few seconds later, Elizabeth Bridge just happened to fall on her husband's knife. And in 1751, a man in Westminster "laid a Wager with a Neighbour that he and his Wife (who was big with Child) could between them" drink "near two bottles of Gin." This they did, only to die shortly thereafter.

Reformers were especially critical of women whose drinking endangered the health or welfare of infants and small children. Three groups of women fell under this broad rubric: pregnant women, nursing women, and women who simply looked after their own or other people's children. It is unclear, however, whether ordinary men and women shared their views. There is, for example, the story of Mary Estwick, an elderly woman who came home one Tuesday "about Two in the Afternoon, quite intoxicated with Gin." While she slept the toddler in her care caught fire. Estwick, however, was by now unconscious, and remained so even as the child burned to death. A coroner's inquest subsequently ruled that the death was accidental, reasoning "that the Woman always used the Child with great Tenderness and Humanity at other Times, and never committed any Act of Cruelty; so that all was owing to that pernicious Liquor."

The sources, however, are overwhelmingly biased in favor of the reformers, who found in drunken mothers and tipsy nursemaids the perfect poster children for their campaign against gin and the people who drank it. Reformers were especially critical of pregnant women who drank gin. As early as 1726, the Royal College of Physicians petitioned the House of Commons to restrict sales of distilled spirits, citing, among other reasons, instances of children born "weak, feeble, and distempered." A pamphlet published in 1732 claimed that gin "murders Infants in the Womb." Thomas Wilson, writing in 1736, complained of "Children coming into the World half burnt up, upon the Livers of some of which are found large *schirrous* Knots," in addition to "other terrible Symptoms." And a few months later, the following warning appeared in a pamphlet celebrating the passage of the Gin Act of 1736:

> *In pregnant Dames gin cou'd Abortion cause,*
> *And supersede prolific Nature's Laws:*
> *Mothers cou'd make the genial Womb a Grave,*
> *And anxious Charge of Education save . . .*

Reformers were no less critical of wet nurses who drank gin. According to Eliza Haywood, drunken wet nurses ran the risk of imparting gin to the infants whom they suckled. "How many," exclaimed Thomas Wilson, "have unhappily drunk this deadly Poison with their Nurse's Milk!" Henry Fielding envisioned a dreadful future for the infant "conceived in *Gin*," poisoned first in the womb and then at the breast. Some wet nurses were even accused of neglecting their duties altogether, and of using gin to sedate the infants in their care:

> *The sucking Brat declines her shrvil'd Pap,*
> *The cordial Bev'rage sips, and takes a Nap.*
> *Hush'd with few Drops he holds his Infant cries,*
> *And spares the maudlin Nurse her Lullabies.*

Reformers took on the cause of infant welfare not because they were sentimental, but rather because they believed that the nation's survival depended on its ability to draw on limitless reserves of manpower for its soldiers, sailors, and common laborers. And this the nation could not do if working-class mothers had small families or gave birth to sickly infants. Even the great philanthropists of the age adopted an essentially utilitarian attitude toward the foundlings whom they rescued, providing them with just enough education to serve later in life as soldiers, sailors, and simple laborers. Jonas Hanway, for example, subsidized a hospital for saving London's foundlings in large part because he believed that the nation was in desperate need of more soldiers and sailors.

Contemporary economic theory also favored an ever growing population. The goal was to ensure that the supply of labor always exceeded demand, the presumed benefits of which were twofold:

because the poor would have to work additional hours in order to subsist, they would have less free time in which to indulge in idle and potentially subversive pastimes; and because wages would be kept low, English exporters could lower their prices and thus undercut their foreign competitors. Hence Thomas Wilson's enthusiastic support for Henry Fielding's plan to "lower workmen's wages and make them labour 6 days in the week when they now hardly work 3." Hence, too, Wilson's assumption that "if the Manufacturers be few, Labour will be dear, and the Value of the Commodity must always be proportioned to the Price of Labour." Low wages, in turn, encouraged the export of manufactures by reducing consumption at home while decreasing their price once exported. This was a core tenet of mercantilism, which was opposed to consumerism and other forms of self-improvement on the part of the poor.

Gin, then, was a threat to both nation and empire because it had the potential to reduce both the numbers and fitness of the next generation of soldiers, sailors, and laborers. This gloomy prospect was especially troubling to Henry Fielding, who doubted that "these wretched Infants" would even survive "to become our future Sailors, and our future Grenadiers." It was bodies that the nation needed for the massed formations that characterized eighteenth-century warfare, both on land and at sea, and bodies, once destroyed by disease or expended in battle, could only be replaced if the working poor continued to reproduce at prodigious rates. They and they alone, certain members of the House of Lords were quoted as saying, provided the recruits to fill the "natural and inevitable Losses" of war while also supplying "Commerce with Manufacturers, Navigation with Mariners, and War with Soldiers." From this it followed that the working poor constituted "the Strength and Riches of every Nation," so much so that with-

To the Mortal Memory of Madam Geneva. *This print was published to celebrate the passage of the Gin Act of 1736, and it makes fun of the people who had the
most to lose from the new taxes on gin. They include a female hawker (at left),
three street urchins, and an old woman whose hat and profile are strongly reminis-
cent of the witches of an earlier era. By courtesy of the British Museum, London.*

out them "Policy would project in Vain...." "The Strength and Riches of a National Community consist in the *Health* and *Numerousness* of its Labourers," Sir Joseph Jekyll reminded his readers in 1736, "for if these be not preserv'd, where will your Produce be? Where will you find Soldiers?"

The rules that have emerged so far are these: young working women were free to drink gin, if only because they were for the most part left to their own devices; married women were also free to drink gin, provided that they were discrete and drank in moderation; and mothers or caregivers who drank gin were strongly discouraged from doing so, if only on eugenic grounds. What working-class men and women thought on the subject of mothers and gin is unclear. At the very least, it is unlikely that they were as invested as their leaders in producing children whose sole purpose was to work at substandard wages or to fight and die in the nation's wars.

That leaves one final group of women: those who could produce neither wealth nor children. Cast sometimes as hags and sometimes as hawkers, older women provided the images that best symbolized the moral and physical decay that contemporary reformers associated with gin. Elias Bockett noted as much in 1730, writing:

> *Lord! What an outcry there has been,*
> *About old women's drinking* Gin!
> *As if it burnt their guts, and shrivel'd*
> *Their skins, and made 'em look bedevil'd.*
> *Meer calumny! for purpose ill*
> *Design'd...*

73

Literary images of Mother Gin and Madam Geneva are strongly suggestive of age without dignity, although actual physical descriptions are rare. In *The Downfall of Mother Gin*, originally published in *The Craftsman* in June of 1736, she is "the *good old Lady*." In *Mother Gin, a Tragi-comical Eclogue*, she is "the happy Dame, the *candid* Madam Gin," and in *The Life of Mother Gin* we read that her mother "was of very mean and obscure Birth, insomuch that she was frequently reproached by those that were no Friends to her, with being sprung from the Dunghill, an Expression generally used to denote a Person of low Rank and Parentage...."

While images of this sort are quite common, actual examples of drinking on the part of post-menopausal women are rare, with the notable exception of the dozen or so older women who are supposed to have spontaneously combusted after drinking distilled spirits. Of these, only two, Grace Pett of Ipswich or Southampton and Mary Clues of Coventry, happened to be English. Mary Clues, described as "much addicted to drinking," was reported to have drunk as much as a quart of rum or aniseed water a day, and was also given to smoking a pipe in the evenings. Grace Pett was likewise in the habit of going downstairs every night to smoke a pipe, but unlike Clues, she appears to have been only an occasional drinker, having shortly before her death "drunk very plentifully of Gin ... on the Occasion of a Merry-making, on account of a Daughter who was lately come home from Gibralter."

While only two of the victims were English, their stories nonetheless titillated polite society, appearing on several occasions in the English press. The first death dates all the way back to 1663. The purported victim was a poor woman in Paris, who supposedly spent the last three years of her life consuming nothing but brandy. As a result, her body "contracted such a combustible Disposition, that one Night, she, lying down on a Straw-Couch, was all burned to Ashes and Smoke, except the scull, and the Extremities of her Fingers." The teller of the tale was the famous Dutch anatomist Thomas Bartholin, and his professional status doubtless lent the imprimatur of scientific proof to the story. Bartholin's account next surfaced in 1717, in a book published in Amsterdam by the physician Joannes Henricus Cohausen.

The next such death, again of an unknown woman, occurred in 1692, in Copenhagen. This was followed by the mysterious death of a Madame Millet in 1725. The first mention in the English press dates from 1731, more than half a century after the first female drunkard supposedly fell victim to spontaneous combustion. The story featured a Tuscan "Lady of Quality," later identified as the Countess Cornelia Zangari de Bandi, who was "burnt partly to a cinder, and partly to ashes." It was published in *The Gentleman's Magazine*, then still in its first year of publication. The incident was of sufficient interest to have been forwarded to the Royal Society of London for its consideration, but at the time it received only passing mention in *The Gentleman's Magazine*. A full version of the same story appeared fourteen years later in the *Transactions of the Royal Society* of London, along with the story of Grace Pett of Ipswich. *The Gentleman's Magazine* carried both stories a year later, this time in full. By now *The Gentleman's Magazine* was a flourishing concern, thanks in large part to the remarkable ability of Edward Cave, its founder and publisher, to select stories and oddities of particular appeal to middle-class readers.

In 1775 there was a new victim, Mary Clues of Coventry or Southampton. She was the second and last of the English victims, quite possibly because women who drank gin had long since ceased to trouble polite society. The next two victims were French, the first bursting into flames in 1779, the second in 1782. Their stories appear in a variety of sources, including an essay on spontaneous combustion published by the French physician Pierre-Aimé Lair in 1800.

With Lair, however, the tone changes entirely. Gone is the pseudo-science that had once made the stories credible, and in its place is the moralizing tone that would soon characterize the great temperance movements of the nineteenth century. Lair fancied himself "un médecin moraliste," and he was hopeful that his horrific stories would discourage women from drinking. Four years later, in 1804, the English physician Thomas Trotter retold the same stories in the hope that they would encourage women to remain sober and set an example for men.

As for the victims, only one, the aging Countess Cornelia Zangari de Bandi, was "a lady of quality," and it was perhaps for this reason that her story attracted the most attention, both in England and on the Continent. It appears, among other places, in The Gentleman's Magazine in 1731 and then again in 1746, in the Transactions of the Royal Society for the years 1744 and 1745, in the Annual Register for the year 1763, and also in Lair's and Trotter's cases of spontaneous combustion. Dickens, too, mentions the countess in the preface to Bleak House, claiming that "the appearance beyond all rational doubt observed in that case, are the appearances observed in Mr Krook's case."

What also distinguishes the countess is that she alone was supposed to have been sober when she burst into flames, consistent, no doubt, with her status as "a lady of quality." Instead, she was supposed to have been exposed to alcohol while bathing in camphorated spirits of wine. The other victims were all supposed to have drunk heavily before bursting into flames, and were decid-edly inferior in social status to the men and women who had the means to subscribe to *The Gentleman's Magazine* and the like. The surgeon Bradford Wilmer thus described Mary Clues as being "of indifferent character, and much addicted to drinking" ever since her husband had died. In Caen, another "woman of the lower classes" was also rumored to have been "much addicted to strong liquors" before mysteriously burning to death. The French physi-cian Claude-Nicolas Le Cat claimed that Jean Millet's wife "got intoxicated every day"—that is, until she, too, conveniently burned to death one night, leaving Millet free to pursue the "pretty young girl" who had long since been running the household.

The known ages of the victims range from forty-five years to about eighty. Two, including Mary Clues, were fifty years old, while most, including the countess, were probably in their sixties. Only one of the victims, Mademoiselle Thuars of Caen, appears to have been a spinster, leaving two widows, and two women who were still married. The number of single or widowed women was probably much higher, if only because all of the women happened to be alone when they died. Lair finds another common thread: the victims were either very fat, as in the case of the widow Marie Jauffret of Aix-en-Provence, or very thin, as in the case of a French octogenarian. Too fat or too thin, all were ugly, old, and in the way.

The most curious detail is this: each of the victims managed to destroy herself without destroying any valuable possessions, let alone the house in which she perished. That is, in each instance a woman who had outlived her usefulness had exited quickly and quietly, leaving her belongings for someone else to retrieve the fol-lowing morning. In the case of the countess, the bed in which her body had smoldered was virtually untouched. In the case of Mary

Clues there was very little damage to nearby furniture. "I did not," the surgeon Bradford Wilmer reported, "observe that any thing was much burnt, except Mrs. Clues...." And the widow Jauffret managed to ignite a chair, but nothing else.

The question that inevitably arises is why these stories were credible, especially since cremation, even at the most intense temperatures, cannot entirely destroy bone. Moreover, a burning house or building cannot generate heat in excess of 1,500 degrees Fahrenheit; a body, by contrast, must be subjected to an initial blast of 2,200 degrees Fahrenheit in order to reduce tissue to ash. Even so, the fact that several physicians were prepared to believe in spontaneous combustion lent considerable credibility to these stories, as did the fact that the case histories were often presented before various learned or scientific societies. The stories also played on contemporary beliefs about spirits as a form of fire-water. In 1593, for example, a satirist wrote how "*Maudlen Moonface*, a merry gentlewoman of *Dublin*," drank "a glasseful, nose high, of *Aquavitæ*, the operation of which is no less monstrous than merveilous, for being drunke in a morning, it so warmeth the heart, as if the body were in a bath...."

At the same time, it is unlikely that stories singling out women who were old and in the way would have made much headway had they not also played to prejudices that were deeply rooted in the larger culture. These prejudices were already several centuries old, and had in an earlier era been directed against women who made a living as brewsters or alewives. From the early Tudor period, for instance, there is the poem "Elinor Rumming" by John Skelton. Elinor Rumming is a brewster "well worn in age," "her youth...far past." Her face is "bristléd with hair"; her nose drips continuously; her skin is "loose and slack"; her back is stooped; her hair is grey; her gums are toothless; her joints are knotted; and her legs are spindly. She is, in short, a witch—hence Skelton's claim that "the deveil and she be sib."

There is also the real-life example of Annis Dell. Dell was almost certainly a widow, and she, along with her son George, kept an inn. One day she quarreled with "a good country yeoman," who, having called her an "'old hag' or some such like name of reproof," died shortly thereafter. Dell was immediately suspected of having used witchcraft, and in 1606 she was hung along with her son.

The example of Annis Dell underscores the precarious status of post-menopausal women in early modern England. Widows were especially vulnerable, all the more so since they were free from the supervision that their husbands and fathers had once exercised. A widow, Eliza Haywood observed in 1750, "is frequently a Sovereign, and that in a very ample and absolute degree... she is free from many Restraints she was under in the Life-time of her Husband; and which, perhaps, in many Instances, obliged her to act in Opposition to her own Sentiments...." Naturally, a widow who took advantage of her newfound independence to indulge in vices forbidden to married women ran the very real risk of becoming the object of malicious gossip and lurid rumors.

There is a further dimension to the story, every bit as ugly as the first. It is not hard to see how there might have been an unconscious connection between the real fates of widows and witches in the sixteenth and seventeenth centuries and the imagined fates of women who were old and alone in the eighteenth century. That is, neighbors and relatives who might previously have denounced "poor melancholike women" as witches now took to spreading ugly rumors that defied all scientific explanation. Hence bodies that burned without so much as singeing nearby objects, and hence, too, fire so intense as to reduce bone to ash. Old and in the way, widows lived in a world no longer willing to care for them, and many would end up cast out as witches because their neighbors were as yet unwilling to acknowledge that the traditional bonds and obligations of charity had been irrevocably broken.

The witches of earlier generations collide with yet another twist in our story: the tidy way in which the victims managed to destroy themselves without doing any serious damage to the possessions that would now fall into someone else's hands. The denouement is so fantastic as to be supernatural, much as one might expect of witches; it also strongly smacks of greed, much as earlier charges of witchcraft effectively masked the desire of many families to dispossess post-menopausal women of their property. As it happens, none of the thirteen women who burst into flames were so destitute as to want for furniture or lodgings; under the circumstances, they were bound to arouse feelings of rapacity on the part of their heirs and survivors.

The fact that twelve of the thirteen women died in cities is also relevant. Witches, too, had been disproportionately culled from the growing urban centers of preindustrial Europe. It was in the cities that unwanted proximity turned neighbor against neighbor, especially when a neighbor happened to be poorly behaved and in failing health; at the same time, the tensions of adjusting to a crowded and squalid urban setting almost certainly fostered a venomous environment in which it became convenient for neighbors to denounce the tiresome old woman next door as a witch. London was no exception. A century or so later, in an environment that was substantially unchanged, neighbors whose accusations might once have sent an unwanted woman to the gallows might still take some comfort in believing that the tiresome woman next door had finally left them in peace and in possession of her worldly goods.

England hanged its last witch in 1685. In 1736, the year in which the most infamous of the gin acts was passed, witchcraft ceased to be a statutory offense, as was only right in a country in which sensible Protestants prided themselves on their contempt for superstition. The good and reasonable men who sat in Parliament were doubtless faintly embarrassed that their countrymen could ever have been so irrational as to persecute old and ill-tempered women as witches.

Less than a hundred years later, good and reasonable men and women would again wonder why their ancestors could ever have been so irrational as to believe that old and ill-tempered women could burst into flames for no good reason. It is perhaps not surprising that drunken women all but drop from the literature of the nineteenth century, consistent with the fact that Victorians worried far more about drunken men than they did about the incidental drunken woman. At the same time, the storytellers change. With Trotter, the physicians exit the stage and the novelists take their place. Between the publication of Charles Bockden Brown's *Wieland* in 1798 and Zola's *Docteur Pascal* in 1893, no fewer than nine fictional characters burst into flames; of these only one, in *Jacob Faithful*, was female. The other victims include, in chronological order, the narrator's father in *Wieland*; William the Testy in *Knickerbocker's History of New York*; a blacksmith in Gogol's *Dead Souls*; the sailor Miguel Saveda in Melville's

Redburn; Sir Polloxfen Tremens in William Edmondstoune Aytoun's story "Glenmutchkin"; and the "whiskey-sodden" and otherwise derelict Jimmy Flinn in Mark Twain's *Life on the Mississippi*. The list does not include the female cook in *Jane Eyre*, who was merely "in a frame of mind and body threatening spontaneous combustion."

But the most famous fictional victim was Mr. Krook of Dickens' *Bleak House*. Krook died as he had lived, which is to say alone and drunk, his hideous death having been "engendered in the corrupted humours of the vicious body itself...." By the time *Bleak House* appeared in serial form, in 1852, very few people were inclined to believe that anyone, no matter how disreputable, might burst into flames for no apparent reason. Dickens' most assiduous critic on this point was George Henry Lewes, an old friend and also George Eliot's lover; for his part, Dickens declined to put up a spirited defense, or so his halfhearted citations of the medical literature would suggest.

By now, too, people had long since ceased to worry about women who drank. The halcyon days of female intemperance were over, and polite society had at long last succeeded in imposing at least some of its habits on working-class women. The path to their moral improvement was sobriety, and their reward was the home. Here women ruled, but at the price of being barred from the public spaces and public houses that their men frequented. The campaign to make this happen was long and hard, and was part of a much larger movement to reform the morals of the working poor and make them live and play by the rules of their social superiors. The crusaders against gin and the people who drank it were among the movement's earliest leaders. What they wanted and why at first they failed are the subject of the second act of our tragicomedy.

Act II

IN WHICH Virtue *TRIUMPHS OVER* Prudence

CHAPTER FOUR
A Lesson in Political Arithmetic

If you but rightly understood,
The nature of these sots, you wou'd,
As soon be hang'd as undertake,
A reformation thus to make.
Reform their manners! make 'em live well!
You may as soon reform the devil.

ELIAS BOCKETT, 1730

IN 1725, THE YEAR WHEN PEOPLE first started to worry publicly about gin, Sir Robert Walpole was just forty-nine years old. He was already at the peak of his powers, having at his disposal a wife, a mistress, and, some said, the fisc itself. He had recently proven his worth when the South Sea Bubble collapsed in 1721, threatening thousands of investors with financial ruin and dozens more with political ruin. Among the latter were the king, his mistresses, and several of his ministers. Walpole himself had lost heavily in the scheme, buying high and selling low. This was as unusual as it was fortuitous, as it was the first and only time in a long and lucrative career that the taint of malfeasance did not attach to the person of Robert Walpole. The same could not be said of his colleagues, many of whom had almost certainly been bribed with blocks of stock in the South Sea Company. Two conveniently died during the ensuing furor, and one, John Aislabie, was offered up as a sacrificial lamb, in which capacity he was sent to the Tower of

London until the storm blew over. (Aislabie had been the nation's chief financial minister at the time of the crisis.) Everybody else, however, managed to avoid public scrutiny, thanks to the machinations of young Walpole. Walpole was duly rewarded with Aislabie's old job, and from this point forward he effectively ran the government in partnership with his brother-in-law, Charles "Turnip" Townshend. Townshend, who was by some accounts more interested in cultivating turnips than in running the government, was forced to resign in 1730, making Walpole, if only in the loosest sense of the word, England's first prime minister.

Wily, greedy, and pragmatic to a fault, Walpole managed to cling to power until 1742, amassing, with each passing year, a private fortune from public funds. He was, one of his many enemies later wrote, "More anxious to keep his power than to raise his frame," knowing that "whatever happened, he could be nothing greater than what he was; and, in order to remain in that situation, his great maxim in policy was to keep everything else as undisturbed as he could, to bear with some abuses rather than risk reformations...." Walpole's wish to maintain the status quo at all costs naturally put him on a collision course with the reformers within his own party, including the faction that wished to curtail sales of gin by imposing prohibitive taxes on it. These reformers offended on two levels: they actually wanted the government to do something, and they failed to appreciate the extent to which the government had come to rely on excises to finance past and current expenditures. The one failing was forgivable; the other was not.

Walpole favored excises for the simple reason that they were far more difficult to evade than customs duties. They had two additional advantages, both of them political: they fell disproportionately on urban workers and tradesmen, the vast majority of whom were effectively barred from voting in parliamentary elections, and they allowed the administration to keep down the land tax, thus ensuring the ongoing support of the landed interest that dominated both houses of Parliament. In 1732 Walpole refused to raise the land tax, even though it had just been reduced to its lowest level in twenty years; instead, he opted to reimpose the excise on salt. This particular excise, not surprisingly, fell disproportionately on the poor. The following year, in 1733, Walpole once again refused to raise the land tax, preferring instead to raid the Sinking Fund that he himself had created for the purpose of paying off the national debt.

The net effect of Walpole's fiscal policies was to transfer the burden of financing the government's past and current expenditures to urban manufacturers, merchants, and consumers in the form of excises. Excises, in turn, were to grow by leaps and bounds as the century wore on and the nation drifted in and out of war. Excises on gin would grow by more than 1,200 percent between 1700 and 1771. This was hardly surprising, given the fact that its drinkers consisted primarily of the urban poor, who, unable to vote in parliamentary elections, could virtually be taxed at will.

Nor did it help that the problems associated with gin were mostly urban problems, affecting the very groups who were on the outs with the current administration. Opposition to Walpole, both among Tories and dissident Whigs, was strongest in the nation's urban centers, where the ministry's policies were widely—and correctly—viewed as highhanded and oligarchic. This was especially true in the City of London, which under the City Elections Act of 1725 was forced to disenfranchise householders whose property was rated at less than £10 a year. The City Elections Act also greatly expanded the powers of the Court of

Sir Robert Walpole (1676–1745), de facto *prime minister of Great Britain, 1721 to 1742. According to Lord Chesterfield, "he laughed at and ridiculed all notions of public virtue," including, most notably, all attempts to tax gin out of existence. For Walpole, gin meant revenue for himself, for the government, and for the landowners who dominated both houses of Parliament. This portrait dates from 1740, by which time Walpole, always a* bon vivant, *had become so fat that his legs swelled. By courtesy of the National Portrait Gallery, London.*

Aldermen (whose twenty-five members were elected for life), giving it an effective veto over the actions of the more broadly based—and overwhelmingly Tory—Common Council. The beneficiaries of these restrictions were the City's great merchants and financiers, the very men whose loans helped keep Walpole and his administration afloat. The men who suffered the most under these policies were the City's tradesmen and small merchants, all the more so when the goods they manufactured or sold were subject to excises that the administration was prepared to raise rather than run the risk of alienating its landed allies in Parliament.

In the end, however, the Court of Aldermen proved to be far less compliant than Walpole had hoped, and by 1737 the balance had definitively tipped in favor of the opposition. Once this happened the City would at long last be in a position to play a leading role in the fight against gin. This was an important development because the City was the most organized and politically well-connected jurisdiction in the metropolis, certainly when compared to the hodgepodge and chaos that characterized local government in Westminster and East London. All of the City's representatives in Parliament also happened to be aldermen, thus ensuring that the agenda set by the Court of Aldermen could be pursued at both the national and local levels. It also helped that the City sent four representatives to the House of Commons, compared to just two each from the far more populous enclaves of Westminster and East London. Among the latter's representatives was Sir William Pulteney, elected in 1734 and reelected in 1741. Pulteney had been passed over for office in favor of the duke of Newcastle, and for this he never forgave Walpole. He quickly emerged as a leading member of the Whig opposition, but unlike his more zealous colleagues he was prepared to tolerate gin up to a point. Aside from Pulteney, however, very few of the men returned from either East London or Westminster could lay claim to the connections and influence enjoyed by the City's representatives in Parliament, with the result that the onus of representing the capital's interests in Parliament—including its worries over gin—fell on the jurisdiction with the lowest concentration of gin shops in the capital. In 1725 and 1726, however, the City was still reeling from the City Elections Act, and the opposition in the Court of Aldermen was as yet too weak to take on the problems associated with gin. The cause of reform was further hampered by the fact that it appealed to Walpole's most intractable foes, namely the tradesmen and small merchants of London.

Walpole's close management of the nation's finances meant that the ensuing battle would in many ways be one of numbers, with one side adding up revenues, and the other adding up losses to both the economy and the nation. These losses could be calculated in any number of ways, the most common approach being to demonstrate the extent to which gin cut into the supply of cheap labor by reducing fertility and contributing to infant mortality. These sorts of calculations were commonly known as political arithmetic, and were based to varying degrees on official or semi-official statistics.

Political arithmetic had its origins in the seventeenth century, at which time men such as John Graunt had scoured the parish registers of greater London, along with reports on navigation and trade, in a quest to prove that a growing population was a source of wealth because it kept down wages and with them the cost of English exports. This was, as we have already seen, a core tenet of mercantilism. The popularity of political arithmetic, in turn, accounts for why there were several attempts—most notably in 1725, 1735, 1736, and 1751—to count the number of gin-sellers in the capital; it also accounts for why the more mathematically minded of the reformers consulted parish registers in an attempt to prove that gin was the real reason why deaths consistently outnumbered births in the capital.

Reactionaries though they were, the reformers were nonetheless sufficiently men of the Enlightenment to make statistics—both economic and epidemiological—serve the cause of moral reform. Once they did so they became a force to be reckoned with. And once they found the right balance between the two their message would remain remarkably constant for the next twenty-five years, that is, from 1726, when the justices of Westminster and East London released their first statistical breakdown of gin shops in the capital, to 1751, when Henry Fielding published his famous *Enquiry into the Causes of the Late Increase of Robbers*.

The essential task facing the reformers in 1725, the year when they launched their first sustained campaign against gin, was to convince legislators that their proposals were in fact fiscally and economically sound. This approach was required because the government's policies toward gin had up to this time been dictated by the desire to tap into a new source of revenue while also providing landowners with a seemingly limitless market for their surplus grain. In order to convince Parliament that their program was the better one for creating prosperity at home and dominance abroad, the reformers had to prove that health itself was a source of wealth, if not for the working poor, then for the nation as a whole. This, along with the need to counter the strictly fiscal arguments that the administration could be relied on to use in any debate about an excisable commodity, helps explain why time and time again reformers focused on gin's potential to undermine trade by undermining the health, fertility, and productivity of the nation's working poor.

The first sustained attempt to restrict sales of gin dates from 1725. In February of that year the justices of Westminster ordered their constables to count and list by name and address all individuals selling gin and other spirits, whether licensed to do so or not. Not to be outdone, the justices of East London followed suit in October, and in combining their totals with those from Westminster they came up with 6,187 "houses & shops wherein geneva or other strong waters are publicly sold by retail." The number, while large, did not include individuals who sold gin "even in the streets and highways, some on bulks and stalls set up for that purpose, and others in wheelbarrows . . . and many more who sell privately in garrets, sellars, back-rooms and other places not publicly exposed to view."

The justices now had a number. Their next step was to use this number to best effect, toward which end they prepared a report detailing the extent to which the proliferation of gin-sellers posed a threat to the health and morals of the working poor. With this in mind, the justices drew particular attention to gin's deleterious effects on workers. The "constant use of Strong Waters, and particularly of Geneva," they warned, "never fails to produce an invincible aversion to Work and Labour," thereby depriving the nation of "great numbers of usefull hands, which would otherwise be imployed to the advantage of the public." Those who actually did work, the justices added, wasted their time and that of their employers by constantly sneaking off to the gin shops. Chandlers who sold gin, they went on to say, were the worst offenders, selling or even giving drams of gin to servants, "which one may reasonably suppose, must be paid for by the masters, either in price, Weight or measure of the Goods they are sent for. . . ."

The points made by the justices in 1726 were to be made again and again in the years that followed. They appeared almost verbatim in a new count commissioned by the justices of East London in 1735 and 1736, and were amplified without being altered in a variety of publications, including, most notably, Thomas Wilson's *Distilled Spirituous Liquors the Bane of the Nation*, published in 1736, and Henry Fielding's *Enquiry into the Causes of the Late Increase of Robbers*, published in 1751. The message did not change, but the statistics did, reflecting the reformers' growing sophistication in using political arithmetic to make their case.

Whether by accident or by design, the justices' initiative was complemented by the literary efforts of Daniel Defoe and Bernard Mandeville, both of whom chose the year 1725 to denounce gin. In a short satire appearing in *Applebee's Journal*, Defoe blasted gin as a fatal "Specifick to cure all the Maladies of Life," adding that there were more than five thousand "gin doctors . . . new set up, in and about this sober City . . . and . . . all or most of them have very good Practice." Mandeville's attack on gin appeared in his *Enquiry into the Causes of the Frequent Executions at Tyburn*. In it he blamed gin for the lack of fear shown by felons condemned to death; gin was, as we have already seen, easily procured both in prison and along the long route to the gallows at Tyburn. Neither writer, however, was a true believer, and their efforts, such as they were, were too thin and too insincere to invite comparison with the publishing frenzies that would occur when the Gin Acts of 1736 and 1751 were making their way through Parliament. In 1726, just one year after his attack on gin, Defoe would write a pamphlet on behalf of the London Company of Distillers, while Mandeville, true to the radical spirit of "Private Vices, Publick Benefits," was likewise capable of arguing out of both sides of his mouth, conceding that in the case of gin, "what seem'd irksome and calamitous to some, was delightful and often ravishing to others."

In January of 1726 the Royal College of Physicians also entered the fray, adding its considerable authority to a campaign designed to convince legislators and the public at large that health was a source of wealth. The petition itself was to fall on deaf ears, but it helped lay the groundwork for the first law ever passed against gin and the people who drank it. This was the Gin Act of 1729, and while the act itself was a failure, the campaign leading up to its passage was in many ways a dress rehearsal for the larger and more elegantly orchestrated campaigns of 1736 and 1751.

At least one of the College's members, George Cheyne, had already spoken out against gin. He was the author of *An Essay of Health and Long Life*, first published in 1724. The book was intended for a lay audience, and was dedicated to Sir Joseph Jekyll, who would later play a leading role in pushing the Gin Act of 1736 through Parliament. Cheyne himself was a reformed drunkard, and in his *Essay* he especially condemned strong liquors, linking their abuse to a wide variety of diseases and disorders, including "Gout, Stone, and Rheumatism, raging Fevers, Pleurisies, Small Pox, or Measles." By 1725, Cheyne's book was already in its fourth printing, and its popularity may have been one of the reasons why the College chose this particular moment to condemn the growing popularity of gin in the capital.

Unlike the justices, the physicians took their case directly to Parliament. The burden of presenting their petition fell on John

Freind, who at the time was the only physician with a seat in the House of Commons. Freind also happened to be a familiar face at court, having treated George II's children since 1724, and his wife since 1727. He was, however, a staunch Tory, as were most of his patients, and it was probably for this reason that the physicians' petition languished in committee, leaving no trace in the *Journals of the House of Commons*.

The physicians had, moreover, chosen the worst possible time to present their petition. The nation was for all intents and purposes at war with Spain, forcing Walpole to raid the Sinking Fund that he had set up just a few years earlier. Under the circumstances Walpole was in no mood to tamper with one of the Crown's most important sources of revenue, especially since a small portion of those revenues was by now being used for the construction of his new manor at Houghton Hall. The physicians' advice would prove far more welcome at the height of the War of Austrian Succession. Sailors, the College assured the Admiralty in 1740, might drink malt spirits "without any Detriment." In 1726, by contrast, the physicians reached an altogether different conclusion, arguing that gin was a source of disease and that it incapacitated "great numbers of both Sexes" for work; the physicians also warned that gin was "the cause of weak, feeble, and distempered Children, who must be, instead of an advantage and strength, a charge to their Country."

Whatever its merit, the physicians' petition was destined to languish in committee. The physicians had, however, established themselves as useful allies in the cause of moral reform, and their testimony would be eagerly sought as the Gin Acts of 1736, 1743, and 1751 made their way through Parliament. In the wake of their failure in 1726, the initiative shifted back to local magistrates, the more zealous of whom harassed gin-sellers as best they could. In October of 1728, it was reported that "Several of his Majesty's Justices of the Peace for the Liberty of Westminster, have order'd the Constables, Headboroughs, and other Peace Officers, to make due Enquiry into the Names and Number of Persons retailing Geneva, &c. together with the Names of all such Persons as are harbour'd in their Houses as Lodgers."

Sir John Gonson led this campaign in his capacity as the chairman of the Westminster bench of justices. Gonson was an ardent supporter of both the Societies for the Reformation of Manners and the Society for Promoting Christian Knowledge, and from 1728 on he put their agendas into action, instructing a succession of grand juries to suppress "Vice, Immorality and Profaneness." Among the vices that Gonson singled out was drunkenness, which, given the enormous popularity of alcohol at all levels of English society, had been a conspicuous failure in the Societies' past campaigns. Undeterred, he instructed the juries "to present all Bawdy-houses, Gaming-houses, disorderly Houses, and unlicensed Alehouses," adding that "Those Houses and Shops, where People frequently get drunk with *Geneva*, or other spirituous Liquors, are Indictable as disorderly Houses, whether they have or have not Licences." Gonson went on to single out gin, noting that:

Nothing is more Destructive either to the Health or Industry of the poorer Sort of People, on whose Labour and Strength the Support of the Community so much depends, than the immoderate Drinking of *Geneva*. It is common for a starving Sot, intoxicated with this or the like Liquors, to behold his Rags and Nakedness with a stupid Indolence, and either in senseless Laughter, or in low and insipid Jests, to banter all Prudence and Frugality, drowning his pinching Cares, and losing, with his Reason, all anxious Reflections on a Wife, or Children, perhaps crying for Bread in a horrid empty Home. In hot Tempers, it lets loose the Tongue to all the Indecencies and Rudeness of the most provoking Language, as well as the most hellish Oaths and Curses, and is frequently followed by Quarrels and Fightings, and sometimes has been the Cause of Murder. Besides all this, these Houses and Shops are the Receptacles of Thieves and Robbers, and often the Original of them too: For when a Wretch has spent and wasted that, which should support himself, and his Family, it is here, that they Associate and turn House-Breakers, and Street-Robbers, and so, by quick Progressions, at last make an Exit at the Gallows.

Even as Gonson was waging his campaign against gin, Parliament was quietly considering a bill designed to limit sales of it to a manageable number of licensed establishments. The bill received very little attention in the press as it was making its way through Parliament, and it is unclear who sponsored it, or why. The likeliest explanation is that it succeeded because it had the blessing of George II, who had succeeded George I in 1727. In October of 1728, Townshend relayed the new king's concern over "the frequent Robberies of late committed in the Streets of London, Westminster, and Parts adjacent," noting that the king himself had recommended "suppressing Night Houses, Geneva Shops, and other tipling Houses and Gaming Tables, &c." The new queen, Caroline of Ansbach, may also have lent her support to the bill, just as she would later lend her full support to the Gin Act of 1736.

In any event the Gin Act of 1729 appears to have encountered little resistance in Parliament, where its supporters, quite possibly as a fob to Walpole, pitched it as a way to raise additional revenues by increasing existing excises on spirits. These increases, they argued, would have the additional advantage of reducing "the great Mischiefs occasion'd among the meaner Sort of People, by the excessive drinking [of] spirituous Liquors, particularly of that call'd *Geneva* or *Gin*." The bill was reported out of committee on 14 April, and by May it had been passed by both houses. The London Company of Distillers asked only that its members be allowed to continue adding molasses to their product, and once the bill was passed the Company actually endorsed it, going so far as to commission "a Representation to be made Publick & Incerted in some Paper, to signify the Company's good inclination to Prevent the Excessive drinking of any Distilled Liquors to the Damage of the common People and likewise do declare the Fallacy that is commonly received of making use of any Ingredients in the Liquors to the Prejudice of the healths of the People." If their dealings with the Court of Aldermen are any guide, the Company's members seem to have welcomed the prospect of restricting the number of retail outlets in the capital, presumably in hopes of increasing their own share of the retail trade in gin. Once the bill was passed, however, the Company soon had cause to regret its ill-considered actions, and in a rearguard attempt to soften the act's clauses, its representatives approached the commissioners of excise, hoping to convince them that some of the new duties might prove "difficult to exploit."

The Company's representatives were referring to the new tax—at the rate of five shillings a gallon—on compound waters.

Compound waters were defined as any spirits that were flavored with additives, and the people who performed this procedure were known as compound distillers. Many of these compound distillers also acted as retailers, and so the new tax amounted to a tax on sales at the retail level. Because compound distillers greatly out-numbered wholesale distillers, the new tax did indeed prove "diffi-cult to exploit," mostly because the Excise Office lacked both the resources and manpower to collect it. Despite this obvious defect, the new tax took effect on 26 December. More immediately, as of 2 July, anyone who wished to retail distilled spirits was required to take out a license at the daunting rate of £20 a year. This particular clause was designed to limit retail sales of spirits to a small and manageable number of licensed establishments.

Almost nobody, however, bothered to take out a license, and this, combined with the impracticality of taxing sales at the retail level, doomed the new act from the very start. All told, only 453 licenses were purchased over the lifetime of the first gin act, and more than half of these were purchased in its first six months, that is, when retailers were still uncertain about the extent to which the new act would be enforced. Their fears were to prove groundless. In their haste to pass the bill, legislators had given little thought to its enforcement, which was sporadic at best. In April of 1730, for example, the owner of a coffeehouse on New Bond Street was convicted for selling spirits without a license, and he was sen-tenced to a month in the local house of correction; it is doubtful, however, that he would have been singled out in this fashion had he not also gone out of his way to insult the justice hearing his case. In August, excisemen seized some 250 gallons of untaxed spirits and fined their owners, but again, this was one of the few times when the act was vigorously enforced.

In the capital, the act was circumvented from its very inception. Just before it went into effect it was reported that compound distillers were "concerting in order to intoxicate the Mob at a cheap Rate," with one distiller writing "over his Door, *Parliament Brandy Sold here* (i.e. Distill'd Spirits) which he sells not much dearer than Gin us'd to be sold." Parliament brandy consisted of raw spirits that had not been compounded; as such they were technically exempt from the new duty on compound spirits. They were, according to Pulteney, as widely drunk as compound spirits had been in the past. In the short term, however, per capita consumption of spirits dropped, from about 1.3 gallons per annum in 1729 to just over one gallon in 1730; after that date, however, it rebounded, stabilizing at just over 1.2 gallons in 1731 and 1732. The drop, modest and fleeting though it was, was just enough for the distillers' allies in Parliament to argue that the act "had been a Discouragement to the distilling of Spirits from Corn in *Great Britain*, and therefore ought to be repealed...."

The motion for repeal was put forward by Sir John Barnard and Micajah Perry, both of whom represented the City of London in Parliament and in the Court of Aldermen. Both had been lobbied by the London Company of Distillers, in whose journals they are mentioned with thanks for "their Great Services done for the Company in Parliament." Barnard, a wine merchant by trade, had broken with the administration over the City Elections Act of 1725, which had given the Court of Aldermen a veto over the actions of the Common Council. An alderman for thirty years, he led the City's tradesmen and small merchants in opposing the financiers and great merchants whose loans helped keep the administration afloat. Perry was a tobacco merchant by trade, and along with Barnard had adamantly opposed the Excise Scheme that

Walpole proposed in 1732. But now, in March of 1733, Barnard and Perry joined with Walpole in a rare display of bipartisanship, adding their names to his and fourteen others in a report favoring repeal of the Gin Act of 1729. The other signatories included several of Walpole's closest friends and allies, among them Sir Charles Turner and Sir William Yonge. Even John Scrope, who in 1729 had favored placing an additional duty on malt "to discourage the pernicious use of Spirits," lent his name to the report, a further indication of just how broadly based its recommendations were.

The bill's timing was curious, coinciding as it did with Walpole's attempt to push his Excise Scheme through a reluctant Parliament. At the heart of the Excise Scheme was a plan to create bonded warehouses for storing imports, starting with tobacco and wine, before they were either sold or re-exported. The proposal was naturally a source of "great alarum to the clandestine dealers in wine and tobbacco" because it was designed to ensure that duties would in fact be paid in full. Walpole had already created bonded warehouses for processing and taxing imports of coffee, tea, and chocolate, and this newest proposal to add to the Excise Office's powers was naturally regarded with suspicion by importers—among them Barnard and Perry—who up to this time had enjoyed considerable success in evading customs duties. In the end Walpole was forced to abandon his Excise Scheme, making it, along with the Gin Act of 1729, one of the year's political casualties.

Repeal may very well have been a bargaining chip in the raucous debates and public demonstrations that greeted and ultimately doomed the Excise Scheme; at the very least it was one of the few initiatives in Parliament that was supported both by Walpole and his opponents in the City, allowing both parties to stage a brief show of unity at a time of political crisis. Walpole supported repeal because he had no wish to undermine an industry that provided him with revenue, and his opponents in the City supported it because in its own modest way it reduced the powers of the Excise Office by eliminating the tax on compound spirits. As such, repeal represented a small victory in the larger campaign to curb the growth of the Excise Office, and with it, Walpole's grip on the nation's finances.

In the meantime dangerous precedents had been established and valuable lessons had been learned. The most dangerous of these precedents would reappear in the Gin Act of 1733. It rolled back taxes on gin, but like its predecessor it sought to curtail sales by hawkers. Toward that end the new act relied on informers for its enforcement, offering them £5 for each conviction. It would neglect, however, to compensate informers when their victims were too poor or too stubborn to do so themselves, with the result that for three years almost nobody was prosecuted for selling gin without a license. In 1736, however, with the passage of a new and much tougher gin act, informers would be richly rewarded for prosecuting retailers caught selling gin without a license, and this time they took the bait, leading to a succession of riots that would further undermine the ministry's authority in the capital. By resorting to informers, the reformers repeated the mistakes made by their forerunners in the Societies for the Reformation of Manners, and in so doing they did enormous damage to their cause.

In that regard, then, lessons had not been learned. The reformers had, however, finally learned how to get Parliament's attention. And they did so primarily by cloaking their ideas in the mantle of political arithmetic, mastering, through trial and error, new and increasingly sophisticated ways to influence the nation's political agenda. Their ideology, far from being progressive or even remotely humanitarian, can be traced back to two seventeenth-century traditions, one puritan, the other mercantilist. What was new was the skill with which the enemies of gin merged and repackaged the two traditions, for in so doing they succeeded not only in appealing to the empiricism of a new age but also in laying the groundwork for a new type of advocacy in public life. This new type of advocacy was both irrational and seemingly rational at the same time: naturally it appealed to the emotions—as, ultimately, all forms of advocacy must—but it also relied on numbers, thus lending the imprimatur of scientific proof to what were in fact highly emotional claims. Political arithmetic had come of age, and its new masters had some very old-fashioned ideas when it came to gin and the people who drank it.

CHAPTER FIVE

A Whig and a Prig

O, J–k–l how immense thy Merit!
How vast those Patriots publick Spirit!
To strip the Poor of their chief Pleasure,
And Thousands leave to starve at Leasure!
  "The Funeral Procession of Madam Geneva," 29 September 1736

SIR JOSEPH JEKYLL, member of Parliament since 1697 and Master of the Rolls since 1717, was nearly eighty years old in 1736. In the evenings, while Walpole drank punch with his cronies and told dirty jokes, Jekyll played host to men bent on making the world a better place. The most earnest of these men belonged to the Society for Promoting Christian Knowledge, which had been founded in 1698 to "counteract the growth of vice and immorality" both at home and abroad. A man of regular habits, immense wealth, and conspicuous virtues, Jekyll was just the sort of man whom the Society wished to cultivate. He was, one of their members later recorded in his diary, "a very exact man in his family," so much so that the earl of Egmont accused him of having "left his next immediate heir... out of his will because he returned from his travels through France and not through Holland, as Sir Joseph had directed him." Jekyll rose promptly at 6:00 every morning, and at 7:50 A.M. he led his family in prayer. Then and only then did they eat breakfast. An hour before lunch he took a walk, followed by another constitutional later in the afternoon. Supper was at

Sir Joseph Jekyll (circa 1662–1738), champion of the Gin Act of 1736 and a major contributor to James Oglethorpe's plan to colonize Georgia. The portrait, by an unknown artist, lends credence to the claim that Jekyll "had a hatchet face and surly look." By courtesy of the National Portrait Gallery, London.

8:00, and at 9:50 he again led his family in prayer. At least some of his prayers were answered, for he lived a long life and died a very wealthy man, leaving, by one account, an estate valued at £100,000.

Toward the end of his long life Jekyll emerged as the natural leader of a Whig faction bent on moral reform; he probably also had allies among the party's "boy patriots," whose power had been growing steadily ever since Walpole had failed to carry the Excise Scheme of 1733. Young, ambitious, and impatient at Walpole's seemingly endless tenure, the boy patriots did everything in their power to weaken and embarrass the aging prime minister; not surprisingly, one of the easiest ways to do this was to attack the venality and corruption for which his administration was notorious. Unlike his younger colleagues, however, Jekyll could claim a certain degree of moral superiority, and with it, just enough political capital to expend in one great cause. Lord Hervey, who thoroughly despised Jekyll, thus remembered that "though no individual in the House ever spoke of him with esteem or respect, but rather with a degree of contempt and ridicule, yet, from his age, and the constant profession of having the public good at heart beyond any other point of view, he had worked himself into such a degree of credit with the accumulated body that he certainly spoke with more general weight, though with less particular approbation, than any other single man in that assembly...." The earl of Egmont was equally uncharitable in his reminiscences. Jekyll, he wrote, "had a hatchet face and surly look, always looking grave and speaking sententiously." The same image appears in a pamphlet published several years after Jekyll's death. In it Jekyll comes back to earth to bemoan the repeal of the gin act that he had shepherded through Parliament:

GUILLELM·CAROLINE·DE · BRANDEBOURG·ANSPACH
REINE DE LA · GRANDE BRETAGNE,
ET ELECTRICE · D'HANOVER.

Caroline of Ansbach (1683–1737), queen of England and wife of George II. Caroline distinguished herself as regent during George II's many absences from England, overseeing, among other things, both the passage and implementation of the Gin Act of 1736. By courtesy of the National Portrait Gallery, London.

His Face was like a Winter's Day
Clad in November's Frown;
And clay-cold was his shrivel'd Hand,
That held his tuck'd-up Gown.

Jekyll may not have had many friends, but the few he did have happened to be very important people. One of these was Lord Hardwicke, to whom he was related by marriage. As lord chancellor and lord chief justice, Hardwicke would play an active role in maintaining public order when the Gin Act of 1736 took effect. Jekyll's most important ally, however, was Queen Caroline, who acted as regent during George II's many absences from England. As regent she was responsible for enforcing the Gin Act of 1736 while George II was away in Germany. Her personal physician happened to be John Freind, who, it will be recalled, had presented the Royal College of Physicians' petition against strong liquors back in 1726. In Mother Gin, Jekyll and the queen found a common enemy. Jekyll believed that gin constituted a "growing *Evil* threatening his Country"; the queen, having witnessed "a great deal of Bestialities and Indecencies" in the streets of Westminster, had let it be known that she was "an hearty enemy to distilled and spirituous liquors."

In December of 1735, Jekyll was approached by Thomas Wilson, a minor bishop and an ardent member of the Society for Promoting Christian Knowledge. Wilson, always on the lookout for lucrative sinecures in the Church of England, was hoping that Jekyll would put in a good word for him with the queen, which he did. At the same time, Wilson discovered that the queen was determined to do something about gin. Shortly after this he was to be found confabulating with Stephen Hales, a close friend and

The R.R. Father in God Tho. Wilson S.T.P. Lord Bishop
of Sodor and Man Consecr: Jan. 16. 1697.

Thomas Wilson (1663–1755), bishop of Sodor and Man, member of the Society for Promoting Christian Knowledge, and author of Distilled Spirituous Liquors the Bane of the Nation. Like his patron Sir Joseph Jekyll, Wilson was a passionate supporter of James Oglethorpe's plan to colonize Georgia, toward which end he wrote an Essay towards an Instruction for the Indians. He also attempted to instruct his own parishioners by having select religious texts translated into Manx. By courtesy of the National Portrait Gallery, London.

author of *A Friendly Admonition to the Drinkers of Brandy, and other Distilled Spirituous Liquors*. Like Wilson, Hales was a member of the Society for Promoting Christian Knowledge.

One month later, in January of 1736, Wilson completed a draft of his own opus, *Distilled Spirituous Liquors the Bane of the Nation*, which he then circulated among members of the Society. He also pressed a copy on Jekyll, who "approved it in the Maine," desiring only "that its Moral Reflections might be kept to the last and not intermixt in the Body of the Treatise." Jekyll also agreed to contribute £20 from his vast fortune toward publishing a thousand copies of Wilson's book. The costs of the second printing were underwritten, in part, by Sir John Philips, who, like Wilson and Hales, was a member of the Society for Promoting Christian Knowledge. It was money well spent, for the book was to have an enormous, if fleeting, impact on public opinion. Much of the book's appeal lay in its exhaustive use of political arithmetic, complete with formulas for calculating just how much beer and gin might be manufactured from a bushel of grain. Long after his book had been published, Wilson would continue to press Jekyll for preferment in the church; Jekyll, however, was already at the limit of his influence, and was turned down flat when he approached Newcastle on the subject in 1736 and then again in 1737.

By 1736, it was clear that organizations such as the Society for Promoting Christian Knowledge could not possibly hope to reform the morals of the working poor on their own. This was especially true of the Societies for the Reformation of Manners, whose reliance on informers had done irreparable damage to their reputation in the capital. The time had come for the reformers to try their luck in Parliament, and it was in this capacity that they approached Sir Joseph Jekyll, asking him to draft a new and tougher gin act.

The bill that Jekyll proposed was, in the words of one legislator, "one of the boldest experiments in politics that was ever made in a free country." It seemed, the same skeptic added, "as if intended to try the submission and obedience of our people." This is exactly what Jekyll and Wilson had in mind, for they wanted nothing less than to effect a general reformation of manners among the lower classes. Their reasoning went something like this: drunkenness was a direct cause of other and far worse offenses, including robberies, assaults, and even murders. From this it followed that a reduction in drunkenness would inevitably lead to an overall reduction in lawlessness, and with it a greater willingness to obey both employers and magistrates. Both Jekyll and Wilson had an essentially conservative vision of the social order: the poor were the bulwark of the social order as long as they produced both children and wealth for the nation. But once they ceased to produce either, they were a threat to it, especially when they found the time and money to indulge in vices that might annoy or frighten their social superiors. Hard work at low wages, in turn, served two goals, one economic, the other social: it kept down the costs of English exports, and it kept the poor in their place.

Like other traditionalists, Wilson also disapproved of luxury and conspicuous consumption on the part of the working classes, who "Instead of being contented with *Beer* and *Ale* brewed at home of their own Malt...must now have *Tea* and *Spirits* at six times the Expence...." For his part Jekyll was genuinely shocked that the poor, given a choice, might choose gin over offal:

Why, the miserable Creatures, in such a Situation, rather than purchase the *coarser Joynts of Meat*, which the *Butchers* use to sell them at a very easy Rate . . . and I may add, good and wholesome in themselves too; I say, rather than do this, they will repair to the *Gin-Shops*, upon whose destructive Commodities they will freely lay out all they can rap or rend, till the *Parish Work-Houses* are fill'd with their poor, starv'd Families, *Trade* and *Country* depriv'd of their *Manufactures* and *Labours*, while the Butchers cannot so much as *give* these *Joynts* to the *common People*, to whom they us'd to sell 'em, but are forc'd, either to bury 'em, or to give 'em to the Dogs.

Far from being even remotely philanthropic, the agenda behind the Gin Act of 1736 harked back to a social vision whose heyday, like Jekyll's, had long since passed. It was mercantilist in an age when mercantilism was losing ground to increasingly complex ways of looking at wealth and its proper distribution. Like the mercantilists who had come before them, Jekyll and Wilson frowned on high wages and consumerism, all the more so when together they threatened to blur social distinctions between rich and poor. This put the two men on a collision course with the rising ethos of consumerism for all classes. It also marked them as curious reactionaries in a culture that was increasingly inclined to see man as a consuming animal.

The second campaign against Mother Gin began in 1734, just one year after the Gin Act of 1729 had been repealed and the much weaker Gin Act of 1733 had taken effect. This time the aldermen of London took the initiative, ordering their beadles to compile a list of everyone who happened to be selling distilled spirits without a license. Several beadles balked at this request, and it was perhaps for this reason that no further action was taken at this time. Then, in June of 1735, the bishops of Bristol and Gloucester, the earl of Scarborough, Sir Joseph Jekyll, and others, "having represented to the Queen the pernicious Consequences of the vending and drinking of such vast Quantities of *Geneva*," drafted a resolution "to suppress most of them in the County of *Middlesex*." The group cited gin's damaging effects on "the Health and Industry of labouring People, particularly of the Soldiery."

For several months, however, nothing happened, although it is clear that the London Company of Distillers sensed that an attack was imminent. In July the Company formed a standing committee to manage its affairs in Parliament and draft "Memorials or Proposals which they may think adviseable . . . to Shew that the Company are desirous to prevent the Irregularities complained of as practised in the houses of several persons distilling and selling strong waters. . . ." The wholesale distillers had, for once, guessed right. In October of 1735, the justices of both Westminster and East London ordered their constables, just as they had back in 1725, to list by name and address all individuals retailing spirits, whether licensed or not. The ensuing report proved to be the single most important document in the rhetorical skirmish leading up to the Gin Act of 1736. In January of 1736, the report's key findings were published in London's leading newspapers; at the same time, Thomas Wilson appended a copy of the report to *Distilled Spirituous Liquors the Bane of the Nation*, which with Jekyll's help was printed at the end of the month.

What contemporaries did not know—or simply chose to overlook—was that the justices' report merely expanded on the report they had released to an indifferent public ten years earlier. Aside from the fact that the totals differed—6,187 retailers in 1726 as opposed to 7,044 in 1736—the conclusions drawn from them were virtually identical, often matching each other word for word. The real difference was one of timing. When the justices first released their report back in 1726, Walpole had been at the peak of his power and could safely ignore initiatives that threatened one of the Crown's most important source of revenue; in 1736, when the same report was reissued with new numbers and a few new details, Walpole was politically vulnerable, making this an auspicious time to push for reforms that were as high-minded as they were impractical. The new number—7,044—was given added urgency by the fact that it was widely viewed as representing just the tip of the iceberg. Geographically it was limited to Westminster, Holborn, Finsbury, and the parishes surrounding the Tower of London, and even in these neighborhoods individuals who sold gin surreptitiously went uncounted, as did any retailers who happened to be friends or relatives of the constables who had conducted the census.

Having first released their results to the press, the justices now proceeded to petition Parliament for a new gin act. This occurred in February of 1736. They were aided in their efforts by London's leading newspapers, which chose this particular moment to run a series of highly sensational articles just as the bill was making its way through the House of Commons. These articles first appeared in February of 1736, that is, when the bill was still vulnerable to being tabled. "There is," one correspondent noted, "hardly a *Week*, I may say a *Day*, that we don't hear of some *Murder*, *Robbery*, *Fire*, or other dreadful *Mischief*, occasioned by People being intoxicated with these inflammatory Liquors." By way of example he cited the story of Mary Estwick, under whose care a toddler by the name of Mary Graves had burnt to death.

Then, toward the end of the month, an overweening publican in Southwark unwittingly provided newspaper editors with still more ammunition by posting the following sign just outside his gin shop:

Drunk for one pence.
Dead Drunk for twopence.
Clean Straw for nothing.

The enemies of gin immediately leapt on this slogan, which with just a dozen words succeeded in conjuring up both the squalor of the establishments that sold gin and the depravity of the people who drank it. Years later the slogan still had the power to mortify polite men and women. In 1751, Hogarth incorporated it into *Gin Lane*, and in 1757 Tobias Smollett quoted it when chronicling the horrors of the recent gin craze.

The press also did its part by drawing attention to gin's potentially fatal effects. This was in fact a complaint of long standing. In 1725, Defoe had claimed that in just one month more than a dozen people had died as a direct consequence of drinking gin. In April of 1728, *The London Evening-Post* had reported that "a Journeyman Pewterer, after drinking largely at a Brandy Shop...fell down the Stairs, broke his Arm, and tumbling into the Thames, was drowned." And in December of 1735, just before the newest campaign against gin began in earnest, *Read's Weekly Journal* reported that "the Wife of a Shoe-Blacker in Fetter-Lane, came home so much intoxicated with Geneva, that she fell on the Fire, and was burnt in so miserable a Manner, that she immediately died, and her Bowels came out."

Up until 1736, however, stories implicating gin in sudden and untimely deaths had been sporadic and quite rare; then, with the push for new legislation, they increased dramatically in both number and intensity, only to drop as soon as the bill passed both houses of Parliament. Nor did they reappear in significant numbers in the early 1740s, when per capita consumption of gin was much higher than it had been in 1736. In just one issue, in March of 1736, *Read's Weekly Journal* reported that "a young Woman died in Isleworth Church-Yard, occasioned by drinking of Geneva," and that four soldiers and a farmer's wife had also died in drinking bouts at about the same time. In the same week, one of the *Journal*'s rivals reported that "one William Thomas having drank nine Quarterns of Geneva in the Catharine Wheel-yard, St. James's, died immediately." Less than a month later, another of the *Journal*'s rivals reported that "two Glaziers and a bricklayer came to a shop in Field-lane, and drank Geneva by half a pint at a draught, till they had exhausted 9 quarts; the two former died in the shop, and the other did not survive them above half an hour." A coroner's inquest subsequently determined that the three men had died as a result of "excessive Drinking." And *The Norwich Mercury* did its part at the end of March by reporting that "four Men drank Gin to such an Excess, in an Alley near Holborn-Bridge, that three died the next Day, and the fourth, a Carpenter, with a large Family, lies so Ill that his Life is despaired of," adding that some of the spirits contained, "as we are credibly inform'd...Soap Lees, Urine, and Quick Lime...."

The bill proposed by Jekyll was controversial from the very start, and it had to be substantially amended before it had any chance of passing. Between its introduction in February of 1736 and its final passage in early May, its key provisions were changed several times in an attempt to make it more palatable to Walpole, who opposed the bill every step of the way. His majority in Parliament was by now too slim to allow him to alienate members who sold grain to the distillers; nor was he willing to sacrifice one of the Crown's most lucrative sources of revenue. He also knew that the act would be resisted, correctly predicting that it would not only fail to achieve its goals but would also lead to riots. It was his opposition to the bill that encouraged the wholesale distillers and sugar-planters to hope for a last-minute reprieve that never came. The bill was also stoutly opposed by Sir William Pulteney, who almost never sided with Walpole. Like Walpole, Pulteney warned that the bill in its present form could only "raise great Disaffection to the present Government, and ... produce such Riots and Tumults, as may endanger our present Establishment...." Events were to prove both men right.

The bill's primary goal was to reduce consumption, and to do this its framers sought to drive small gin-sellers out of business by forcing them to purchase licenses. The new fee, having originally been proposed at £40 a year, was almost immediately raised to £50, an amount that vastly exceeded what most retailers made in an entire year. At the same time, however, even the most sanguine of the moral reformers were loathe to destroy the wholesale distillers by forcing them, too, to purchase the new licenses. This meant that Parliament had to set some minimum quantity of spirits to be sold without a license, the trick being to agree on an amount acceptable to wholesalers but prohibitive to most retailers. Representatives from the City naturally wanted to ensure that wholesale distillers who lived and worked in the capital would still find a market for their product, and with this in mind they held out for the lowest possible minimum. Richard Lockwood, who represented Worcester but earned his living in London, wanted none at all, while Alderman Micajah Perry, who had intervened on behalf of the London Company of Distillers back in 1733, wanted just one gallon, as did Sir John Cotton, a known Jacobite sympathizer, and Charles Calvert, baron of Baltimore. For his part Jekyll wanted a minimum of five gallons, as did the Tory Thomas Gore and the former Tory Thomas Winnington, who, unlike Jekyll, had a sense of humor and got along with Walpole. Once the bill was in committee, Jekyll, at the urging of the physician Charles Cotes, was prepared to compromise, dropping his initial bid from five gallons to three. Walpole held out for a minimum of two gallons, and after much wrangling, prevailed. A final agreement, however, was not reached until the first week in April, after which Walpole attempted to soften the bill's other provisions. It was at this time, too, that the sugar-planters and their allies made a last-ditch appeal to Parliament to exempt rum from the pending act. Both Walpole and the sugar-planters failed, and early in May the lords passed the bill without amendment. Jekyll and the moral reformers had won a stunning victory at the expense of a weakened ministry and a disorganized industry.

Only four groups had a direct stake in opposing the bill. These were the compound distillers, the small gin-sellers, the wholesale distillers (as represented by the London Company of Distillers), and the sugar-planters, whose exports of molasses and rum were now at risk. The first two had neither the resources nor the social standing to lobby Parliament, leaving the onus of defending the entire British distillery to the wholesale distillers. The wholesale distillers, in turn, were perfectly prepared to sacrifice their lesser brethren, and may even have hoped to profit at their expense by moving into the retail end of the trade. A letter published in *The London Daily Post* in October of 1736 implies as much. It promised the wholesale distillers increased profits because gin could now only be sold in large quantities; at the same time it dismissed "your little peddling Retailers" as people who lived "from Hand to Mouth." The wholesale distillers, in turn, were abandoned by the sugar-planters, who asked only that rum be exempted from any restrictions. By defining their respective interests in the narrowest terms possible, the wholesale distillers and sugar-planters effectively yielded the high ground to Jekyll and his allies, who had consistently maintained that "the interest of every particular man must give way to the general interest; and where the preservation of the society was so essentially concerned, the prejudice of some few particular persons was not to be regarded." It was a successful argument for the simple reason that their opponents failed to make a coherent case for protecting an industry that was still far from respectable.

The London Company of Distillers did not, however, fail for lack of trying. On several occasions it commissioned hacks to write on its behalf. One of these hacks was a Mr. Crawford, who was probably responsible for a series of uninspired broadsheets appearing early in 1736. The Company also spent considerable sums lobbying members of Parliament, so much so that in April of 1736 its governing body was forced to forgo the purchase of two hundred shares in the South Sea Company "by reason of the great Sums which the Company have already Expended at and are like further to Expend in the Managing their Affairs now depending in Parliament." By July the Company had spent upwards of £200 in Parliament, both on solicitors and on copies of tracts to be delivered to individual legislators. It was money poorly spent. In the end, the Company succeeded only in delaying the start-date of the act by two months; it was also the recipient of two other concessions, both of them token. The minimum quantity of distilled spirits that could be sold without a license was, as we have already seen, reduced from five to two gallons, and ruined distillers would be allowed to enter trades from which they might otherwise have been barred by gild restrictions. This last concession, it was noted with some bitterness in their journals, was "not like to be of any particular Service" to the Company's older members.

Even after the act had passed both houses of Parliament, the wholesale distillers as a group still failed to appreciate just how serious the threat to their industry was. Over the next several months they fought a rearguard battle against the new law, confident that it would never actually be implemented. In July, for example, it was reported that they had, "since the Rising of Parliament, applied to some in the Administration, that some Alterations may be made in their Favour next Session of the said Act, and having Hopes thereof, are for keeping up their Working, Stills, Houses, &c." They continued to be hopeful just two weeks before the new act took effect, at which time *The London Daily Post* reported that several distillers were prepared "to wait the Issue of the next Sessions of Parliament, thinking the Gin Act will be either repealed or amended." Three weeks later, their livelihood now virtually proscribed, the Company still persisted in its folly, hoping against hope that the new act would be amended by Parliament once its consequences were fully appreciated. The Company had badly miscalculated. It was only after resistance to the Gin Act of 1736 became widespread that the administration would in fact intervene, not to repeal the act, but rather to close its many loopholes. This it did in 1737 and then again in 1738.

The Company's lobbying efforts were further undermined by its failure to join forces with the West Indian sugar-planters. The planters were directly affected by the bill because it proposed placing restrictions on the sales of all distilled spirits, including rum. Their lobby was by far the most powerful of the colonial lobbies, and it was perhaps for this reason that they felt that rum would somehow be spared. The planters may even have welcomed the bill in the beginning, seeing an opportunity to increase their exports at a time when French and Spanish rivals were underselling them. In any event, they asked only that rum be exempted from any restrictions on spirits, ostensibly because the people who drank rum were wealthier and better behaved than the rabble who drank gin.

Because of their influence and perhaps because so many members of Parliament were themselves inveterate punch-drinkers, the sugar-planters had reason to hope that rum would be exempted from the act. But like the London Company of Distillers, they completely misread the mood of Parliament. Their petition, presented on 6 April, went unheeded. Two supporting petitions, one from Bristol's Society of Merchant Adventurers, the other from Liverpool's seafaring merchants, also died in committee. Stunned, the planters then appealed to the influential readers of *The Daily Gazetteer*. At the time the newspaper received generous subsidies from the ministry, making it the most logical place to publish last-minute appeals to Walpole and his inner circle. There the planters published a succession of letters, starting in June and ending only after the Gin Act of 1736 had taken effect. The London Company of Distillers and the sugar-planters had both badly overestimated their position, believing up to the last minute that Walpole could and would rescue them.

In its final form, the Gin Act of 1736 required publicans to purchase licenses for selling gin and all other spirits in quantities less than two gallons. At £50, the fee amounted to a virtual prohibition on retail sales, the idea being to limit these to the few establishments whose owners could afford the new rate and whose customers could afford the costs that would inevitably be passed on to them. Toward the same end the act specifically forbade the hawking of gin and all other spirits about the streets, and instead limited the trade to licensed establishments only. It also imposed a prohibitive tax of twenty shillings a gallon on all retail sales of spirits. By themselves these clauses merely represented a newer and tougher version of the failed Gin Act of 1729, which had taxed retail sales at the rate of five shillings a gallon while also requiring publicans to take out a license at the rate of £20 a year.

Like the Gin Act of 1733, the Gin Act of 1736 relied on paid informers for its enforcement. Informers served an important function at a time when both the burden and cost of prosecution fell on private individuals, and with the proper rewards they could be relied on to detect and denounce victimless crimes at a time when municipalities were still without police forces of their own. The Societies for the Reformation of Manners had employed them in this capacity over the past several decades, and more recently, when the Gin Act of 1729 was replaced with the Gin Act of 1733, informers had been given carte blanche to prosecute men and women who continued to hawk gin without a license. Few, however, had taken the bait, if only because the Gin Act of 1733 made no provision for compensating them when their victims were too poor or too angry to do so themselves. The same flawed clause was carried forward into the Gin Act of 1736, with one important difference: the new act also allowed informers to denounce established publicans to the commissioners of excise, where their odds of collecting rewards were much better. This did the trick, so much so that just two weeks after the act took effect there were already "upwards of twenty Informers about Town, who make it their sole Business to give Informations against Persons who presume to sell spirituous Liquors...."

Despite its misgivings, the ministry took every possible step to prevent riots as the start-date for the new act approached. It did so not out of any particular enthusiasm for the new act, but rather out of fear that any riots against the government might easily be co-opted by Jacobite sympathizers. This is exactly what had occurred earlier in the year when riots against Irish laborers had very nearly become "a generall disorder." At the time the government had been caught off guard, and this time it was determined not to repeat past mistakes. Its options, however, were very limited. For one thing, it could not rely on local justices to keep the peace. Eighteenth-century justices were unpaid, and to the extent that they had roots in their own communities they were for the most part reluctant to enforce foolish and manifestly unpopular laws. Lord Hardwicke, in his capacity as lord chief justice, met with only limited success when he called on local justices to be especially vigilant as the start-date for the new act approached. One in particular, a justice by the name of Mitchell, "Seem'd very cool, of giving any Assistance in the Affair, Saying 'twas much better in his Opinion to take no Notice at all, by reason it might put outragious People in Mind of doing Mischief...." The one notable exception among the metropolitan justices was Colonel Thomas De Veil, who used the occasion to curry favor in Whitehall. "I will," he assured the ministry, "be watchfull at this Criticall time in which, and upon all other Occasions, the Government may rest Secure that they have in me a trusty and indefatigable Servant...."

Fearing the worst, the ministry took the extraordinary step of calling out the army. The order came on 28 September, just two days before the act was to take effect. Walpole's spies had intercepted four letters showing that publicans in the capital were conspiring to incite riots against the act by providing free gin to all comers. Armed with this information, Walpole easily prevailed on the queen, who was acting as regent at the time, to deploy troops at key positions in the capital. These included her residences at Kensington Palace and Somerset House, the government offices at Whitehall, and Jekyll's office on Chancery Lane, along with Covent Garden and Hyde Park. Jekyll, who was widely and correctly blamed for the new act, had the most to fear. He had already received several threatening letters, and on the night before the act took effect sixty foot soldiers had to be dispatched to Chancery Lane in order to disperse the mob that had gathered there. After that and for the next several days, guards, their bayonets fixed, remained posted just outside the side entrance to Jekyll's office, the main entrance having already been bolted shut. Newcastle, a born survivor, wisely decided to abandon the prime minister and the capital at this crucial juncture, ostensibly to oversee local elections in Chichester. Having left for a "short Stay in the Country," he hastened to assure Walpole that he had taken "Care to have constant Accounts sent me of all that passed, That if there had been the least Occasion, I might have returned on a Minute's Warning."

On the day before the new act was to take effect, hundreds and probably thousands of people assembled "at the Gin-shops, Distillers, and Publick-houses about the Town, and in the Suburbs" and got extremely drunk on gin; they did not, however, cause any disturbances aside from occasionally insulting passersby. The following morning several of the revelers "lay in the Streets dead drunk, with their taking Leave of that Liquor." Many of these gatherings took the form of mock wakes to mark the passing of Mother Gin. In one, staged just after the new act had taken effect, "several People made themselves very merry on the Death of Madam *Gin*, and some of both Sexes got soundly drunk at her Funeral, for which the Mob made a formal Procession with Torches, but committed no Outrages." Mock funerals were also staged in Bristol and even in Bath, much to the amusement of the political hacks whom Walpole paid to publish *The Daily Gazetteer.*

The Funeral Procession of Madam Geneva. *The print, which dates from 1736, was reissued to celebrate the passage of the Gin Act of 1751. While the distillers, dressed in white aprons, consist entirely of men, their customers are mostly women. Drunk on gin, the women in the foreground are reduced to begging and fighting. In the meantime their children starve, much to the alarm of the ratepayers who will now be called on to support them. By courtesy of the Guildhall Library, London.*

The Exit of Mother Gin in Bristol, has been enough bewail'd by the Retailers and Drinkers of it; many of the latter, willing to have their Fill, and to take the last Farewell in a respectful Manner of their beloved Dame, have not scrupled to pawn and sell their very Cloaths, as the last Devoir they can pay to her Memory. It was observ'd, Monday, Tuesday and Wednesday, that several Retailers Shops were well crowded, some tippling on the Spot, while others were carrying it off from a Pint to a Gallon, and one of those Shops

The Lamentable Fall of Madam Geneva. *This print, dating from 1736, shows a street clogged with hawkers and paupers. To the left, the brewers rejoice, hopeful that the Gin Act of 1736 will pick up their business. To the right, the vintners also rejoice. At bottom left a woman vomits, having drunk gin under the guise of "A Cure for the Cholick." By courtesy of the British Museum, London.*

had such a good Trade, that it put every Cask they had upon the Stoop; and the Owner with sorrowful Sighs said, *Is not this a barbarous and cruel Thing, that I must not be permitted to sell them again?* And pronounc'd a heavy Woe, on the Instruments of their drooping. Such has been the Lamentation, that on Wednesday Night her funeral Obsequies was perform'd with Formality in several Parishes, and some of the Votaries appeared in ragged Cloaths, some without Gowns, and others with one Stocking; but among them all, we don't hear of any that have carried their Grief so far, as to hang or drown themselves, rather chusing the drinking Part to finish their Sorrow; and accordingly a few old Women are pretty near tipping off the Perch, by sipping too large a Draught.

In the capital, at least, the wakes for Mother Gin were organized and financed by aggrieved publicans in hopes of inciting riots against the new act. Their subversive intent was not wasted on Walpole's spies, whose reports had prompted the queen to deploy troops in the capital. Nor was their intent wasted on local authorities. When, for example, Mother Gin lay in state at a distiller's shop on Swallow Street, a neighboring justice, fearful of "the ill Consequences from such a Funeral," "took the Undertaker, his Men, and all the Mourners into Custody." Local authorities were also quick to apprehend "a few rascally Fellows" who upon getting drunk in Newgate Street "cry'd out, *No Gin, no King.*"

All told, the government had deployed well over five hundred troops. It was an impressive and effective show of force, and its success was a source of considerable relief to Walpole and his inner circle. Newcastle returned to London just in time to take some of the credit for Walpole's hard work, remarking with unwarranted pride how a vigilant government had forestalled riots in the capital. By the fourth of October, less than a week into the new act, the troops posted outside Jekyll's office on Chancery Lane were discharged. "All remains very quiet," *The London Daily Post* reported, "there not being the least Disturbance, on Account of Mother *Gin*." The government had, for the moment, prevailed.

Having succeeded in avoiding any civil unrest in the first few weeks of the act, Walpole wanted nothing more than to let it lapse. The fact that virtually no one in the capital actually complied with the act doubtless amused him to no end: Jekyll now looked like an old fool and the Crown continued to profit from wholesale sales of distilled spirits, which suffered only a temporary setback in the act's early years. Its most important clause, requiring publicans to purchase a license to sell distilled spirits, was almost universally ignored. As already noted, the new licensing fee amounted to a virtual prohibition on retail sales, and naturally only the largest and most respectable public houses could possibly afford it. Two of these, Amos Wenman's Punch House on London Bridge and the London Punch House of Ludgate Hill, immediately took out licenses, but only because eight excisemen had been posted at each establishment "to prevent their acting contrary to the Tenour" of the new act. Indeed, only twenty licenses, each good for only one year, were ever purchased over the lifetime of the act, meaning that the vast majority of the nation's publicans were breaking the law every time they sold distilled spirits.

And break it they did. Some publicans made little or no attempt to conceal the fact that they were still selling gin, while others either sold substitutes or simply continued to sell gin under new and often defiant names. Less than one week after the act had taken effect it was reported that "tho' the Common People are deprived of *Gin*, there are various Drams invented and sold at the

Gin Shops, in lieu thereof...." These included a variety of hasty wines concocted from berries and other fruits, in addition to spirits sold under such fanciful names as "sangree," "tow-row," "cuckold's comfort," "Parliament gin," "Bob," "makeshift," "the last shift," "the ladies' delight," "the baulk," and "King Theodore of Corsica."

Distilled spirits also continued to be sold by apothecaries, who in the first two weeks of the act took shameless advantage of a loophole allowing them, along with physicians, surgeons, and chemists, to continue dispensing liquors for the treatment of medical complaints. Not surprisingly, these complaints increased exponentially just after the new act took effect, with the result that apothecaries were mobbed by customers demanding "Gripe and Cholick Water, &c." Other retailers quickly followed suit. One, described only as "A certain Person near St. James's-Market," added red dye to a bottle of gin, and, tongue in cheek, prescribed "two or three Spoonfuls...four or five Times a Day, or as often as the Fit takes you." The London Company of Distillers naturally received a sympathetic hearing when they reported these abuses to the commissioners of excise, who quickly ruled that apothecaries could not sell distilled spirits under "the Pretence of Medicine, Cordials, and such." It was at this point that the Society of Apothecaries also intervened, asking for a list of all members who had violated the act.

Having prevailed in Parliament, Jekyll and his coterie were now anxious to prove that they had in fact succeeded in reforming the morals of the working poor. This, however, proved considerably more difficult than taking advantage of a weakened administration and a disorganized industry. Just two weeks after the new act became law, soldiers posted to the Tower of London were supposedly new men, so "generally amended in their Conduct; that whereas there us'd to be frequent Court martials held (sometimes two in a Week) for the Trial of Offences generally committed from the miserable Effects of that pernicious Liquor, there had not been Occasion for above this Fortnight past . . . to appoint any Court Martial." At the same time it was reported that the "lower Sort of People" had already regained "their Reason and Strength," and that "many Houses of Debauchery are shut up in the Hundreds . . . the Spirit of Rioting ceases, and Slothfulness is observ'd to vanish by Degrees." These happy effects, however, were short-lived. As early as April of 1737, gin was again being sold "in all the Towns round London as much as ever," while in October of the same year it was reported that "*Gin is as much sold as ever, it being to be had almost every where.*"

Because the act pursued an agenda of blatant social control, it had the unintended consequence of transforming an unthinking indulgence into a conscious act of political protest against an already unpopular government. This sudden transformation almost certainly broadened gin's appeal, thus contributing to the sharp and almost willful increase in consumption that occurred shortly after the act took effect. Most importantly, because the act relied on informers for its enforcement, it was doomed from the very start. Their activities naturally sparked riots all across London, and since the ministry lived in mortal terror of disorder, it was forced—in 1737 and then again in 1738—to strengthen rather than scuttle the act. It was only in 1739, when the nation was at war with Spain, that the ministry could at long last do like everyone else and simply ignore the act.

In 1736, however, virtue had triumphed over prudence, and because of this the ministry would for the next several years fight a failed rearguard action as it attempted to restore order in the capital. The anger of the people was in many ways misplaced—Walpole, after all, had opposed the bill all along—but because of their spirited resistance the act continued to be a source of acute embarrassment to the ministry even after the death of Jekyll in 1738. These events played into the hands of Walpole's opponents; not surprisingly, the riots and general disorder that the act provoked would for several years figure prominently in leading opposition newspapers, most notably in *The London Evening-Post*. For their part the editors of the pro-ministerial *Daily Gazetteer* increasingly chose to ignore or gloss over the same events, and instead ran stories set as far away from London as possible.

In the end, the Gin Act of 1736 was as ill-conceived as it was out of touch with the people whom it sought to control. It owed its existence to a small and very determined group of moral reformers, and owed its enactment to the naked ambition of dissidents within the party. It was, in a quote attributed to Lord Bath, "well intended, but...dictated by Anger, and ratified by Zeal; and, therefore,...too violent to be executed." Like Jekyll and Wilson, many of its supporters were associated with a variety of other worthy causes, the net effect of which was to increase their moral stature relative to that of a ministry whose corruption and venality were notorious. By the same token, the removal of key players, starting with the death of Queen Caroline in 1737, would seriously undermine their efforts. Jekyll died one year later, by which time the act that he had shepherded through Parliament was all but a dead letter. Of the original core group of moral reformers only Thomas Wilson and Stephen Hales would survive to play a key role in the next campaign against Mother Gin. In the meantime the enemies of gin had succeeded only in sewing the seeds of mistrust and suspicion in neighborhoods all across London. The reign of the informers had begun.

CHAPTER SIX

Enter the Informers

> *...the practice of drinking was become so general among the common people, that it certainly required great skill and caution to have eradicated it, which this act was so far from doing, that it really heightened the evil by the addition of many others, as dangerous and detestable; for on the one hand, it let loose a crew of desperate and wicked people who turn'd informers merely for bread; and on the other, it exposed numbers of unhappy people, who before the selling of spirituous liquors by retail became a crime, had got a livelihood thereby, to be distressed, beggared, and sent to prison.*
>
> *Memoirs of the Life and Times, of Sir Thomas Deveil, Knight*, 1748

IN THE EIGHTEENTH CENTURY, distilled spirits were still widely used as a cure-all, so much so that the Gin Act of 1736 placed no prohibitions on spirits used by physicians, apothecaries, surgeons, or chemists "in the preparation or making up of medicines for sick, lame, or distempered persons." Knowing this, informers would approach kindhearted publicans and ask for gin on behalf of a loved one, claiming that he or she was ill. This gin could then be used as evidence against the person who had sold it. The most audacious of these frauds was perpetrated by a farrier turned informer, who in April of 1737 bought a dram of gin "under Pretence of a Horse's being ill."

The more common ploy, however, was for an informer to ask for gin on behalf of a bedridden wife, accompanying each such request with a conspicuous display of uxorious solicitude. This is exactly what a man known only as Michael did in August of 1737. Michael was a peddler, and after drinking several cups of liquor, quite possibly gin, it occurred to him that he could make a great deal more money as an informer than he ever could as a peddler. And so he approached Mrs. Howe, a publican in Westminster, and asked for a dram of gin, claiming that his wife was sick. Moved by his story, Mrs. Howe foolishly filled a bottle with gin and sold it to him. It was then, bottle in hand, that Michael made his big mistake. According to an account published in both *The London Evening-Post* and *Read's Weekly Journal*, he "told three or four of his acquaintance . . . of his design, and let them see the liquor; they desired him to let them taste it, which he did; some of them amused him whilst the others drank it up, and one of them piss'd about the same quantity in the bottle and return'd it to him. . . . " None the wiser, Michael took the vial to a justice of the peace, who as luck would have it insisted on tasting its contents before passing judgment.

A few months later, in Bristol, another would-be informer approached a publican, again claiming that his wife was sick and required gin. This time, however, the publican was wary, and sold him a bottle filled with vinegar. Once again the presiding magistrate insisted on tasting the bottle's contents before passing judgment. The judgment, predictably enough, went against the plaintiff, who was sentenced to sit in the town's stocks. While he languished there, a mob "brought a Pitch-Kettle, pitch'd him all over, and afterwards roll'd him in Feathers, by which Means he was made a most Grotesque Figure."

Over the lifetime of the Gin Act of 1736, at least four informers, including one woman, were beaten to death by angry mobs; dozens more very nearly lost their lives; and countless others were subjected to what one source blandly referred to as "the rough Discipline of the Rabble." Bad things happened to informers because they made it impossible for ordinary men and women to trust each other, and when this happened the community itself was at risk. And because informers targeted gin and the places where it was sold, they threatened the one place where working men and women were able to meet, share a drink, and perhaps even find a job in hard times. Above all, informers threatened the very notion of hospitality, and with it the lavish displays of generosity that cemented friendships, tided people over in hard times, and helped make bearable the stark inequalities in status and income that existed side by side in eighteenth-century London.

If the risks associated with informing were enormous, so, too, were the rewards. Consider the options of a young woman newly arrived in London in 1737 or 1738. She could work for a year as a maid and earn £5 in addition to receiving room and board, or she could inform against just one gin-seller, and upon securing a conviction collect a reward of £5. There were two ways to make money, one hard, the other easy, and many people naturally chose the latter. Most did so only once, collecting their reward and then attempting to hide as best they could. A few, it appears, acted out of spite, but they were in a distinct minority. One of these was a journeyman shoemaker who in December of 1737 was ostracized by his fellow journeymen for "having given an Information to a Magistrate." In his defense he "own'd the Charge to be true, but insisting that it was done merely in Revenge to an Injury done his Wife, rather than for the sake of Reward, he therefore hop'd they would excuse it, and he would never be guilty of the like again."

But again, most informers acted out of nothing more than simple greed, and it was for this reason that there had been so few prosecutions under the Gin Act of 1733. Its primary goal was to drive small gin-sellers out of business, and to do this it required them to take out a license at the prohibitive rate of £20 a year. Those who refused to do so and continued to sell gin faced two stark choices: spend one to three months at hard labor in the local house of correction, or pay a fine of £10, with £5 going to the informer or informers who had prosecuted them, and £5 to the local overseer of the poor. The problem, as we have already seen, was that the Gin Act of 1733 failed to compensate informers when their victims were too poor to do so themselves. And since most of the people who hawked gin as a sideline did so because they were poor, there was little point in prosecuting them.

The same fine of £10 was carried forward into the Gin Act of 1736, and this time those who refused to pay it were to be sentenced to two months' hard labor at the local house of correction. (In the past, justices had enjoyed some discretion in sentencing offenders; this discretion was now removed, presumably because justices had been too lenient in the past.) As in 1733, these clauses were only supposed to apply to individuals who retailed gin in public places, and not to individuals who sold it out of fixed establishments. Individuals in the latter category fell under the jurisdiction of the commissioners of excise, and were subject to a fine of up to £100 for each violation. In practice, however, the distinction was frequently blurred, with the result that established retailers who should have been tried before the commissioners of excise were often tried by one or more justices of the peace. Unlike the petty hawkers targeted by the Gin Act of 1733, most retailers in this class had the means to pay £10 when caught selling gin without a license, with two predictable results: informers now had sufficient incentive to go after larger retailers, and per capita consumption momentarily declined as nervous retailers curtailed their operations.

In balance, however, the Gin Act of 1736 failed to achieve its objectives. Per capita consumption of gin dropped only temporarily, in large part because the act provided no financial incentive for prosecuting the thousands of poor people who hawked cheap spirits in public places. At the same time, prosecutions of middle-class retailers were sufficiently numerous to provoke a backlash against informers and the various excisemen and constables who assisted them. The resulting attacks were a source of growing concern to the ministry.

Parliament responded by enacting two supplemental gin acts, the first in 1737 and the second in 1738. The two acts specifically targeted "persons of little or no substance," toward which end they authorized the commissioners of excise to pay informers £5 when convicted retailers refused to do so themselves. The same retailers were now to be whipped before being discharged from the local house of correction, although this particular clause, apart from attracting sporadic attention in the press, appears to have had no effect whatsoever in deterring hawkers. The Gin Act of 1738 also made it a felony to attack an informer, the punishment for which was seven years' exile in America.

The Gin Act of 1737 and the addendum made to it the following year succeeded in attracting informers without, however, dampening sales of gin. By August of 1737, 127 petty hawkers had been convicted and incarcerated in greater London; two months later the number had jumped to 432, with an additional 83 individuals avoiding prison by paying £10 each. Prosecutions peaked in 1738, by which time "about 12,000 Persons in all" had reportedly been tried and convicted in and around the capital. Of these, 4,896 individuals are supposed to have been convicted by the commissioners of excise (the commissioners' own records list only about 900 convictions for the same period of time, with a total of 1,642 over the lifetime of the Gin Act of 1736); another 3,000 or so had reportedly paid £10, leaving approximately 4,000 individuals who were convicted and sent to prison by local justices of the peace. After 1738, however, prosecutions by informers came to a virtual halt, even as per capita consumption continued to rise. By 1741, the Gin Act of 1736 was a dead letter, although it and the amendments made to it in 1737 and 1738 would remain in force until March of 1743.

The Gin Act of 1743 continued to impose a penalty of £10 on illegal hawkers, and continued to award half of the amount to informers. At the same time, the act reduced the fee for licensing distilled spirits to just twenty shillings a year, and made no provision for paying informers when convicted retailers were too poor to do so themselves. The first provision effectively reduced the population of unlicensed gin-sellers to the very poor, while the second effectively removed any financial incentive for informers to prosecute them. The clock had, for all intents and purposes, been set back to 1733.

Money naturally mattered to most informers, but few were willing to risk their lives for the sake of £5. Wittingly or not, each informer performed a complex calculus in which the variables were profit, opportunity, and risk. The object, of course, was to maximize profit and opportunity while minimizing risk. And the most obvious way to minimize risk was to attract as little attention as possible. An informer was especially vulnerable after going public with his or her evidence, and most chose this juncture to move as far away as possible from the neighborhood in which they had just operated. When, for example, the "wicked Design" of an informer in Southwark became public knowledge she "thought proper since that to abandon her Dwelling." And when another woman "fail'd in the Proof of her Informations exhibited before the Commissioners of Excise against four...Persons," she "craftily convey'd herself out of the Court" and decamped across the Thames to Southwark.

The need for anonymity, in turn, effectively barred informers from all towns except London. By 1750, the capital had a population of about 675,000; by way of contrast, Bristol, the nation's second largest city, had a population of only 50,000, leaving Norwich a distant third, at about 36,000. These small numbers naturally mitigated against anonymity, although some intrepid souls were still willing to take their chances outside London. In Norwich, for example, two women, described as "very expert in their Business," took "several Top-Distillers, and a great number more of petty Traders" to court in May of 1738; two other female informers, described as strangers belonging to a gang, are known to have operated in Bristol at the same time.

The odds, however, overwhelmingly favored informers operating in London. The capital had two obvious advantages: it was the nation's largest market for distilled spirits, and it had the highest concentration of potential victims of any city in the country. Numbers mattered because professional informers always worked under a system of diminishing returns: of the total population of potential offenders, only some would make the mistake of being caught in violation of the law, and of these, fewer still would actually be convicted. Moreover, once an informer was known in a neighborhood, prudence dictated that he or she move on; in the meantime, the victims were sadder but wiser. It is, for example, highly unlikely that Mrs. Howe in Westminster ever sold gin to a stranger again.

In the end, the odds worked against informers, even in a city as large as London. By the summer of 1738 informers were already running out of people and places to target. In the parishes of Horsney and Highgate, for example, it was reported that "there were not five Publick Houses in both Parishes, but what had been inform'd against, and had paid Ten Pound. . . ."

Until that happened, however, London was an ideal place for informers to operate because the sheer size and concentration of its population allowed informers to form gangs and collaborate, if only in order to exchange information about potential victims in distant neighborhoods. These informal networks allowed informers to operate in relative anonymity in neighborhoods where they were as yet unknown, thus prolonging their careers and allowing them to secure more convictions. In order to exchange information many informers entered into loosely knit gangs, the first mentions of which date from 1738. Before that time, informers had tended to operate either on their own or in pairs, entering into partnerships only as the risks associated with informing increased and the pool of potential victims began to shrink. The gangs were active for only a brief period—the first eight months in 1738—and whether by cause or by effect, this flurry of activity happened to coincide with the peak of prosecutions under the Gin Act of 1736. By the fall of 1738, both the informers and their gangs were already in full retreat: several of their leaders were under indictment or already in prison for perjury, while their more active members had already left town or gone into hiding.

Very little is known about the internal workings of these gangs. On one level, they probably provided their members with a sense of community. This was an important consideration, given the fact that informers were otherwise shunned. When, for example, Elizabeth Gardiner decided to join the gang headed by Charles Darley, she met him, Elizabeth Armstrong, Mary Jackson, and several others at a public house in the suburban parish of St. Giles-in-the-Fields. There they asked her, "Are you one of our Clan, and will you be true?" Gardiner responded in the affirmative, upon which "they all shook Hands with each other, and sat down and drank to one another."

The gangs' primary function, however, was to exchange information about potential victims. It was information that Charles Darley and his confederates wanted from Elizabeth Gardiner once she had agreed to join them. Did she, they asked, know "any Persons that sold Liquors"? Information of this sort was useful because informers were safest when they operated outside their own neighborhoods, and for this they needed to be in touch with people in distant parishes. The surviving records only occasionally identify the addresses of both informers and their victims, but when they do they often show the former and latter to have resided in separate parishes, often at a considerable distance. This was true in at least 17 out of 42 cases in Westminster; moreover, at least 16 of the 109 informers known to have operated in Westminster lived elsewhere.

Gangs also allowed informers to work in twos or threes, with each informer corroborating the other's testimony before a magistrate. Charles Darley asked Elizabeth Gardiner "if they could not drink together"; they then proceeded to the "Room of a House" in Hammersmith, where, they later testified, they bought gin from a woman by the name of Margaret Tyson. Luke Burgis and Henry Devon testified together that they had bought a quartern of gin "in a roome" from Elizabeth Maletrat, and Sarah Jones and Elizabeth Armstrong testified that they had bought gin in a "Room of a House situate in the parish of St. Giles's in the fields." Partnerships of this sort constituted the least risky of the stratagems employed by the informers, but their drawback was that any profits had to be split two or even three ways.

Since most eighteenth-century Londoners rarely ventured outside their immediate neighborhoods, informers faced formidable obstacles in forging social networks that spanned the entire metropolis. This was where the excisemen came in: their existing jurisdictions covered large geographical areas, putting them in touch with widely dispersed individuals; they were, moreover, authorized "to detect and inform against all persons that retail Spirituous Liquors." In this capacity excisemen were able to enlist individuals whom they had already met in the course of collecting duties. This was almost certainly true of John James, who ordinarily collected duties from barbers and the sellers of hair powder. His partner in informing just happened to be Thomas Kingston, a barber-surgeon.

The minutes of the Excise Board name several excisemen who were specifically employed in "detecting of Retailers of Spiritous Liquors." They included, most notably, Edward Parker, Robert Smith, William Colebrook, and Samuel Davis. Of these,

Parker was the most notorious. Between 1737 and 1738, he enlisted informers, coordinated their activities, and corroborated their testimony when they went before local justices of the peace. He was present when Elizabeth Gardiner joined Charles Darley's gang, and Darley probably reported to him. Unlike Gardiner and Darley, who were subsequently convicted of perjury, Parker managed to stay out of prison. He was, however, the target of several violent attacks. In November of 1737, two men were sent to prison for having assaulted him, while two months later, in January of 1738, he, along with William Mitchell and the notorious justice Thomas De Veil, was jostled for more than two hours while a thousand or so rioters gathered outside De Veil's house in Westminster. By the time of his death in December of 1738, he had, according to one account, been "instrumental in giving Informations against upwards of 1500 Persons," for which he was owed £1,535 by the Excise Office. According to another account, he had amassed "upwards of 1000 £ by swearing against People," which, if true, would link him to at least two hundred prosecutions under the Gin Act of 1736.

In March of 1738 the Privy Council asked local justices to redouble their efforts in enforcing the gin act. This set the stage for Parker to play a leading role in assisting the justices of Westminster, in which capacity he was identified as "the Excise Officer who has constantly attended the Justices." His primary role was to "enquire into the Characters of the Persons who give Evidence upon Informations." Parker very quickly managed to make himself indispensable, so much so that when he fell ill early in December of 1738 the justices were forced to adjourn; when he died a few weeks later their first order of business was to appoint a successor "to attend their Meetings as Informer in the Room of the said Parker." Shortly thereafter it was discovered that Parker had pocketed a portion of the fines paid to the court, with the justices' clerk, Joseph Porter, receiving "half a Guinea out of each ten pounds he received." In the meantime, Porter had already fled, taking with him £50 of the fines paid by convicted retailers. Faced with these revelations, the justices decided to end their special sessions, assuring Newcastle that "notwithstanding the Difficulties which have of late arisen from the Considerations abovementioned, yet the Business of the said Meetings has been carried on diligently...."

The name Lawrence Parker also shows up, both in the minutes of the Excise Board and in local newspapers. He may or may not have been related to Edward Parker. He appears to have organized a gang of informers as a sideline, and like Edward Parker, he was assaulted on several occasions. The most celebrated of these attacks occurred while Parker was visiting the house of correction at Tothill Fields in September of 1737. He was probably looking for gin-sellers who operated inside the prison—a common enough practice—but he was either too well known or too obvious in his inquiries to pass unnoticed. Six inmates, quite possibly individuals who had been sent there under the Gin Act of 1736, surrounded and attacked him, and it was only with great difficulty that he was rescued. One of his attackers was a woman by the name of Rose Biquall. Her husband, Marmaduke, happened to work in the prison, and when Parker was attacked he "obstinately and contemptuously" refused to come to his aid.

Lawrence Parker next surfaces a year later, at which time he was indicted for attempting to suborn perjury. The text of the indictment suggests that he was attempting to recruit informers. He had, it was alleged, asked John Smith and Walter Dorand to testify against a man by the name of Richard Worth. By now, things were starting to go terribly wrong for Parker. He had, according to *Read's Weekly Journal*, employed "near 30 persons," fifteen of whom were now prepared to testify against him. Bail was set at £100—an unusually high amount and one indicative of just how unpopular he had become—but two months later he was acquitted. Even so, the jury had deliberated for seven hours, which was an eternity by contemporary standards. (When the notorious arsonist John Aitken was put on trial for his life in 1777, the jury, having heard the judge's summation of the facts in evidence, declined to leave the courtroom and "almost immediately pronounced the Prisoner, Guilty.") Parker drops from the record at this point; he had had a very close call, and given the black mood of the public, he had been very lucky.

Excisemen who recruited informers and corroborated their testimony were able to do so only as long as they had the blessing of the officials responsible for enforcing the gin act, and this was by no means a given. These officials consisted of the commissioners of excise and local justices of the peace, and neither group was entirely comfortable with the act's reliance on informers. The commissioners, who ordinarily tried individuals of some standing, tended to give defendants the benefit of the doubt when, as was so often the case, they outranked the people who informed against them. In one of the earliest cases tried by the commissioners, dating from November of 1736, the case was dismissed because "The main Witness to prove the Fact was a vagrant Boy, who serves the Hackney Coachmen's Horses with Water at their Stand, and such other service Offices...." And in July of 1738 the commissioners

Sir Thomas De Veil (1684–1746), the son of a Huguenot minister, a soldier in the wars against Louis XIV of France, and perhaps the most notorious of London's "trading justices." As the leading magistrate in the capital, he convicted hundreds and possibly thousands of gin-sellers who fell afoul of the Gin Act of 1736. By courtesy of the National Portrait Gallery, London.

dismissed the case against Nicholas Reynolds, a victualler in Islington, when it was discovered that "the Informers were in Jail for several notorious Crimes"; it also helped that there were "many Persons of Reputation" prepared to testify on Reynolds's behalf.

With time, the commissioners also became uneasy with the activities of their own men. The first signs of this date from February of 1738, when the commissioners very publicly dismissed a senior excisemen who, having once "been very diligent in detecting the Retailers of Spirituous Liquors," was now "under the Displeasure of the Board for some indirect Practices." In January of 1740, Robert Smith and David Bartlett were dismissed for perjury, and in 1741, three more excisemen were dismissed, this time for extortion; a fourth, appropriately enough, managed to avoid dismissal by informing against his colleagues.

Many local justices were from the very beginning suspicious of informers and the excisemen who supported them. Excisemen had never been popular among justices outside London, while within the capital they were generally only tolerated in Westminster, thanks in large part to the presence of several justices intent on making a name for themselves. These justices included, most notably, Thomas Cotton, Nathaniel Blackerby, and Thomas De Veil. Of these, De Veil was by far the most active. From 1729 or 1730 until his death in 1747, De Veil was the ministry's point man in the capital, and this made him a very unpopular man. In 1734 he was stabbed while on the job; two years later, when the Gin Act of 1736 took effect, his house on Bow Street became a target, and was the scene of at least three separate riots between 1737 and 1738. In his memoirs, which were written in the third person and published posthumously in 1748, De Veil complained bitterly of the hardships that the act had imposed on him and his fellow justices.

"There was scarce one day passed," he wrote, "without the most flagrant riots . . . not only to the danger of the justice, but to the annoyance and disturbance of the whole neighbourhood." "Colonel *De Veil*," he added, "was sensible of this, but at the same time, he could not help being provoked at it. . . ."

De Veil was, however, handsomely compensated for his pain and suffering. When he was stabbed in 1734 he received a bonus of £250; in 1738, after he had tried and convicted hundreds of gin-sellers and had been threatened on numerous occasions, he was appointed Inspector-General of Imports and Exports, with a salary of £500 a year; in 1740 he was awarded £100, presumably for his diligence in convicting gin-sellers; and in 1744 he received an additional award of £400. In the same year he was also knighted, having long since arrogated to himself the title of colonel.

De Veil, along with Thomas Cotton and Nathaniel Blackerby, routinely furnished the press with the names of people whom they tried and convicted under the Gin Act of 1736. In all probability, they did this in order to make a name for themselves and curry favor with Walpole and his inner circle; at any rate, De Veil's name appears on an almost daily basis in London's newspapers for the years 1737 and 1738, that is, at the peak of prosecutions under the Gin Act of 1736.

De Veil's close ties to the ministry predisposed him to working with excisemen and tolerating informers. The same cannot be said of his colleagues in East London, who in the absence of a salary, often exacted fees—and sometimes took bribes—from the people who came before them. De Veil himself resorted to these practices, as did most of his colleagues in Westminster, but as a rule most of these "trading justices" had neither the stature nor the resources to enforce a manifestly unpopular law. Their reputation was—and remains—very poor. Edmund Burke, writing in 1780, remembered that they "were generally the scum of the earth—carpenters, brickmakers, and shoemakers; some of whom were notoriously men of such infamous characters that they were unworthy of any employ whatever, and others so ignorant that they could scarcely write their own names." This was perhaps harsh. Most of the justices in Westminster and East London at this time seem to have been modest men with modest motives, wishing nothing more than to maintain their already tenuous standing in the community. And to do this they had to protect their friends, neighbors, and clients from the informers and excisemen in their midst.

The story of Clifford William Phillips illustrates the point. Phillips was a justice of the peace for the Tower Hamlets; he was also a distiller, and one of the hawkers whom he supplied was a housekeeper by the name of Mary Bryan. In October of 1737, Bryan was arrested for selling gin without a license, and was taken before justice Richard Farmer. Farmer, however, was eating dinner at the time, and ordered Bryan to be held at the Angel Alehouse. Upon hearing of this, Phillips sent his clerk to the alehouse with the demand that the prisoner be released. Farmer's clerk refused, upon which a second messenger appeared, claiming that he had come to take Bryan to Farmer. This, however, was a ruse, and once again Farmer's clerk refused to hand over the prisoner. In the meantime Phillips had managed to assemble "a vast Councourse of People" who "began to Murmur and say that Mr. Phillips... would not punish her and she ought to be set at large." Undaunted, Farmer came to the alehouse, intent on trying Bryan then and there. Phillips made his appearance at about the same time, and in "a very insulting manner" told Bryan, "Woman I discharge you, go about your Business for you have Committed no

Offence Cognizable before a Magistrate." Farmer, however, succeeded in outshouting Phillips, and, having found Bryan guilty and unable to pay the fine mandated by the gin act, sentenced her to two months' hard labor at the local house of correction. It was at this point that Phillips became positively enraged, telling everyone within earshot that "no Magistrate in this Division would Act in such Dirty work but Mr Farmer."

This was not entirely true. It is true that one month later, in November of 1737, Farmer ruled on behalf of two excisemen, one of whom happened to be Edward Parker, but Phillips himself had on at least one occasion assisted excisemen in their hunt for gin-sellers. This happened back in October of 1736, at which time *The Norwich Mercury* reported that "the Officers of Excise made Complaint to Clifford Wm. Phillips. Esq...that several Vagabond Persons took upon themselves publickly to sell Distill'd Liquors in Buckle-street...whereupon the said Justice ordered a Constable to attend them, and went in person with the Officers into Buckle-Street, and caused several Persons there to be apprehended for selling Distill'd Liquors...."

In 1737, however, no fewer than five excisemen testified on behalf of Farmer, suggesting that their relations with Phillips had soured in the intervening year. They were Edward Parker, Robert Smith, William Colebrook, Samuel Davis, and Benjamin Marshes. Not surprisingly, all five took particular exception to Phillips's claim "that he knew more than any of the Commissioners of Excise and that by their... Employing such Scoundrels and Rascals as we are made the Excise stink in every persons Nostrills...."

For his part Farmer took the extraordinary step of attempting to have Phillips removed from office. He ultimately prevailed, notwithstanding Phillips's complaint that "being left out of a Commission when once in leaves an Odium upon the person as if guilty of malepractice...." In 1743, in a gesture that can only be described as pathetic, Phillips nominated himself to serve on the commission of peace in Middlesex. He also sued Farmer for libel; in this, too, he appears to have been unsuccessful. As for Bryan, she was trundled off to the house of correction at Clerkenwell. To his credit, Phillips saw to it that she was "exempted from hard labour" and was "treated favourably" while incarcerated. A few months after she was released, she was again convicted, this time by Anthony Chamberlain. The conviction was in all probability designed to send a message to Phillips; in any event, Bryan took the unusual step of appealing her newest conviction. Appeals were unusual because they were costly and only rarely successful; under the circumstances it is doubtful that Bryan could have sued Chamberlain without Phillips's help. In a census dating from 1736 she is listed simply as a "Retailer"; moreover, like most working women of the time, she was illiterate, signing a subsequent deposition with a mark. Perhaps, though, Mary Bryan had the last laugh, for in the eventful weeks between her conviction in October of 1737 and her second conviction in January of 1738, she found the time to marry a man by the name of Daniel Harrington.

Phillips's behavior stands in marked contrast to that of Sir Edward Hill and Pierce Griffith, both of whom served as justices in Westminster. Unlike Phillips, they were prepared to work with and tolerate informers. This was underscored in a case dating from 1739. It started when Thomas Loach and Letitia Heathcoate, two of London's most notorious informers, entered a public house in Westminster. There, they claimed, Catherine Croft sold them gin. Upon hearing their testimony, Hill and Griffith ordered her arrest.

Her husband, Thomas, accompanied her as she was led away, intent on proving his wife's innocence. At the trial he asked Loach and then Heathcoate to describe the room where the incident took place. Loach remembered seeing several men drinking beer from clay pots, while Heathcoate remembered seeing several men drinking beer from pewter pots. At this point Croft "begged of the Justices to take Notice how they contradicted one another," only to be told by Hill "that was not material; a Man might be mistaken." Croft then asked that he "might have Liberty to inquire after the Informers Characters," believing them to be "Vagabonds & of no Credit at all." The justices again rejected Croft's request, telling him in no uncertain terms that he "had no Business to enquire after the Kings Evidence for that they (meaning the said Justices) were satisfyed as to their Character." At this point the justices had Croft ejected from the room, and threatened to send one of his witnesses to Newgate for testifying against Loach.

It was by now inevitable that Catherine would be convicted, and her husband, having been allowed back in the room, grumpily paid her fine. He was still very angry. Later that night, Croft, along with three of his regular customers and a local overseer of the poor, went to Hill's house, demanding that he refund half of Catherine's fine. (This was the portion earmarked for the poor— hence the presence of the local overseer of the poor.) Croft also wanted Hill to have Loach and Heathcoate arrested for perjury. By now Hill was thoroughly irate, warning Croft that he "was in the Water by the Knees away & wanted to plunge himself over head & Ears." Croft, however, was determined, and a week later he approached De Veil himself, who complied with his request and issued a warrant for Loach and Heathcoate's arrest. Croft also put himself to the trouble and expense of suing Hill and Griffith;

the case was ultimately thrown out, but not before the two justices were themselves put to a great deal of trouble and expense.

As for Loach and Heathcoate, they were never found. In his frustration Croft went to their last known address, only to be "informed by a person then in the House that they were gone away from there and had robbed their Lodgings of several things." Between them, they succeeded in convicting at least thirteen unlucky retailers, sometimes working together, sometimes with other informers.

The cases of Mary Bryan and Catherine Croft were by no means atypical. They highlight a simple truth: justices in Westminster were far more willing than their colleagues in East London to cooperate with informers and convict the men and women who continued to sell gin to their friends and neighbors. This was brought home when in March of 1738 the Privy Council contacted justices in the capital, "recommending an exact and vigorous Execution of the Laws to prevent the selling [of] Geneva, and to put the Laws in Force against Riots and Tumults." Westminster's justices responded by holding special sessions over the next ten months; by way of contrast, their colleagues in and around the Tower of London had stopped all special sessions by the middle of June.

Westminster's justices were also far more eager to convict defendants than were their colleagues in East London. Between April and June, 89 percent of the people appearing before them were convicted, compared to less than 38 percent of those appearing before justices operating in and around the Tower of London. Even worse, more than half of all defendants never bothered to show up for trial; nor did the Tower justices make any attempt to apprehend them. The spotty attendance of defendants paralleled that of the justices themselves, who on five separate occasions failed to attend their own sessions; on seven other occasions only one justice bothered to appear. Attendance was especially lax in the Liberty of the Tower of London, where, just one week after local justices had agreed to hold special sessions they scaled them back to "Mondays, Wednesdays, and Frydays only." They did so because, as their clerk noted with each passing day, "Nothing Occured." All told, over the course of two months, they charged only two individuals, neither of whom appeared for trial.

On the south bank of the Thames, in Southwark, local justices seem to have taken a middle course, breaking neither with the ministry nor with their community. The records show that Southwark's justices convicted 236 individuals over the six and a half years in which the Gin Act of 1736 was in effect; assuming these records are complete, the number is quite modest. Southwark's justices were also prepared to make occasional symbolic concessions in enforcing an unpopular law. This was especially true of Sir John Lade, who, in addition to being a justice, was a brewer and a former member of Parliament. In February of 1738 he convicted a publican after an informer produced a punch bowl containing gin; upon paying his fine the publican turned around and accused the informer and his partner of having stolen the bowl, upon which Lade sent the pair to the county jail. In another incident, dating from May of 1738, a mob gathered outside Lade's house while he tried an informer for extortion; Lade was forced to read the Riot Act, but later that evening, after the mob had dispersed, he dispatched the informer to jail under cover of darkness. Two other informers were less lucky. They were, according to *The Country Journal*, committed to the New Gaol [jail] in Southwark, for extorting Money from several Persons under Pretence of stifling Informations lodged against them for retailing Spirituous Liquors.... Their Company would have been very acceptable in Bridewell, where there are now eight Persons confined upon the Informations of these very Fellows. They were escorted in their Passage to the Goal by a Mob of upwards of 1000, mostly boys and Girls, some of whom carry'd on the Top of Mop-Sticks, &c. as Trophies or Flags, old Aprons, white and blue, huzzaing as they went, god save the King....

Justices like Lade, however, appear to have made little effort to keep excisemen from operating in Southwark. In January of 1738, it was reported "one very vigilant Superior Officer of Excise in Southwark has been instrumental in convicting to the Number of 96 Persons." This may very well have been the same exciseman who in March of the same year was attacked by a mob, "under the Notion of his being an Informer." There are also hints that one or more gangs of informers operated in Southwark, although it is unclear whether they were organized by excisemen. Sarah Clewley, for example, belonged to a gang of counterfeiters for whom informing was probably a lucrative—if highly risky—sideline. Her career, like those of so many other informers, was short-lived, coming to an abrupt end when she was charged with perjury in the summer of 1738.

By 1737 the Excise Office had assigned up to thirty of its men to finding and prosecuting retailers who sold gin without a license. The real work, however, was done by hundreds of ordinary men and women posing as customers. And the first thing that stands out is how very similar they were to the people they preyed on. This is hardly surprising: most of the people who broke the law and sold gin did so because they were poor, and most of the people who betrayed them also did so because they were poor. And like most people who sold gin, most of the people who informed against them did so as a sideline. In East London, for example, at least six informers were employed in construction of one form or another, while six more were employed in the manufacture of apparel. Both trades were subject to sharp seasonal fluctuations, forcing workers to support themselves as best they could in the off-season. The same trades are also heavily represented in the census of gin-sellers that was conducted between 1735 and 1736, with 22 carpenters, 12 bricklayers, and 119 weavers.

Another fact stands out: there were nearly as many female as male informers. This, too, is not surprising, given the freedom with which younger women frequented gin shops in the capital. Female informers also found it easy to pose as customers, and, like legitimate female customers, they often descended on the gin shops in groups, sometimes with men, sometimes with other women. Women accounted for nearly half, or 82 out of 198, of the informers known to have operated in Westminster over the lifetime of the Gin Act of 1736; in East London, where the records are spottier and limited to just two months in 1738, women accounted for slightly more than half, or 45 out of 81, of all known informers. In both jurisdictions, women were just as likely as men to enter into partnerships with other informers, whether with men or women.

Because the vast majority of informers were ordinary working people it was easy for them to pose as the sorts of people who drank gin. And because informers consisted primarily of ordinary working people, the day would come when polite society would turn on them, just as it had already turned on the unseemly gin-sellers who plied their trade in the streets of London. And when this happened the Gin Act of 1736 was doomed. This point was reached in 1738. In January of that year, *The London Daily Post* published a highly inflammatory poem under the title "*Invitation to* Joe Clincher, *to leave the Highway and turn* Informer."

> *Come Brother* Joe, *my sturdy Lad,*
> *Foresake the Road, and quit the Pad;*
> *Informer turn if you'd be wise,*
> *And boldly swear for the—*
> *I'll Voucher for you ever stand,*
> *And play the Game into your Hand,*
> *No one can better cogg a Die,*
> *Or any faster clench than I;*
> *When first this Trade I did begin,*
> *I dauntless swore thro' thick and thin;*
> *And now my Word is oftner ta'en,*
> *Than Sacred Vows from Honest Men,*
> *Five Pounds I've gain'd by ev'ry Oath,*
> *And Thousands shall, between us both;*
> *No Calling sure can better suit ye,*
> *You'll keep your Trade and do your Duty.*

By unleashing informers on the working population of London, polite society had traded one evil for another. Informers, it turned out, posed an even greater threat to law and order than did the motley people who sold and drank gin. Informers turned neighbor against neighbor, and, what was worse, they brought still others together in riot and protest. And neighbors who coalesced against the informers in their midst posed a far greater threat to law and order than did scattered drunken individuals acting out on their own. It was once again time for polite society to enter the fray, this time to undo the damage of its good intentions.

CHAPTER SEVEN

Exit the Informers

The summary Power of receiving Informations, judging upon them, and carrying Sentence into Execution without the Interposition of Juries, or any of the usual Forms of Law, was in this Case widely extended, notwithstanding so much had been said but a very little time before, as to the Danger, and Illegality of such a Practice. This shews how subject all Men are to be hurried away by their Passions, and how easy a thing it is to sanctify very bad Measures, by pretending to apply them to a good purpose.

> *A Letter to a Friend in the Country in Relation to
> the New Law Concerning Spirituous Liquors*, 1743

IN APRIL OF 1738, in the parish of St. Giles-in-the-Fields, a woman, described only as "an Informer against Persons for retailing Spirituous Liquors," took her own life. Upon finding out where she had been buried, her neighbors, not content to let her rest in peace, disinterred her corpse and drove a stake through her heart. Four months later, in August, Sir Joseph Jekyll died, and by December, Edward Parker, who by one count had masterminded some fifteen hundred convictions under the Gin Act of 1736, lay dying. Two weeks later he, too, was dead, bringing the justices' sessions to a complete standstill. Unlike Jekyll's funeral, Parker's funeral was a quiet affair, but not so quiet as to escape the attention of several newspapers. He was, it was reported, "interred in a private Manner...for fear the Mob should tear his Corpse to pieces." This was, given the fate of the woman in St. Giles, a reasonable precaution.

By the end of 1738, death, starting with the demise of Queen Caroline in 1737, had removed several of the key players associated with the Gin Act of 1736. With their passing the impetus for moral reform foundered, and the networks of informers that men like Parker had helped organize quickly fell apart. The Gin Act of 1736 was well on its way to becoming a dead letter. Had the act been more popular or more successful, other men might have come forward to champion it at this point, but none did. Even so, the act failed not because several of its champions happened to die at roughly the same time, but rather because it relied on informers. The activities of these informers sparked a popular backlash that created a political crisis for both the ministry and the magistrates responsible for enforcing the act. For two years, from 1736 until 1738, hardly a day passed in which an informer was not attacked on the streets of London; during the same two years hardly a month passed without a major riot. The cumulative effect of these outbursts was extraordinary: by the end of 1738, ordinary Londoners had succeeded in cowing both the men who judged them and the men who governed them. It was a rare and singular triumph for ordinary men and women, and the story of how they triumphed, like all good stories, contains elements of passion, wit, and drama.

Almost everybody had anticipated that there would be trouble when the Gin Act of 1736 first took effect, but almost no one, with the conspicuous exception of Sir Robert Walpole, had predicted that the real trouble would come several weeks later and would last as long as the act was conscientiously enforced. "I am,"

Walpole wrote in October of 1736, "not without apprehensions, that a non-observance of the law in some form may create great trouble; and a sullen acquiescence and present submission in others, in hopes of gaining redress by parliament, may lay the foundation of very riotous and mobbish applications...."

Events would prove Walpole right. Although the act itself took effect without incident, once it began to be actively enforced the situation rapidly deteriorated. Four months into the act, riots, including those against the informers now operating in London, were very much on the king's mind when he addressed the House of Commons; in the same month, February of 1737, they were also the subject of an extended debate in the House of Lords. By August of 1737, excisemen operating in the capital were in fear of their lives, noting that "several Mobs have of late assembled themselves in a riotous manner and have greatly insulted and abused divers persons concerned in detecting the Retailers of Spirituous Liquors contrary to Act of Parliament, some of which have been in great danger of losing their lives...." It was at this point that a reward of £20 was offered "for discovering the Persons, who have been or shall hereafter be guilty of the like riotous and disorderly proceedings"; no one, however, stepped forward to collect the reward, and in the meantime attacks on informers and those who assisted them continued unabated, so much so that the following year Parliament made it a felony to attack informers.

Women played an important role in the riots that shook London between 1736 and 1738. More often than not, it was women who incited riots by noisily announcing the presence of informers, each time drawing large and menacing crowds from nearby houses and shops. A woman in the Strand "cry'd out *Informers*, on which the Mob secur'd" the alleged informer "and us'd him so ill, that he is since dead of his Bruises." Mary Brown and Susanna Fritter routinely harassed Anne Furth, each time causing "great numbers of People to assemble themselves and gather together about her in the Street, calling her Informer, whereby she was severely pelted with Stones and Dirt." Mary Burt was sentenced to twelve months' hard labor for having set "a Mob in the streets on two Persons, signifying they were Informers, on which Occasion they were ill treated...." And Elizabeth Burt was committed to the Westminster house of correction for having assaulted Elizabeth Parker and for having given her "the Title of an Informer and threatening her so that she goes in danger of her Life."

Then there was the example of Sarah Miller, who in August of 1738 stationed herself outside the house of Anne and George Adams and started screaming. She was, it was later claimed, there to deter Anne Adams from testifying against gin-sellers and "thereby to defeat the Execution" of the Gin Act of 1736 "and to render the same useless and ineffectual." Miller did not mince words. "Damn you, you informing Bitch," she shouted, upon which "great Numbers of Persons...to the Number of Twenty did then and there Assemble themselves" outside the Adams' residence. Miller next sought "to Excite the said persons...to do some Bodily harm to the said Anne Adams," toward which end she called Adams an "informing Bitch who goes partners with the Informers." "You bitch," she added, "you had Share of the money...which you bought your Scarlett cloack with." It was at this point that Adams, who was pregnant, became truly frightened. A few minutes later she miscarried. Unmoved, Miller, along with the assembled crowd, continued to heap abuse on Adams. When it was all over, Adams took Miller to court, only to lose her case two months later.

In some instances women went one step further and joined in the ensuing fray. Anne Bray, Margaret Reilly, a man by the name of Plant, and his wife were accused of "unlawfully and Riotously Assembling themselves together" for the purpose of "Breaking...Peter Sneath's Window and calling him Informing Dog, and forcing open his Door and Cutting his Face." Susanna Harold, wife of John Harold, and Henrietta Wells, a spinster, were indicted along with six men for "violently assaulting and beating" John Hill, a constable in Saffron Hill. In the course of attacking Hill they managed to grab hold of an informer then in his custody, raising "a great Mobb" by "calling out Informer against Ginn."

Actual attacks on women were quite rare. This is interesting because roughly half of all informers were in fact women. That said, when women were attacked they were treated just as roughly as men. A crowd treated one woman "with such Severity, by beating, kicking, and cramming Dirt into her Mouth," that she subsequently died of her wounds; "even her own Sex," it was reported, "exposed her to great Indecencies." Within a week of this incident, "an elderly Woman having inform'd against a Retailer of Gin, was severely us'd by the Populace, who dragg'd her through the Kennel in Brewer-street, St. James's, and then threw her into a Horse Pond...." Another woman, described as "well dress'd," "fell into the Hands of the Mob, near Cheapside, and [was] treated in such a manner that her Life was thought to be in danger." And then there was the case of Letitia Heathcoate, the especially notorious informer who was set upon after testifying against Catherine Croft; Croft's husband, along with several of his trusted customers, were alleged to have "made a great Riot and Disturbance, and Some of them tore the said Heathcote's Cloaths, and threatened to murder her...."

London mobs were capable of showing extraordinary discipline, whether in dispensing street justice to the informers in their midst or in rescuing gin-sellers who had been placed under arrest. In the case of the former they were true to their rural roots, subjecting their victims to the highly ritualized "rough music" that had in the past been used to shame and ostracize villagers caught violating the community's most basic rules. Rough music could take several forms. A transgressor might, for example, be placed backwards on a horse or ass, attracting hoots of derision and worse as he or she was paraded about the streets. This is exactly what happened in 1738, when an informer was "set upon an Ass...whilst others beat and pelted him, leading him up and down Bond-street..." At least eight other informers were dunked in a trough or open sewer; this particular form of punishment was known as "riding the staing." In yet another variant of rough music, a transgressor might be burnt in effigy. Hence the punishment meted out to an informer by the name of Pullin. According to *The London Evening-Post*, he was "carry'd in Effigy about the several Streets, Squares, &c. in the Parish of St. George Hanover-Square, for informing against a Victualler in Princess-street...and after the Procession was over he was fix'd upon a Chair-Pole in Hanover-Square, with a Halter about his Neck, and then a Load of Faggots placed round him, in which Manner he was burnt in the Sight of a vast Concourse of People."

Crowds were just as prepared to come to the aid of neighbors when constables or informers came to apprehend them. Incidents of this sort speak to just how difficult it was to arrest gin-sellers: not only were friends and neighbors likely to be at hand when a warrant was served, cornered gin-sellers could easily enlist the support of casual onlookers by crying out, "Informers!" When some bailiffs arrested a man in Audley Street "the Prisoner cry'd out Informers," upon which "the Mob rose immediately and almost killed the Bailiff and his Follower, and rescued the Prisoner." When an informer attempted to apprehend a woman in the Strand she immediately "cry'd out *Informers*, on which the Mob secur'd, and dragg'd [him] thro' the Streets; and making Water in a Pot, which they borrowed, pour'd it down his Throat; in short they us'd him so ill, that he is since dead of his Bruises." When two gin-sellers in Southwark cried out, "Informers!" they were immediately "rescued out of the Hands of the Constable, who with his Assistants narrowly escap'd the rough Discipline of the Rabble." And when two constables came to arrest Thomas Lockwood in Covent Garden, a man by the name of Abraham Maudley "rais'd a very great Mob on the Constables and Informers"; Lockwood, it turned out, "had divers times been taken up for the like Offence, and made his Escape, so that the Constables were afraid of him."

Incidents such as these naturally tended to discourage constables from enforcing the Gin Act of 1736. The Gin Act of 1738 acknowledged as much, conceding that "for want of a constable, or other ministerial officer of the peace being at hand to apprehend such offender or offenders, he, she, or they do often escape unpunished." Constables were reluctant to arrest gin-sellers for two reasons. First, many of the people who sold gin were their friends and neighbors. Second, they received no compensation for performing a thankless task. On the contrary, constables were ordinary citizens who were forced to volunteer their time, holding public office for a year while continuing to work their regular jobs. At the end of their brief and generally unwelcome tenure they took up where they had left off, and those who had been overzealous in enforcing unpopular laws could expect to be shunned by their neighbors.

When the Gin Act of 1736 took effect, London's constables had to choose between duty and loyalty. Many, and probably most, naturally chose the latter. In one incident, dating from May of 1738, a constable was actually called on to serve a warrant against his wife for selling gin; it is unknown whether he ever did so. In another incident, dating from November of 1737, two informers, James Dover and William MacCullock, went before justice Thomas De Veil and obtained a warrant for the arrest of Anne Woodham. Their next step was to take the warrant to a constable, who in this case happened to be Oliver Hill. Upon being shown the warrant, Hill threw it down "in a contemptuous manner," stating that "he would not be concerned in such villainous and scandalous Affairs, that they might go to some other Constable, for that the Character of a Highwayman was much more preferable than that of an Informer." "Their business," he added, "would be done for them before the Thing was over."

Hill made good on his threat. He knew that the easiest way to cause trouble was to let everyone know that Woodham was about to be arrested. And so the first thing Hill did was to tell a passing neighbor that he had a warrant for Woodham's arrest, adding that "*those* (pointing to these Informants *with Contempt*) *are the Informers.*" Upon reaching Woodham's house, Hill again did his best to attract a crowd, crying "out aloud, *Mrs. Woodham come out, I have got a Warrant against you for selling Gin.*" This had the desired effect. Four or five men rushed to the scene; MacCullock wisely fled at this point, leaving Dover to fend for himself. Hill, not surprisingly, made no attempt to rescue him, and shortly after the beating began he left the scene. Dover's ordeal, however, had just begun. At one point he was dragged along the streets of Westminster while locals pelted him with stones and dirt; at another he was beaten with a whip; and at yet another he was very nearly drowned in a watering trough.

Westminster was ground zero. There were more riots here than anywhere else in the capital, and because they occurred so close to the center of government they were a source of particular concern to the ministry. Of the riots known to have occurred in the capital, no fewer than thirty-seven occurred in Westminster, compared to eight in London proper, and just four each in East London and Southwark. This is hardly surprising. Informers, as we have already seen, were especially active in Westminster, thanks to the willingness of local magistrates to work with them; the city also had a tradition of rough-and-tumble politics, and its publicans were openly unhappy with Walpole and his regime.

The worst of these riots occurred in January of 1738. It started when Martha Beezley and another informer went to justice Thomas De Veil and testified against a man by the name of Edward Arnold. Incensed, Arnold went to Beezley's lodgings and threatened to kill her. Someone, probably Beezley, then went straight to justice De Veil, who promptly issued a warrant for Arnold's arrest. As Arnold made his way to De Veil's house, people rushed out of their houses and shops to join him; by the time he reached his destination he was at the head of a large mob numbering a thousand or more. In the meantime, both Beezley and her accomplice had taken refuge in De Veil's house. This placed De Veil in an untenable position; he could not, he later wrote, turn out the pair "without sacrificing their lives, or keep them without hazarding his own." His only option was to read the Riot Act, upon which a man named Roger Allen stepped forward and encouraged the crowd to tear down De Veil's house and kill the two informers. This impasse continued until troops appeared and escorted the two informers to safety and Allen to jail.

In February, Allen was charged with violating the Riot Act. In theory, this meant that he could be hung if convicted; it is unlikely, however, that Allen worried much while awaiting trial. Prosecutions under the Riot Act were extremely rare, and convictions were even rarer, in large part because jurors were notoriously reluctant to uphold a law that was widely regarded as too harsh. The case of Roger Allen would prove no different. On the morning of his trial, in May of 1738, a huge crowd gathered outside the court at Westminster Hall; inside, the courtroom was reportedly "so full you might have walk'd on the People's Heads." Allen played to the crowd, babbling and otherwise playing the fool; as he later confessed, "My own life had certainly been lost, if I had not *Wit* enough to prove myself a *Fool*." Allen's mother was in on the act, testifying that her son was "*an Idiot*, and *a silly weak Fellow*"; the defense also managed to produce a shoemaker who testified that Allen "was so weak and silly he could be of no Service to him in his Trade, nor would he ever learn it, &c." The jurors held out for an hour, but in the end they were completely cowed, acquitting Allen and breathing a collective sigh of relief as his supporters hoisted him on their shoulders and carried him away in triumph.

The acquittal of Roger Allen had a chilling effect on De Veil and his colleagues in the Westminster justiciary. That Monday, nine justices sat in Westminster Hall, the scene of Allen's triumph just five days earlier, and not a single defendant was brought before them. This was because "the Constables were afraid to go out with Precepts as they had done, least the Populace, encouraged by his Acquittal shou'd rise on them." For his part the exciseman Edward Parker complained that "Witnesses were so terrified on Allens Acquittal that he could not prevail on many of them to appear as usual." As for Allen, he became a local hero, receiving gifts and money from victuallers and publicans in the heady days following his trial. His wife Mary was less fortunate. Back in February, while Allen was in Newgate awaiting trial, she was hauled before De Veil on a charge of stealing from her former employer. De Veil took his revenge, and to no one's great surprise, Mary Allen was sent to join her husband in Newgate.

By the end of 1738, London's justices were in full judicial retreat. Many of their constables were in open revolt, and they themselves had been battered, insulted, and challenged every step of the way. In Westminster, for example, Judith Walmsley had intruded "her self in a forceible and Contemptuous manner before the Bench of Justices...insulting them in the Execution of their Office, and threatening the Informers that she wou'd wait their coming out." In Westminster, too, a distiller had berated justice Thomas De Veil, behaving, according to one account, "in a very audacious insolent Manner, insulting the Justice in his House."

In the end, however, it was the sheer volume of cases that overloaded the criminal justice system and exhausted its officials.

By August of 1738, it was widely reported that "about 12,000 Persons in all" had been convicted under the act in and around London. Of these, the majority, or about 7,000, had been tried by justices of the peace. These numbers naturally placed an enormous burden on the magistrates responsible for enforcing the act, forcing them to work extra hours in circumstances that were frequently trying. For a brief period of time, local magistrates rose to the occasion, agreeing to hold extra sessions. The commissioners of excise took the lead, agreeing in October of 1737 to set aside "every Tuesday and Thursday, for trying all Offenses against the Spirituous Liquors Act." In March of 1738, the justices in the capital, responding to a request from the Privy Council, agreed to redouble their efforts and hold special sessions. They were not, however, prepared to work additional hours for an indefinite length of time, especially since they were not paid for their efforts. In Westminster, the average number of justices attending these special sessions dropped from ten in April of 1738 to just four in January of 1739. Had they continued for two more months, the number may very well have dropped to zero; this, at least, is implied by the following announcement, published in *The London Evening-Post* in March of 1739: "The Trade of informing against Persons *for retailing spirituous Liquors* against law, seems almost at an end, few Magistrates caring to trouble themselves about it; for not one in twenty are able to make out their Informations, but by downright Perjury; none but the very Scum of the People following so scandalous a Trade."

It was at this moment that London's justices chose to declare victory in the face of overwhelming evidence to the contrary. Their manifest failure did not, however, prevent them from indulging in expressions of unwarranted self-congratulation. The justices of Westminster, as might have been predicted, were the worst offenders, confidently informing the Privy Council in August of 1738, "That it appears to them that the selling [of] Spirituous Liquors is now mostly in Private Places and there only to such as they think they can trust."

In the meantime, the commissioners of excise had already slackened in their enforcement of the act. An act dating from the reign of Charles II allowed them to exercise discretion in assessing penalties, and in the case of the Gin Act of 1736, they appear to have first exercised this option in May of 1737. This stands in sharp contrast to their earlier behavior. In the early days of the act, in November of 1736, they had denied all requests to reduce fines. "Their Hounours," it was reported at the time, "stick close to the Letter of the Act." Six months later, however, the commissioners chose to reduce the fines of no fewer than thirteen women and ninety-one men. In most cases, the fine was reduced from £100 to just £10; wealthier defendants were fined at proportionately higher rates, typically in the range of £20 to £40. In June, the commissioners went one step further, and actually summoned "all the Persons before them, who had paid in their Fines of 100£ . . . and after admonishing them . . . they were pleased to mitigate their Fines, some to 20£ and others to 30£ according to the Nature of their Offences; and the remaining part of their several Sums were returned to them." The commissioners continued to commute fines over the next two years, as is variously recorded in the board's minutes and in local newspapers.

At the same time the commissioners took steps to discourage prosecutions brought by professional informers. In February of

1737, they refused to issue any summons "without the Matter of Complaint first being exhibited to them, and supported by undoubted Evidence," while two years later, in March of 1739, the commissioners put further obstacles in the way of professional informers, resolving "not to receive any more Informations against persons for retailing Spirituous Liquors, unless the Informers Characters are supported by reputable Persons, which doubtless will prevent innocent Persons from becoming a Prey to those People who live upon their Spoil."

Three points bear emphasis in accounting for the commissioners' growing disenchantment with the Gin Act of 1736. First, they had not been consulted in drafting the act, and like Walpole, they probably had serious misgivings about its fiscal impact. Second, the act put the commissioners in the awkward position of having to judge distillers and middle-class publicans whose enterprises had until this time been actively encouraged by Parliament. And third, many informers appearing before the commissioners were clearly disreputable, the net effect of which was to tarnish the commissioners' own status and social standing.

The revolt of the commissioners was followed by the revolt of several key vestries in London. The revolt of the vestries was highly significant because the vestries had always been the natural allies of moral reform. Moreover, the Gin Acts of 1733, 1736, 1737, and 1738 had all enlisted the vestries' ongoing support by making churchwardens and overseers of the poor the recipients of half of all fines paid by gin-sellers upon conviction. This is why it was so remarkable that, in August of 1738, the vestry of St. Giles-in-the-Fields elected to return £500 of the £750 already paid to the parish's churchwardens; around the same time, the vestry in Highgate also elected to return the fines paid by unfortunate parishioners. And one week later, it was reported that several parishes in greater London had returned most of the fines recently paid by their respective parishioners.

The growing disenchantment of London's vestrymen makes sense on two levels. First, the vestrymen were recruited from the middle classes, and as such they were uneasy when the Gin Act of 1736 took direct aim at both the status and the livelihoods of middle-class publicans. The second reason why the vestrymen broke ranks with the reformers was purely fiscal. While the Gin Acts of 1733, 1736, 1737, and 1738 all provided the vestries with a new source of funds, they also threatened to add to the poor rates by depriving the poor of a livelihood. In the end, the vestrymen may very well have calculated that they were losing more money than they were taking in. In March of 1738, for example, the justices meeting in Hick's Hall complained that "some churchwardens or overseers of the poor, instead of applying such conviction-money to the use of the poor of their parish, have returned it to the parties so convicted, upon pretence of their being poor...." There is also the example of justice Clifford William Phillips, who, as we have already seen, got into a great deal of trouble by accusing one of his colleagues of depriving "a great many Poor Familys from honestly getting their Bread," thus earning "the Curses of all poor persons." This view was shared by at least two overseers of the poor, who subsequently wrote to the lord high chancellor on Phillips's behalf, claiming that he was much loved by the parish's poorer residents.

The vestrymen constituted one bellwether of middle-class opinion; jurors constituted another. The typical London juror was probably a tradesman, and by law he had to own property worth £10 or more a year. In the case of Roger Allen, the jurors were almost certainly intimidated by the presence of so many noisy partisans. In less sensational cases, where there were no immediate threats, jurors seem to have been unfavorably disposed toward individuals who participated in riots or who assaulted informers and the various officers assisting them; this bias, however, must be balanced against the fact that there were very few prosecutions for this particular type of offense, consistent with a general reluctance to prosecute rioters, or to proceed past indicting conspicuous ringleaders. Of the seventy-two individuals on record for participating in a riot or attacking an informer or constable, only thirty were actually indicted. (The actual number of rioters was of course much higher, as the vast majority of these individuals were never prosecuted in the first place.) And of those indicted, only thirteen were ever tried. Ten were found guilty, and three, including Sarah Miller, were acquitted.

At the same time, however, jurors took a dim view of the dirty tricks used by informers, and in a majority of cases they convicted informers charged with perjury or extortion. Of the thirty-one informers known to have been indicted for perjury, seventeen were ultimately convicted and nine were acquitted. In the case of extortion the ratio is even higher, with nineteen individuals indicted, fourteen convicted, and just one acquitted. These convictions succeeded, if nothing else, in ending the careers of the individuals in question: they were, on average, sentenced to a year in prison, along with a small fine, and none appears to have returned to informing upon release. In the final analysis, hardened informers could expect to meet with either street justice or with a more formal kind of justice. The result was always the same: to end the informer's career.

And so they all walked away—the constables, the justices, the commissioners of excise, the vestrymen, and, to a lesser extent, the jurors who were called upon to uphold an unworkable law. The unmaking of the Gin Act of 1736 is a testimonial to the power of ordinary people: they could not make laws, but they could, given sufficient provocation, unmake them. The people did not, however, unmake the law on their own. What both obscures and explains the fate of this particular gin act was the quiet pressure exerted by middle-class intermediaries with ties to both the plebeian culture of the people who sold and drank gin and to the patrician culture of the nation's political elite. They were the men who variously served as churchwardens, jurors, and magistrates, and as a group they had the most to lose as lawlessness swept their neighborhoods and threatened to lay bare the weakness of social controls in the capital. Their dissent, quiet and cumulative though it was, allowed the nation's political elite to back away from a bad law without appearing to give in to the rabble.

The Gin Act of 1736 was a study in unintended consequences. Far from curbing sales of distilled spirits, it created, from the perspective of an already unpopular government, a far more serious problem in the form of open contempt for the law and its agents. For two years, from 1736 to 1738, the ministry did what it could to make the law work; when that failed, it spent the next five years allowing an unpopular law to die a quiet death, even though the act would not be formally repealed until 1743.

By 1740, sales of gin had reached an all-time high, with the average adult drinking nearly two gallons a year. It was at this point that the commissioners of excise made one last attempt to enforce the Gin Act of 1736. The first hints of this date from March of 1740, at which time the *Craftsman* reported that "Prosecutions on the celebrated Gin-Act, which seem to have slumber'd for a good while, were recommenc'd before the Board of Excise"; at this time, however, only one person was actually convicted. Then, in September of 1740, *The London Evening-Post* reported that eleven people had been convicted by the commissioners, and that more than two hundred cases were pending. The following month, in October, the same newspaper reported that the commissioners were trying cases put on hold since 1739, and by June of 1741 the conviction of several more people by the commissioners led the newspaper to warn its readers that "the old Trade of informing seems to be reviv'd." In November, it was widely rumored that the act was about to be enforced again in earnest; this, however, proved to be a false alarm, and once again the commissioners lapsed into lassitude. Over the next two years, sales of gin continued their merry climb, peaking at just over 2.2 gallons per capita in 1743. By now, however, the nation had more important things to worry about. War had come, and with it, the need to raise taxes and coerce the rabble who drank gin into serving as sailors and soldiers.

Act III

IN WHICH Time Passes *AND* Wisdom *IS* Gained

CHAPTER EIGHT

Mother Gin Grows Old

We are endeavouring to reform a Vice almost universal, a Vice which, however destructive, is now no longer reproachful. We have tried the Force of violent Methods and found them unsuccessful; we are now therefore to treat the Vulgar as Children, with a Kind of artful Indulgence, and to take from them secretly and by Degrees what cannot be wholly denied them, without exasperating them almost to Rebellion.

FROM SAMUEL JOHNSON'S TRANSCRIPTION
OF A SPEECH BY LORD BATHURST, 1743

IN 1743, AT THE HEIGHT of the War of Austrian Succession, several notorious informers were pressed into military service and shipped off to an uncertain fate. They were placed in harm's way at the instigation of their neighbors and victims, who cheerfully betrayed them to the press gangs that were once again scouring London's dockside parishes in search of able-bodied seamen. One, John Markham, was taken out of a gin shop in St. Katherine's by a press gang "who had Notice given them of the Affair, and carry'd on board a Tender, where probably he may be of some Service to his Country." Another, a man by the name of Spence, had the misfortune of running into one of his victims on Tower Wharf, upon which the aggrieved publican prevailed on the lieutenant of a press gang to force Spence into service. For this "Favour he promis'd to give his Men as much Strong-Beer as they would drink: The Affair was accordingly executed, and the Fellow carry'd on board a Tender at the Tower amidst the Acclamations of the Populace." And in another incident, two excisemen, disguised "in Sailors Jackets and Trowsers," were "met by a Press-Gang, who thought them two sturdy Fellows, fit to serve in the Royal Navy, impress'd them, and, notwithstanding their Commission, carry'd them on board a Tender at Woolwich"; there the two men languished until the commissioners of excise ordered their release. War had come, and among its many casualties were the Gin Act of 1736 and the informers that it had unleashed on the people of London.

For three years, from its enactment in 1736 to the start of war with Spain in 1739, the gin act that Jekyll and his coterie had championed had been a source of acute embarrassment to Walpole and his administration. After 1739, the act was openly ignored by magistrates and retailers alike, and while Parliament made no attempt to change this state of affairs, it was still too politically risky to admit defeat and call for repeal, especially for an administration that was growing weaker with each passing year.

Walpole had been able to survive a succession of domestic crises, starting with his failure to carry the Excise Scheme of 1733, but with the outbreak of war in 1739 his days were numbered. Three years later, following a string of military setbacks, he was at long last forced to resign. Many of his colleagues, however, remained in office, while the old man, having been kicked upstairs into the House of Lords, continued to exercise considerable influence behind the scenes. He was succeeded by a shaky triumvirate consisting of John Carteret, the duke of Newcastle, and Newcastle's brother, Henry Pelham. Carteret, however, was forced to resign just two years later. For this he could thank his old enemy, Sir Robert Walpole. Years earlier, back in 1724, Walpole had ousted Carteret from his position of secretary of state, effectively exiling him to Ireland. There Carteret served as lord lieutenant until 1730. Once back in London, Carteret quickly reestablished himself as one of Walpole's most implacable critics. Carteret's revenge came in 1742, when he was appointed high secretary of state; even then he continued to be hounded and undermined by his old rival every step of the way.

Thanks to Walpole's machinations, Carteret's grip on power was shaky at best, and throughout his brief administration he was plagued by bad news from the front, forcing him to widen the search for both money and men. The despised informers were among the first men to be swept up by the press gangs; at the same time the new administration, desperate for additional funds, was considering a bill that would raise excises on distilled spirits while also repealing the more objectionable clauses of the Gin Act of 1736. That bill, in its final form, was the Gin Act of 1743.

By January of 1743, almost everyone was waiting for Parliament to pass a new and less restrictive gin act. Even the London Punch House, one of the few establishments to purchase a license under the Gin Act of 1736, neglected to renew its license, as was widely reported in local newspapers. The bill itself moved swiftly through the Commons, where its passage was widely regarded as a foregone conclusion. It was put forward by Francis Fane, an eminently practical man who was also counsel to the Board of Trade. Early in January, the Excise Office gave its input, and in the middle of February, after several amendments had been tacked onto the bill, it was forwarded to the House of Lords for their approval. There the bill encountered unexpected resistance.

The ensuing debates were among the most elegant in the history of Parliament, thanks in large part to the skill and imagination of young Samuel Johnson, who in transcribing the sessions embellished and otherwise improved on the original speeches. Years earlier, in 1734, Johnson had approached Edward Cave, the editor of the newly launched *Gentleman's Magazine*, offering to write a regular feature for the magazine. At the time Johnson was a nonentity, having recently failed as a schoolmaster; Cave, not surprisingly, turned him down flat. Four years later, however, Cave gave Johnson his first big break, and Johnson became a regular—if poorly paid—contributor of both poetry and prose, including highly polished transcriptions of the more important debates in Parliament between 1741 and 1744. There was just one problem: Johnson rarely attended the actual sessions, relying instead on secondhand accounts and his own considerable literary imagination. In the case of the debates over the Gin Act of 1743, Johnson was laboring under yet another prejudice: he, like so many men of taste, despised gin, defining it in his famous *Dictionary* as "A distilled spirituous water, made with no better an ingredient than oil of turpentine, put into the still, with a little common salt, and the coarsest spirit they have, which is drawn off much below proof strength." Elsewhere he stated his preference for Scotch whiskey, pronouncing it "preferable to any English malt brandy."

Because it was illegal to publish speeches given in either house, Johnson modified the orators' names in perfectly obvious ways and published their speeches under the coy rubric of "Debates in the Senate of Lilliput." These appeared in installments in *The Gentleman's Magazine* between November of 1743 and February of 1744, long after the matter had been laid to rest. Not to be outdone, the magazine's chief rival, *The London*

Magazine, ran its own version of the debates, which, while more prosaic than Johnson's, was almost certainly more accurate.

The coalition opposing the bill was formidable. It included all of the nation's bishops, and several of its most capable lords, starting with Philip Dormer Stanhope, fourth earl of Chesterfield, and the redoubtable Lord Hervey. Chesterfield, who is best known for his *Letters to his Son* and *Letters to his Godson*, was by now quite deaf. He had been one of the dissident Whigs opposing Walpole, although his own moral standards left much to be desired. As Samuel Johnson once remarked, Chesterfield's *Letters* taught "the morals of a whore, and the manners of a dancing master." Johnson, however, was a far from impartial observer, having attempted and failed to enlist Chesterfield as his patron; and so while Chesterfield was on record elsewhere as opposing the Gin Act of 1743, Johnson's version of his orations cannot be taken too seriously.

Chesterfield ostensibly opposed an increase in the excise on gin because it gave the appearance of sanctioning drunkenness. By way of analogy he argued that no nation had ever imposed "a Tax upon Theft or Adultery, because a Tax implies a License granted for the Use of that which is taxed, to all who shall be willing to pay it." The argument was of course sheer sophistry. Taken to its logical conclusion it would have left legislators with no other option than to shut down the entire British distillery, and this was farther than anyone wished to go. Having made his point, Chesterfield proposed what he really had in mind, namely, that spirits be "removed out of the Reach of the People . . . by the heaviest Taxes levied with the utmost Rigour."

Chesterfield was both eloquent and elegant; Hervey was both of these things, and dangerous, too. He was a favorite with the royal family, having served as the vice chamberlain of the royal household between 1730 and 1740; he was also known for his caustic wit, making him a formidable adversary in debates. It was with a pen dipped in acid that he had written his *Memoirs of the Reign of King George the Second*, which bear an uncanny resemblance to Suetonius's *Lives of the Caesars*. Hervey gave a total of three speeches in favor of keeping the existing gin act, and while he essentially reiterated what Wilson and Jekyll had said back in 1736, he almost certainly did so with a great deal more wit. In Johnson's version of the debates, Hervey comes across as cold, clever, and heartless, showing not the least bit of sympathy for the plight of the masses who sold and drank gin. In the end it was Hervey who lent the imprimatur of class and snobbery to the simple and in many ways archaic conservatism of Wilson and Jekyll. Hence this marvelous passage, as doctored by Johnson:

> We know that they [strong liquors] produce in almost every one a high Opinion of his own Merit; that they blow the latent Sparks of Pride into Flame, and, therefore, destroy all voluntary Submission, they put an End to Subordination, and raise every Man to an Equality with his Master, or his Governour. They repress all that Awe by which Men are restrained within the Limits of their proper Spheres....

While Hervey and Chesterfield lent their famous names and considerable talents to the cause, it was the bishops who lent it the tincture of *gravitas*. Most had been handpicked by Walpole or Newcastle in an attempt to pack the House of Lords with men dependent on the administration for their advancement, and some, such as Francis Hare (bishop of Chichester), and Benjamin

Hoadly (bishop of Winchester), had even written pamphlets and articles on behalf of the administration while Walpole was still in power. With the old man now on the sidelines, the bishops took the opportunity to engage in a conspicuous—if short-lived—display of virtue.

True to the spirit of the age, the bishops opposed the bill on strictly secular grounds. Their first step, like the reformers who had come before them, was to find useful facts and figures. With this in mind they summoned three eminent physicians, Doctors Mead, Lee, and Barker, "to give their opinions of the fatal consequences of these poisonous liquors." Their next step was to summon the commissioners of excise and ask them why the Gin Act of 1736 had failed. The commissioners naturally protested their innocence and instead blamed certain justices who "had not always been equally zealous in seconding their endeavours...."

The bishops failed, however, in their attempt to derail the bill by bottling it up in committee. With this obstacle cleared, the ministry pressed once again for the bill's passage in the House of Lords. When the bill was again blocked after its second reading, the ministry pulled out all stops lest it experience yet another embarrassment in what had already been a calamitous year. Carteret himself spoke on behalf of the new bill, and, if Johnson's version is to be trusted, he did so with some wit, confessing at one point that "I myself suffer by some Indulgence which yet I cannot prevail upon myself to forbear; this Indulgence is the Use of too much Snuff, to which it is well known that many Persons of Rank are not less addicted...." On a more serious note, Carteret acknowledged that no government could prevail when the people were united against it; in the case of the late gin act the people had been "determined...not to be governed by this Law; and have consequently endeavoured to hinder its Execution; and so vigorous have been their Efforts, that they have at last prevailed." Carteret understood, better than most, that ordinary gin-sellers were widely regarded as "carrying on a lawful Employment for supplying the Wants of the Poor, relieving the Weariness of the Labourer, administering Solace to the Dejected, and Cordials to the Sick."

In the end, however, the bishops and their allies only succeeded in delaying passage of a new gin act by a few weeks. On 25 February the lords passed the bill eighty-two to fifty-five, and by March, with the new gin act about to take effect, there was a sudden rush to buy licenses to sell beer and ale, as these would be required of anyone seeking to sell spirits. The contract to print the new licenses was itself eagerly sought, with Newcastle, ever the dispenser of patronage, recommending two stationers of his acquaintance to the Excise Office. In the meantime the commissioners of excise, anticipating a run on licenses, reassigned several of their officers to the distillery division.

On 26 March 1743, the new gin act took effect. Its framers openly acknowledged that the Gin Act of 1736 had been plagued by "great difficulties and inconveniences," and had not "been found effectual to answer the purpose thereby intended...." The first thing the new gin act did was repeal the excise on compound spirits. These had proven impossible to collect, as the Excise Office had neither the resources nor the manpower to tax the tens of thousands of individuals and establishments that continued to sell spirits in open defiance of the law; moreover, what little manpower the commissioners could spare had been diverted to ferreting out publicans who refused to purchase licenses under the terms of the Gin Act of 1736. By contrast, the framers of the new act had the good sense to insist that all taxes be levied at the point of manufacture, and in so doing acknowledged what everyone else already knew, namely, that the Excise Office was at its most effective in monitoring and taxing operations that were large, conspicuous, and relatively few in number. The old licensing fee was reduced from £50 a year to just £1; at the same time, however, existing excises on spirits were nearly doubled in an attempt to provide the Crown with much-needed funds for the war effort. Enforcement continued to be split between the commissioners of excise and local justices of the peace, and sales continued to be limited to licensed establishments only. Informers, while not precluded from bringing charges, were effectively put out of business by reducing licensing fees to a level that most publicans could afford. The clock had, for all intents and purposes, been set back to 1733, the only difference being that taxes on spirits had been doubled.

As in 1736, the commissioners of excise were at first very active in enforcing the new act. They may even have done so with considerable enthusiasm, having been asked for their input while the bill was making its way through Parliament. For one thing, they did not issue licenses to all comers. When, for example, the keeper of a notorious gin shop in Southwark petitioned local justices for a license to sell gin and was turned down, he "hang'd himself in his Chamber" because "he had no Hopes of getting one from the Commissioners of the Excise...." Trials of retailers operating without a license began in May, just two months after the Gin Act of 1743 had taken effect. In the first round, twenty-two retailers were tried before the commissioners of excise; all were convicted. Less than one month later, in June, there were nearly a thousand cases pending before the commissioners, but by March of 1744 that number had fallen by more than half, to about four hundred.

Local justices were generally desultory in enforcing the new act, just as they had been in the late 1730s. There was, as before, an initial flurry of activity, followed by a spiral into utter lassitude. Shortly after the new act took effect the justices in the Westminster parish of St. Martin-in-the-Fields refused numerous applicants, putting them "entirely out of Hopes of obtaining" licenses to sell gin. Actual convictions under the act were quite rare, however. The justices in Southwark were the first to act, sentencing two retailers to the local house of correction in May of 1743; they also convicted several more people in December of the same year. By March of 1744, however, there were already hints that the metropolitan justices were falling behind the commissioners in upholding the new act, and it was at this time that the Privy Council intervened, asking Newcastle, in his capacity as chief justice of the peace for Middlesex, to order the justices of both Westminster and East London to redouble their efforts. Nothing came of this, however, and so the onus of enforcing the new act increasingly fell on the commissioners of excise, who from this point forward were to be found convicting retailers large and small.

In the end, however, the Gin Act of 1743 satisfied neither those who had pushed for it nor those who had opposed it. Much to almost everyone's surprise consumption actually began to fall once the new act took effect. Indeed, it was not until the early nineteenth century that consumption would again reach the heroic levels achieved in

1743. These effects were already apparent just four months after the new act became law, at which time *The London Evening-Post* reported that revenues from excises on distilled spirits were unexpectedly off by about £2,000. This was the largest such decrease over the previous seven years, exceeding any single drop in revenues over the lifetime of the Gin Act of 1736. This downward trend is borne out in records kept by the London Company of Distillers: in its halcyon days of the 1720s and '30s, an average of eight new members were added to the Company each year; by the 1740s this average was down to just under four a year; and by the 1750s it was down to just under three. At the same time, purchases of licenses skyrocketed, with newspapers reporting that publicans had purchased upwards of 200,000 annual licenses by January of 1744, and a total of 481,400 between March of 1743 and June of 1747.

The fact that so many publicans took out licenses goes a long way toward explaining why the Gin Act of 1743 succeeded where its predecessors had failed. In effect, the new act placed the onus of policing customers on licensed publicans. This was a sensible step, given the fact that metropolitan magistrates had neither the manpower nor the inclination to do so themselves; publicans, by contrast, now had a stake in keeping their licenses, and the best way to do this was to turn away customers whose activities or behavior might bring their establishments into disrepute. The result was that sales suffered. Lord Bathurst had predicted as much in 1743, arguing that "when the Cheapness of Licenses shall make it convenient for every Man that pleases to retail Spirits in a publick Manner, they will be generally drank in Houses visited by publick Officers, observed by the neighbouring Inhabitants, and frequented by Persons of Morals and Civility, who will always endeavour to restrain all enormous Excesses, and oblige the

Masters of the Houses to pay some Regard to the Laws." By 1747, Lord Bathurst's prediction had come to pass, with the London Company of Distillers observing that under the new act publicans "could not suffer any Enormities to be committed in their Shops, without the Observation of the Civil Magistrate. . . . "

Sales of gin continued to be soft in 1747. Even worse, the war was still going badly, and the budget, at just under £10,000,000, was at an all-time high. And so once again lawmakers resorted to the time-honored expedient of raising excises on spirits while making it easier to buy and sell them. Combined excises had already been raised to just under a shilling a gallon back in 1746, an increase of more than 22 percent. The following year, Parliament allowed wholesale distillers back into the retail trade, provided only that they purchase a special license at the rate of £5 a year. This was done at the behest of the London Company of Distillers, whose timing—for once—was spot on.

Although this most recent concession to the wholesale distillers led to howls of protest, and provided much-needed fodder for the campaign leading up to the Gin Act of 1751, it had surprisingly few takers. By their own accounts, the commissioners of excise issued special licenses to only 598 wholesale distillers in 1748; in 1749 this number actually dipped, to 573, rising to 648 in 1751. The largest number of these, 150, were issued to distillers in Westminster, with another 45 going to distillers operating in the infamous parish of St. Giles-in-the-Fields. At the same time, overall demand was already steadily inching downward, with per capita consumption of British spirits declining by nearly 28 percent between 1743 and 1750. It was against this backdrop of sagging sales that the moral reformers launched their third and final campaign against Mother Gin.

For nine long years, from 1739 to 1748, the reformers had bided their time, upstaged by war on the Continent and, in 1745, by rebellion at home. This was the worst possible time to tackle strictly domestic issues; nor was this the time to suggest that the Crown place restrictions on an industry that provided it with much-needed revenue. Then, in October of 1748, the War of Austrian Succession came to an end with the signing of the Peace of Aix-la-Chapelle, and between 1749 and 1750, 79,000 soldiers and sailors were abruptly released into a jittery civilian population. With their return the public's attention naturally turned to the crimes that unemployed veterans might commit once back in England. These fears persisted into the early 1750s, and since gin was widely believed to be a leading cause of crime and immorality, respectable society was easily swayed by arguments that promised to reduce both by suppressing gin. Hence the claim that gin was the root of all evil, "the Author of all Sin: The DEVIL himself, in a vile Dram of GIN." Hence, too, the following verse, as published in *The London Evening-Post* in March of 1751:

> *This* wicked *GIN, of all* Defence *bereft,*
> *And* guilty *found of* Whoredom, Murder, Theft,
> *Of rank* Sedition, Treason, Blasphemy,
> *Should* suffer Death, *the* Judges *all agree.*

Henry Fielding, author, lawyer, and magistrate, played a leading role in this campaign. As a young man in the 1730s, he had contributed articles to opposition newspapers, most notably to *Common Sense*, *The Champion*, and quite possibly *The Craftsman*;

he had also savaged Walpole in a succession of otherwise forget-table plays. During the Jacobite rebellion of 1745, however, he had proven his worth to the government by publishing two newspa-pers on its behalf, and in 1748 he was rewarded by being appointed chief magistrate of Bow Street. This was the position formerly held by Colonel Thomas De Veil, who, it will be recalled, had played a major role in enforcing the Gin Act of 1736. During his brief tenure as the chief magistrate of Westminster, Fielding was responsible for creating the first professional police force in the capital, the famous Bow Street Runners. These impressively diverse credentials help account for why his *Enquiry into the Causes of the Late Increase of Robbers*, which appeared in March of 1751, had an enormous and immediate impact on public opinion, convincing an already nervous public that gin was the source of "so many temporal Mischiefs...amongst which are very frequently Robbery and Murder itself." Fielding may even have been asked to comment on the Gin Act of 1751 as it was making its way through Parliament; this, at least, can be inferred from Horace Walpole's *Memoirs of King George II*.

Fielding's contribution, important though it was at the time, pales beside that of his close friend William Hogarth, who less than one month earlier had released two of his most celebrated prints: *Gin Lane* and *Beer Street*. These, along with *The Stages of Cruelty*, were "calculated to reform some reigning Vices peculiar to the lower Class of People," toward which end "the Author had pub-lish'd them in the cheapest Manner possible," selling them at just one shilling each. Hogarth had almost certainly read Fielding's *Enquiry* while finishing *Gin Lane* and *Beer Street*; Fielding, in turn, repaid the compliment by publishing *A Dissertation on Mr. Hogarth's Six Prints* shortly after they were put on sale.

Hogarth would later record that *Gin Lane* belonged to a time when "the dreadful consequences of gin-drinking appeared in every street," adding that "In Gin Lane, every circumstance of its horrid effects is brought to view *in terrorem*. Idleness, poverty, misery, and distress, which drives even to madness and death, are the only objects that are to be seen; and not a house in tolerable condition but the pawnbroker's and Gin-shop." At the center of the scene is a besotted mother whose infant, a boy, is about to plummet to his death. The boy's eyes are strongly suggestive of fetal alcohol syndrome, as are those of the infant on the right margin of the print. In the background another infant sits and bawls as its naked mother is placed in a coffin. It was this cumulative image, of failed motherhood, that most horrified contemporaries, prompting Edward Cave to run the following verse in the March issue of *The Gentleman's Magazine*:

I must, I will have Gin!—that skillet take:—
Pawn it:—No more I'll roast, or boil, or bake.
This juice immortal will each want supply,
Starve on, ye brats! so I but bung my eye.
Starve? No!—This Gin ev'n mother's milk excels;
Paints the pale cheeks, and hunger's darts repels.
The skillet's pawn'd already.—Take this cap;
Round my bare head I'll yon brown paper wrap.
Ha! half my petticoat was torn away
By dogs (I fancy) as I maudlin lay.

In *Beer Street*, by contrast, tradesmen and laborers are fat and well-dressed. To the left a man fondles a woman's breast; she, in turn, dangles a key between her legs. These are all obvious allu-

Gin Lane *by William Hogarth, 1751. By courtesy of the Guildhall Library, London.*

Beer Street *by William Hogarth, 1751. By courtesy of the Guildhall Library, London.*

The Enraged Musician *by William Hogarth, 1741. Hogarth's street scenes teem with people whose sounds, smells, and bad manners were a source of constant annoyance to the well-heeled men and women who made their homes in London's West End. This scene, which dates from the very height of the gin craze, is curiously devoid of gin; the harrowing scenes of* Gin Lane, *by contrast, date from a time when the mania for gin was already abating.*

sions to lust and fertility, which are conspicuous by their absence in *Gin Lane*. In *Beer Street*, Hogarth later recorded, "all is joyous and thriving. Industry and jollity go hand in hand. In this happy place, the pawnbroker's is the only house going to ruin; and even the small quantity of porter that he can procure is taken in at the wicket, for fear of further distress."

Working alongside Fielding and Hogarth were several men who have long since faded into obscurity. They included Isaac Maddox, bishop of Worcester, and the economist Josiah Tucker, in addition to Thomas Wilson and Stephen Hales, both veterans of the campaign for the Gin Act of 1736. The connections between these men were close and for the most part friendly, allowing them to pool their considerable talents and coordinate their efforts in the final campaign against Mother Gin. Wilson, for example, met with Fielding in December of 1750; he also "wrote an account of the conversation to the Bishop of Worcester." Wilson, Hales, and Tucker all assisted in printing the bishop's most recent sermon against gin, under the title of *The Expediency of Preventive Wisdom*, while Tucker, in addition to praising Fielding's *Enquiry*, also contributed his own *Impartial Enquiry into the Benefits and Damages Arising from the Present Very Great Use of Low-priced Spirituous Liquors*, published early in 1751. And Fielding cited Wilson's *Distilled Spirituous Liquors the Bane of the Nation* in his *Enquiry*, along with Maddox's sermon.

Of the lesser known players, Isaac Maddox was by far the most important; indeed, as far as the editors of *The London Magazine* were concerned, his contribution, in the form of a rousing sermon preached on a cold morning in January of 1751, overshadowed the efforts of both Fielding and Hogarth. This sermon, like most, would almost certainly have gone unheeded had

Maddox not already established himself as a man with impeccable credentials, both moral and political. He was a prominent bishop, in addition to being a patron of several worthy causes, including infant welfare. He had also been active in the now moribund Societies for the Reformation of Manners, and in 1737, while still bishop of the obscure diocese of Saint Asaph, he had spoken in favor of the gin act passed the previous year. In 1743, he had adamantly opposed the gin act then making its way through Parliament, and he had added his name to a protest once the bill passed the House of Lords. At the time Maddox could safely be ignored; by 1751, however, he was the spiritual leader of one of the nation's most important dioceses, and this time people took note of what he said. The sermon was in many ways a reprise of the speeches given by the bishops back in 1743, which is to say that Maddox made virtually no appeal to scripture, and instead relied on political arithmetic in making his case against gin. "I speak," he assured his audience, "from evidence." And that evidence, according to the good bishop, proved beyond the shadow of a doubt that gin was "Destroying in the Course of a few Years more Lives than Sword, or Plague, or Famine; lessening the Number of our People by daily Slaughter; diminishing and enfeebling Posterity; and in every respect both as to Number, Health, and Vigour, keeping down the Offspring and Breed of the Nation."

Maddox had almost certainly read *The History and Survey of London*, whose author, William Maitland, had made extensive use of the parish registers kept for greater London by the Company of Parish Clerks. These registers showed, among other things, that the average annual number of christenings for the years 1748 through 1750 was 14,320. This compared to an average of 17,694 for the years 1731 through 1733, that is, "when Spirituous Liquors were not so General as at present." These alarming figures were useful because they seemingly proved what moral reformers had suspected all along, namely that gin posed a direct threat to the nation, weakening the current generation of laborers while also diminishing their "prolific Faculties." Even worse, if this disturbing trend continued unabated, England would inevitably fall behind France in the race to produce babies, and here Maddox was no doubt at his most persuasive when he informed his audience that babies born in Paris had a much higher chance of surviving than those born in London. In the same breath he also asked his audience to consider the plight of infants who were exposed to gin, whether *in* or *ex utero*, for these, after all, were the nation's "real Strength and riches," that is, its next generation of soldiers, sailors, and laborers.

The use of political arithmetic was, of course, nothing new. It had figured prominently in the campaign leading up to the passage of the Gin Act of 1736, with the justices of Middlesex publishing the number of individuals then selling spirits and grouping them by occupation. The parish registers had been consulted as early as 1732, when it was claimed that gin was responsible for two-thirds of all infant mortality in the capital. Maitland, however, was far more exacting in his use of the parish registers, and this greater precision, combined with Maddox's considerable influence and the public's heightened anxiety over crime, gave new urgency to the cause of moral reform.

The one problem, which Maitland himself acknowledged, was that the registers were by no means an infallible guide to births and deaths in the capital. It is likely, for example, that deaths were more routinely recorded than births, with perhaps one-third of all births going unrecorded. For obvious reasons, the births of foundlings were especially prone to falling between the cracks.

Moreover, the registers did not include individuals who were born or who died outside the Church of England. This particular population was substantial, for it included traditional nonconformists as well as the increasingly numerous followers of Methodism. And there was the additional problem of attribution: assuming that the numbers were in some way representative, they did not by themselves prove that gin—and not disease—was the culprit.

In the end, though, all that really mattered was that the men who heard Maddox's numbers were prepared to believe them. The audience that cold January morning included the lord mayor and aldermen of the City of London, in addition to the governors of the City's hospitals; the setting, St. Bride's, was one of Wren's finest churches, all of which doubtless added to the solemnity of the occasion. Shocked and deeply moved by what they heard, the aldermen voted unanimously to draft a petition to Parliament "to prevent the pernicious Use of Spirituous Liquors." This they presented on 21 February. Other jurisdictions—including several local parishes, along with Bristol, Norwich, and Manchester—quickly jumped on the bandwagon, the net effect being to place an enormous amount of pressure on Parliament in a very short period of time.

Legislators were also under considerable pressure from the press, which ran, among other things, a series of forgettable verses about gin. In February, for example, *Read's Weekly Journal* featured the following verse, which had allegedly been "*Chalk'd on the Shutters of an infernal* GIN SHOP":

> BRITTON! *if thou wou'dst sure Destruction shun,*
> *From these curst Walls, as from a Serpent, run:*
> *For there a thousand DEATHS in Ambush lie;*
> *Fatal to ALL, who dare approach too nigh.*

The same issue featured a "LABEL for a GIN-BOTTLE," to wit:

When fam'd Pandora to the Clouds withdrew,
From her dire Box, unnumber'd Evils flew.
No less a Curse this Vehicle contains:—
Fire to the Mind, and Poison to the Veins.

Overall coverage in London's newspapers peaked in March, coinciding, naturally enough, with the presentation of petitions to Parliament and the publication of several pieces against gin, including *Gin Lane*. This time the press was united behind the bill, and was, if anything, even cruder in its attacks on gin than it had been in 1736. *The General Advertiser* was perhaps the worst offender, at one point going so far as to pander to the anti-Semitism that was so ingrained in eighteenth-century English society:

In merry, musty Chronicles we read,
The Sow of David, was a Sow indeed.
Muddled with Hebrew Grains, from Hebrew Gin,
She grunted, snorted, reel'd thro' thick and thin.
Foul Type of Britons, in their sad Decline,
When half of them should be transform'd to SWINE.

For its part, the London Company of Distillers failed to oppose the bill in any meaningful way. In March its representatives took their case to the commissioners of excise, on the assumption that they would receive a more sympathetic hearing there than before Parliament. They pleaded with the commissioners that the Company was willing "to concur in any Measures which might conduce to the Welfare of the Community," including a proposal that would effectively ban the consumption of spirits on premises, and set the minimum that could be purchased at one pint. Nothing, however, came of this proposal, and the commissioners did not, as the Company had so earnestly hoped, recommend it to Parliament. Having been turned down by the commissioners, the Company next made a halfhearted attempt to make its case in the press. Thus toward the end of March its representatives prevailed on the editors of *The General Advertiser* to run a piece warning that the bill now pending before Parliament would lead to widespread smuggling. It was, however, too little too late, for by now the bill was unstoppable. The Company's efforts in Parliament also came to naught, with one of its solicitors cheating it of a bribe earmarked for the housekeeper of the Commons. By May the Company was so demoralized that the members who had been nominated to oppose the bill declined to do so, whereupon its "Court did not think fitt to Appoint any Committee or to proceed any further thereon."

The bill was shepherded through the House of Commons by Francis Fane, who just eight years earlier had championed the Gin Act of 1743. Helping him was Slingsby Bethell of Tower Hill, who in 1747 had sponsored a petition to suppress hawkers and peddlers in the City, and who in 1755 would become lord mayor of London. Because he was an alderman of the City of London, Bethell had almost certainly been among the luminaries attending Maddox's sermon back in January. The committee considering the bill was exceptionally thorough, summoning before it a succession of eminent physicians, in addition to two high constables and representatives from the Excise Office. Despite the enormous pressure that had been brought to bear on Parliament, the bill proceeded at a leisurely pace, quite possibly because Henry Pelham, who was prime minister at the time, was at first opposed to it. Early in June, when two last-minute amendments were added to the bill, it was even rumored that it might "not pass into a Law this Session of Parliament." On 10 June, however, the House of Commons passed the bill, and one week later the House of Lords passed it without amendment. In the end the Gin Act of 1751 was passed because both Houses chose to believe, contrary to all evidence, that consumption was on the rise, and that the wholesale distillers, who in 1747 had once again been allowed back into the retail trade, were in large part to blame for this unhappy—if nonexistent—state of affairs.

The new law took effect almost immediately, on 1 July. It raised excises on British spirits by 4.5 pence a gallon, an increase in excess of 50 percent. At the same time the new act barred distillers from retailing spirits, and for good measure it also barred all sales in prisons, poorhouses, and workhouses. Naturally, hawkers continued to be barred from the trade, and to discourage wholesale distillers from doing business with them the new law removed legal remedies for collecting debts of less than £1. To ensure that licensed establishments in the capital were respectable, the new law limited licenses to publicans whose premises were assessed at £10 or more a year. Justices were still authorized to try petty hawkers, but because they had proven unreliable in enforcing previous gin acts, the new act authorized the commissioners of excise to try petty hawkers in addition to established publicans.

The act also raised the licensing fee for retailing spirits to £2. By showing uncharacteristic restraint in raising this particular fee, Parliament broke with past policy, which in 1729 and 1736 had focused on restricting sales by making it virtually impossible to purchase a license to retail spirits. Once the fee stipulated in the Gin Act of 1751 took effect, purchases of licenses dropped, but not dramatically, from 31,254 in the fiscal year ending in 1752, to 25,438 in 1753; after that purchases slowly edged up at a rate that more or less kept pace with the growth of the population.

With the passage of the Gin Act of 1751, the practice of informing briefly came back to life. Less than two weeks into the new act, "twenty-two Distillers, and upwards of seventy others, were convicted for retailing Spirituous Liquors; the former suffering Tippling in their Shops, and the others for selling without a License." This was, the same report concluded, "Rare news for the Informers, some of whom, it is said, made their Morning's Work worth upwards of 50 £." Toward the end of July, a woman was "detected by the Turnkey of the Fleet Prison carrying some spirituous Liquors into that Gaol...." She was tried and convicted by none other than Slingsby Bethell, one of the architects of the recent act; the woman also had the dubious distinction of being the first person in the City of London to be convicted under the Gin Act of 1751. In August three more women were convicted by Bethell, and all were sentenced to varying terms of imprisonment in the local house of correction. In September, a prominent distiller on Fleet Street "received a threatening Letter from two Pettyfoggers in the Law, in which they pretended they would lodge an Information against him"; the distiller agreed to meet with them, having taken the precaution of bringing along two constables to arrest the pair for extortion. After September, however, the newspapers lost interest in covering enforcement of the new act, even though it is clear that many publicans evaded it as best they could. Early in 1752, for example, casks containing approximately two hundred gallons of "geneva, anniseed, plague-water, cinnamon, and mint-water, cherry and raspberry brandy" were confiscated from a shop off Ratcliff Highway and were unceremoniously staved.

In the short run, though, everything more or less went as planned. The people, for once, were silent, and there was no repeat of the mock funerals and other noisy protests that had greeted the Gin Act of 1736. Just one week after the new act took effect, it was widely reported that "several eminent Malt Distillers have come to a Resolution to decline that Branch of Business." As in 1729 and 1736, consumption dropped in the years immediately following enactment. By 1756, however, it was once again on the rise. If the history of the Gin Acts of 1729 and 1736 is any guide, this reversal would almost certainly have continued had the government not intervened in 1757 and banned the manufacture of spirits from domestic grains. The ban came on the heels of a series of crop failures, and remained in effect until 1760, at which point Parliament again raised excises on spirits. Throughout the ban, per capita consumption of British spirits remained relatively stable, suggesting that a new baseline level of demand had been established, the best efforts of Parliament notwithstanding. Indeed, even in 1759, a year of acute dearth, per capita consumption of spirits was still nearly 25 percent higher than it had been in the halcyon days of the early eighteenth century. English drinking habits had clearly undergone a profound and seemingly irrevocable change over the last sixty years, begging the question of whether the Gin Act of 1751 had any lasting effect.

Most contemporaries acknowledged that the Gin Acts of 1729 and 1736 had been conspicuous failures. In the case of the Gin

Act of 1751, however, not only did consumption drop in the years following enactment, it also remained significantly lower than it had been over the previous two decades. Contemporaries naturally credited the Gin Act of 1751 with these happy effects, for here at last was positive proof that legislation could prevent debauchery. Jonas Hanway, who is best remembered for his failed attempts to rescue London's foundlings, claimed that thanks to "the hand of Providence interposed by the instrumentality of His Majesty's ministers . . . the people themselves seem at length to have discovered, that health and pleasure, food and raiment, are better than sickness and pain, want and wretchedness." Hanway, however, was writing in 1759, a year when real wages were severely depressed and the price of bread was high, leaving the working poor with precious little disposable income to spend on alcoholic beverages.

In the final analysis, however, the calamitous drop in real wages that occurred in the second half of the century had no more effect on consumption than did the gains that had occurred in the first half of the century. Nor, for that matter, did the price of gin, as variously measured by excises and the costs of the materials used in its manufacture, have a significant impact on consumption. The most that can be said is that the cheapness of gin in the early decades of the century encouraged people to try the beverage; from that point forward, however, the gin craze followed the trajectory of other and more recent drug epidemics: that is, it lasted for the span of one generation, and once its peak had passed, demand was still higher than it had been before gin entered the mass market. In 1751, then, the moral reformers merely caught a wave that was already on its downward slope, which is to say that in the end they succeeded by accident rather than by design. Mother Gin had simply grown old.

CHAPTER NINE

The Author Also Grows Old,
and, Reluctant to Conclude the NARRATIVE,
Meditates upon RECENT EVENTS

What must become of the Infant who is conceived in Gin? with the poisonous Distillations of which it is nourished both in the Womb and at the Breast? Are these wretched Infants (if such can be supposed capable of arriving at the Age of Maturity) to become our future Sailors, and our future Grenadiers?   HENRY FIELDING, 1751

... this insanity ... is a greater threat to our national security than communism because it is taking our children away from us and having them come into this world without parents by their side, with permanent physical and brain damage ...

REPRESENTATIVE CHARLES B. RANGEL, 16 October 1987

IN OCTOBER OF 1987, at the height of the so-called "crack epidemic," Congressman Charles B. Rangel took a trip to Broward County, Florida. He was there in his capacity as chairman of the Select Committee on Narcotics Abuse and Control, and with him were several other congressmen. They came from both sides of the aisle, but whether Democrat or Republican, none seemed quite prepared for what awaited them in the county hospital's neonatal clinic. There they saw several prematurely born infants. Like most infants born before their time, they were not an attractive sight. These infants, however, had an additional blemish: they had been born to mothers who were known or suspected users of crack cocaine. Rangel was very nearly reduced to tears by the sight, exclaiming at one point, "This has shattered the myth of mother-hood as we know it." Not to be outdone, his Republican colleague, E. Clay Shaw, Jr., read the following statement into the record: "When you look at these tiny, tiny babies, it is enough to make you cry, but it is enough to make you so damned mad that we are going to have to get tough with this, we are going to have to do more...."

Rangel and Shaw were by no means alone. In the late 1980s, politicians from both sides of the aisle vied with each other in denouncing the singular evils of crack cocaine and the depravity of its users, while reporters, many of whom should have known bet-ter, characterized crack cocaine as a drug that was instantly addicting, transforming its users into dangerous and inhuman monsters. One unwary reporter, citing "specialists in drug addic-tion," was completely taken in by the claim that, "Crack can over-whelm one of the strongest forces in nature, the parental instinct." And another reporter, citing yet another specialist, simply accepted as truth the claim that, "The addiction to cocaine is so strong that it often overrules the maternal instinct a mother has."

Ultimately, of course, many editorial boards came to their senses. In July of 1991, for example, the editorial board of the *San Jose Mercury News* observed that, "The image of bad women destroying their babies in the womb fits perfectly with the politics of demonizing drugs and of regulating pregnancy." "Crack babies," the editors added, are not "destined for inevitable fail-ure—unless our expectations make that a self-fulfilling prophecy." Politicians, however, did not come to their senses. Like gin, crack cocaine just happened to become news in an otherwise dull politi-cal season, and like gin, it was very quickly transformed into the poster child for everything that was frightening about cities and the people who inhabited them.

It is at this point very difficult to resist the temptation to draw comparisons between the gin craze and more recent drug scares, and yet it would be wrong to do so without first sounding a cautionary note: drugs affect the minds of their critics just as much as they affect the minds of their users. Reason, in other words, is always the first casualty in any debate about drugs and their use in a liberal society. The breakdown of reason, in turn, has given rise to some curious fallacies, especially among the nation's more conservative politicians.

The flip side of this observation is that while politicians and moral reformers often exaggerate, only rarely do they lie outright. People, in other words, drink alcohol or take drugs precisely because they *do* have effects. (Some politicians, of course, simply lie. George W. Bush, Sr., who went on national television and claimed that he was holding up a bag of crack cocaine seized in Lafayette Park, constitutes a conspicuous example. In their initial search, agents from the Drug Enforcement Agency had been unable to find anyone dealing crack cocaine in the vicinity of the White House; it was only after they had lured a dealer from a distant neighborhood to the park that they were able to make a seizure in seeming proximity to the seat of government.)

But again, just because politicians and moral reformers make exaggerated and even misleading claims about drugs, it does not stand to reason that drugs are inherently harmless. Gin really did have adverse effects on the health of many of its drinkers, if only because so many of them were already poorly nourished and lived in neighborhoods that were as squalid as they were insalubrious.

The real fallacy lies in assuming that any drug, including gin and crack cocaine, is by itself responsible for the poor health and poor behavior of its users. This is casuistry at its very worst. The corollary is no less attractive, for by singling out drugs and the people who use them the state effectively absolves itself of the responsibility to do something about the sorts of environments that make drugs attractive in the first place. To quote from a column written by Ellen Goodman back in 1990, "Communities that are slow and stingy with support may be quick to prosecute. In retreat from principles of communal responsibility, we are trying to force individual responsibility."

The casuistry that worked for the Reaganites and their successors in the first Bush administration also worked for men like Thomas Wilson and Sir Joseph Jekyll. Eighteenth-century reformers were right when they said that gin was undoubtedly bad for a good many people, but they neglected to add that its effects would probably have been relatively minor had they not been compounded by overcrowding, disease, and disgustingly poor sanitation. And it was these factors, just as much as gin itself, that appalled polite men and women, without, however, motivating them to share their wealth with people less fortunate than themselves—or to pay them anything approaching a decent wage. Hence the enormous appeal of the campaign against gin, for here, at last, was a simple solution to a devilishly complex problem.

Hence, too, the enormous appeal of Hogarth's *Gin Lane*. The print is many things, but at its most literal it is really nothing more than a succession of shocking tableaux. A carpenter pawns the tools of his trade for gin; an infant falls to its death; a mother or nursemaid silences another infant with gin; a dead or dying ballad-seller sits unobserved and unattended; a suicide hangs from the rafters, exposed to public view; and just outside an under-taker's shop, a woman's body is lowered into a coffin while her orphaned child bawls uncontrollably.

It is a remarkable print—easily Hogarth's best—and it suc-ceeds as propaganda because it identifies cause and effect in terms that are as stark as they are seemingly irrefutable. Gin is cause and poverty its effect. It is a very appealing equation: take away gin and away goes poverty and in comes the jolly prosperity of *Beer Street*. The converse is a little trickier, for it forces us to look deeper for the causes of poverty; it may even force us to do something about it. This approach was, of course, even less popular in eighteenth-century England than it is today.

Poverty and gin were inextricably linked, but which came first? Most of London's working poor led lives of unspeakable misery before the advent of gin; moreover, their lives, as measured by real wages, were even more wretched after its demise. It was not gin that made people poor; it was poverty that made them drink.

If reason fails, as it most certainly has in the so-called "war on drugs," then skepticism must suffice. The gin craze, although it occurred so very long ago, provides us with some pointers in pre-dicting when the next big drug scare will occur. The first point is obvious enough: the drug should be new or newly rediscovered. At the same time, it must also be both affordable and widely avail-able. Distilled spirits had been available in England since the late Middle Ages, but their use only became problematic when advances in distilling and real wages allowed ordinary men and women to purchase gin and other cheap spirits in large quantities. The same is true of cocaine, which has been available in the

United States since the late nineteenth century. Although its use gave rise to periodic panics in the late nineteenth and early twentieth centuries, none could compare to the shock that greeted the proliferation of crack cocaine in the mid-1980s. The same, presumably, will also be true of synthetic or "designer" drugs of the future as they make their appearance one after another.

The second point is a little trickier. The drug, whether new or not, must be perceived as being stronger and more dangerous than any of its predecessors. In the case of gin, this really was the case. Crack cocaine presents a more ambiguous example. Smoking cocaine is certainly more efficient than snorting it, but there is no conclusive evidence that crack cocaine is any more addicting than powdered cocaine. There is even less evidence, beyond the purely anecdotal, that crack cocaine is instantly addicting. Even so, the only way to rouse a public that has seen drugs come and go in rapid succession is to say that the newest drug to hit the streets is several times stronger than its predecessors. Hence this claim, as made in a pamphlet written for adolescents: "As dangerous as cocaine powder is, it's nothing compared to its smokable forms.... Whereas addiction to cocaine powder usually develops gradually, crack can quickly hurl you onto the carousel of addiction." Hence, too, this claim, as put forth in a book written on behalf of the first Bush administration's war on drugs: "Crack...is highly addictive. Users have been known to become addicts within only a few days of steady use...."

It is not, however, enough merely to demonize a particular drug. Ultimately, the drug must have a human face. There are two obvious candidates for the position: the people who sell the drug, and the people who are victimized by them. In this, the eighteenth-century crusaders against gin were true pioneers, demonizing not only the petty gin-sellers who clogged the streets of London, but also the women who chose the pleasures of gin over the travails of motherhood. Next to these failed women they placed their neglected and unhealthy infants. Together, mothers and infants made the perfect poster children: one invited censure, and the other invited pity. Each, in its own way, horrified polite society. It was a motif that would be repeated to great effect. In Victorian England, for example, mothers who worked in factories were criticized for using opium to sedate their infants, while more recently, images of "crack babies" have served to galvanize public opinion against crack cocaine. "These mothers don't care about their babies and they don't care about themselves," Dr. Jing Ja Yoon was quoted as saying in 1989.

The quote appeared, conveniently enough, in an article by Douglas J. Besharov, a member of the right-wing American Enterprise Institute. This point of view has naturally attracted a great deal of criticism from the left, which in this case is perfectly justified. Katha Pollitt perhaps put it best when she observed that, "The focus on maternal behavior allows the government to appear to be concerned about babies without having to spend any money, change any priorities or challenge any vested interests. As with crime, as with poverty, a complicated, multifaceted problem is construed as a matter of freely chosen individual behavior."

Poster children are useful, but only up to a point. New drugs are most likely to take on a problematic status when all or most of their users happen to belong to a marginal group or race. In the case of gin, its drinkers consisted overwhelmingly of London's working poor, many of whom were recent immigrants to the city. As a group, they had worried their social superiors long before gin became widely available. Very similar concerns animated the early

American temperance movement, which effectively pitted native—and generally rural—Protestants against recent immigrants to the nation's growing cities. And like the Scots and Irish who came to eighteenth-century London in search of work, many of these recent immigrants just happened to be Catholic. Illicit drugs have also been the victims of guilt by association. Opium, for example, was originally associated with Chinese immigrants to the American West, while marijuana was originally associated with Mexican-Americans. These unsavory associations, in turn, ultimately led to bans on both substances.

Cigarettes present yet another example. As the socioeconomic status of smokers continues to decline relative to that of their critics and other non-smokers, it becomes easier and easier for public health advocates to propose and sometimes even impose increasingly extreme restrictions on people who are, for all intents and purposes, their social inferiors. Among their victims is the fictional Rumpole, who, banned from smoking in chambers, is reduced to lighting up outdoors. There he finds himself in the company of secretaries, "Short-skirted, high-heeled, with cigarettes dangling from their lips, they would seem to any passer-by to be ladies of the street. . . ."

A new drug must also be given a putative home, preferably an unsavory one. Enter the "gin shop," the "opium den," and the "crack house." Each, of course, belongs to a different era, but they all have one thing in common: they are, both literally and metaphorically, synonymous with the slums and dark places that have always frightened polite society.

Nobody, of course, wishes to be accused of hysteria or pandering. This is where the experts come in, be they doctors, epidemiologists, or law-enforcement officials. No congressional hearing about illicit drugs is complete without them. Rangel, for example, summoned several such experts before his select committee in October of 1987, including two physicians and a registered nurse. And here we can thank Mother Gin for a new form of advocacy in public life, one that both enlists and manipulates statistics and other forms of scientific evidence in the cause of reforming the morals of the working poor.

The next point follows logically from its predecessors: Because a drug is new or has returned after years of lying in wait, and because its effects are trumpeted as unprecedented, extreme measures must be taken. These measures are made all the easier by barraging the public with frightening images of the drug's villains and victims. Extreme measures are the consequence of extreme rhetoric, and in the case of the gin craze, legislators responded by unleashing an army of informers on the people of London. Even so, eighteenth-century legislators were in fact more cautious than their modern counterparts, who have managed to trample on a far wider range of civil liberties in fighting the war on drugs. Informers, ironically, have also made a comeback, with informants getting reduced or suspended sentences in return for what New York City police officers call "testalying." It is, however, simplistic to blame legislators and legislators alone for hasty and ill-conceived expedients. Legislators, after all, are under enormous pressure to make quick fixes, thanks in no small part to the dubious role of the media in magnifying drug scares.

If legislation cannot prevent debauchery, it can most decidedly contribute to it. It can do so by focusing the public's attention altogether too much on a particular substance, thus imbuing the substance with far more significance than it might otherwise merit. Perversely, this has been the case with both crack cocaine and the so-called designer drugs of late: many people, it turns out, are very keen on trying out drugs that are touted—albeit incorrectly—as inducing a "whole body orgasm," or, better yet, a rush that is "better than sex."

And when this focus is initiated by an unpopular government or is accompanied by penalties that are regarded by many as harsh or unfair, the substance can become something more than itself, emerging as a symbol of a counterculture or political protest. This is exactly what happened when the Gin Act of 1736 effectively sought to outlaw sales of gin: for two years, from 1736 until 1738, the capital was rocked by a series of popular protests that posed a much more immediate threat to public order than gin ever had; moreover, sales, after a momentary slump, actually increased, in part because selling and drinking gin now constituted a form of political protest against a wildly unpopular government. By the same token, one of the reasons why sales actually dropped after the Gin Act of 1743 took effect was because its reversal of the much harsher Gin Act of 1736 effectively stripped gin of its symbolic value among London's proletariat.

The essential point is that drugs can very easily become exaggerated symbols in what are in fact cultural skirmishes. Because alcohol and other drugs invariably give rise to elaborate social rules of their own, it is virtually impossible to attack either without also attacking the larger culture in which they are consumed and from which they derive much of their meaning. Gin is no exception. And because gin was overwhelmingly the beverage of choice among London's proletariat, it was altogether too easy for polite men and women to associate it with all of the other things that they found distasteful and frightening about cities and the people who inhabited them.

And with that we come full circle. Two final points stand out. The first is that skirmishes over drugs are necessarily skirmishes over how people live—and sometimes seem to waste—their lives. When we react against a new drug and the effects it might have on other people's behavior, we are also reacting against the culture in which the drug has taken root. This is what makes the rhetoric of eighteenth-century reformers so refreshing: unlike modern reformers, they were unabashedly elitist. What they had to say may not have been attractive, but at least it was honest.

The second lesson follows from the first. Eighteenth-century London was a huge, complex, and often very frightening place, especially for people whose ideals were still very much rooted in a rural and increasingly mythical past. To the extent that cities are complex and often very frightening places, we are apt to attach rather too much meaning to the drugs that take root in them; we are also too easily seduced by the notion that the complex problems that come with complex places boil down to a simple and single source, be it gin, heroin, or crack cocaine. This is perhaps especially true of modern America, whose core ideals are still very much rooted in a rural and by now entirely mythical past. Instead, we find ourselves drawn, both literally and esthetically, to the simplicity and homogeneity of the suburbs; in this we are perhaps not so very different from the polite men and women who flocked to the stately squares and crescents of London's West End, decrying, in their precipitous flight, the vices of those less fortunate than themselves.

The Gin Acts Laid Bare for All to See

> *To inflict a Penalty upon a real Crime, to punish an Action which is generally thought pernicious and scandalous, is not only necessary but popular; but to inflict Penalties upon Actions which are thought neither pernicious nor scandalous will always be thought oppressive; and consequently must alienate the Affections, at least of those who actually suffer by such Regulations.*
>
> *The London Magazine*, January, 1737

PARLIAMENT PASSED A TOTAL of eight "gin acts" between 1729 and 1751. Each of these laws naturally had a more formal name, and some were simply inserted as clauses into legislative acts of an altogether different nature. But to refer to each of these acts by their proper name would serve no particular purpose, other than to convince the reader that the author is a bore. And so, for the purposes of wit and brevity, the laws by which Parliament alternately sought to tame and tax Mother Gin have been called the gin acts. In the end, none of them quite worked the way their framers had intended.

THE GIN ACT OF 1729

The first of the gin acts dates from 1729. It sought to reduce sales of gin by raising taxes on cheap spirits flavored with fruit and other additives, and by raising the licensing fees to be paid by publicans. It failed miserably, and so a new gin act was drafted and passed just four years later, in 1733.

THE GIN ACT OF 1733

The second gin act became law in 1733. While repealing the taxes and licensing fees mandated by the Gin Act of 1729, the Gin Act of 1733 nonetheless had the stated goal of putting an end to street sales of gin, and for this it relied on professional informers. It, too, failed miserably.

THE GIN ACT OF 1736

The Gin Act of 1736 was the most notorious of all the gin acts. Like its predecessor, the Gin Act of 1733, the Gin Act of 1736 relied on professional informers for its enforcement, and like the Gin Act of 1729, it raised taxes on spirits while also raising the licensing fees to be paid by publicans, this time by astronomical amounts. It briefly succeeded in reducing sales of gin by licensed publicans, but it did little to deter gin-sellers who operated without a license and in open defiance of the law.

THE GIN ACT OF 1737

The Gin Act of 1737, which was actually a clause in the so-called "Sweets Act" passed that year, plugged a major loophole in the Gin Act of 1736 by authorizing the commissioners of excise to reward informers for going after the petty hawkers who sold gin in the streets and alleys of London. As a result, thousands of Londoners, most of them women, were convicted of selling gin without a license; even so, sales of gin continued to rise, while the unwelcome activities of the informers provoked a backlash not only against the Gin Act of 1736, but against the government itself. For the next two years, from 1737 to 1739, hardly a day passed in which an informer was not attacked on the streets of London, sometimes by mobs of a hundred or more people.

THE GIN ACT OF 1738

By 1738, the government was prepared to let the Gin Act of 1736 lapse. It could not, however, ignore attacks on informers, especially since many of these attacks occurred very close to the seat of government in Westminster. And so in 1738 Parliament passed a new gin act that made it a felony to attack an informer; the new law also allowed private individuals to arrest gin-sellers. In doing so, the government acknowledged that many constables were by now refusing to arrest friends and neighbors who happened to sell gin.

THE GIN ACT OF 1743

The Gin Act of 1743 was passed at the height of the War of Austrian Succession (1740–1748). It had two goals: to undo the damage done by the Gin Acts of 1736, 1737, and 1738, and to raise new revenue for the war effort. Toward that end the new gin act reduced the licensing fee to be paid by publicans to an amount that most of them could afford to pay, thus putting informers out of business; it also increased the excise on gin. Much to almost everyone's surprise, sales of gin actually started to drop.

THE GIN ACT OF 1747

In 1747, England was still at war, and the government was still very short of funds. Parliament responded by passing the Gin Act of 1747. The new act raised excises on gin once again, and it also allowed wholesale distillers to take out licenses to retail gin. Far from raising new revenue for the government, the law actually succeeded in further reducing the demand for gin.

THE GIN ACT OF 1751

With the return of peace in 1748, the reformers once again entered the fray. They did so even as the demand for gin was already in decline. This time, however, the reformers hit their stride, expertly playing on the public's fears of crime. And so they offered a simple formula with an equally simple solution: gin, they said, led to crime; take away the first and away goes the second. This time no one stood in the reformers' way as they pushed the eighth and final gin act through Parliament in the spring of 1751. The Gin Act of 1751 raised excises on British spirits by more than 50 percent; it also banned sales of gin in prisons and other lockups, while barring both distillers and street hawkers from retailing gin.

Parliament needn't have bothered. Sales of gin were already dropping, while rapid population growth, coupled with a succession of disastrous harvests, would soon drive down wages while driving up the price of basic foodstuffs; as a consequence, most men and women were now simply too poor to buy gin. The era of the great gin acts was over, and with its passing gin began its slow climb out of the gutter and into the liquor cabinets of polite society.

NOTES AND SOURCES

AN HISTORIAN IS not unlike a pirate's parrot. Both perch on the shoulder of someone whose intellect dwarfs their own, and both squawk out bits and phrases picked up somewhere else. And neither creature fully understands what it is that he or she is saying. In the case of the gin craze, I have played the role of both pirate and parrot, relying very heavily on four important and impressive works: M. Dorothy George's *London Life in the Eighteenth Century*, first published in 1925; George F. E. Rudé's "'Mother Gin' and the London Riots of 1736," published in 1959 in the *Guildhall Miscellany*; Peter Clark's "'Mother Gin' Controversy in the Early Eighteenth Century," published in 1988 in the *Transactions of the Royal Historical Society*; and Lee Davison's "Experiments in the Social Regulation of Industry: Gin Legislation, 1729–1751," published in 1992 as a chapter in *Stilling the Grumbling Hive*.

All four scholars made extensive use of archival materials, and it was in their footsteps that I followed as I made the rounds of London's rich archives and libraries. I have supplemented the research of my predecessors with a detailed reading of eighteenth-century legal documents, including lists of gin-sellers convicted under the Gin Act of 1736. These documents are to be found, in varying states of completeness, in the Public Record Office, the London Metropolitan Archives, the Corporation of London Records Office, and the Surrey Record Office. I have also made extensive use of eighteenth-century newspapers, which are to be had on microfilm in any major university library. I am referring, of course, to the famous Burney Collection of British newspapers.

Much has been written about the so-called "war on drugs," and it would be a mistake to believe that the conclusions reached in chapter nine are either startling or entirely new. On the contrary. At most, they build on the earlier work of both historians and sociologists, including, most notably, Harry Levine, Craig Reinarman, David Musto, and Philip Jenkins. In particular, Jenkins's *Synthetic Panics* is must-reading for anyone who is already thinking beyond the drug scares of the past and imagining the drug scares of the future.

INTRODUCTION
PAGE

1. Bockett epigraph: Elias Bockett, *Blunt to Walpole* (London: Printed for J. Wilford, 1730), p. 26.

1. "A Mob, hearing of this Affair": *Read's Weekly Journal*, 3 April 1736, p. 2.

3. The figures include only the population: E. Anthony Wrigley and Roger S. Schofield, *The Population History of England, 1541–1871. A Reconstruction* (London: Edward Arnold, 1981), pp. 528–529; T.S. Ashton, *An Economic History of England: the 18th Century* (London: Methuen & Co., 1961), p. 243.

3. Although there were as yet no formal restrictions: Jessica F. Warner, "Historical Perspectives on the Shifting Boundaries around Youth and Alcohol. The Example of Preindustrial England, 1350–1750," *Addiction* 93, no. 5 (1998), pp. 641–657.

3. "A Man . . . no time to recollect or think": Josiah Tucker, *An Impartial Enquiry into the Benefits and Damages Arising from the Present Very Great Use of Low-priced Spirituous Liquors* (London: Printed for T. Trye, 1751), p. 21.

3. A man described as a "Plush Weaver": *Read's Weekly* Journal, 14 July 1750, p. 3.

3. "Drank a Pint of Gin off at a Draught": *Read's Weekly Journal*, 21 July 1750, p. 4.

3–4. "He fell down, and died immediately": *The London Evening-Post*, 20–22 January 1741, p. 2.

4. A man and his pregnant wife died: *The London Morning Penny Post*, 26–29 July 1751, p. 2.

5. The burden of prosecuting offenders fell on their victims: John M. Beattie, *Crime and the Courts in England 1660–1800* (Princeton: Princeton University Press, 1986), p. 40.

5. William Goudge spent £24: Reay Sabourn, *A Perfect View of the Gin Act* (London: Printed for W. Thorne, 1738), p. 39.

6. It has been estimated that of the some fifteen thousand bills: Joanna Innes, "Parliament and the Shaping of Eighteenth-century English Social Policy," *Transactions of the Royal Historical Society* 40 (1990), p. 69.

6. The former consisted primarily of officeholders: Paul Langford, *The Excise Crisis. Society and Politics in the Age of Walpole* (Oxford: Clarendon Press, 1975), pp. 11–14.

6. It was from the ranks of these country squires: J.H. Plumb, *The Growth of Political Stability in England 1675–1725* (London: Macmillan, 1972), pp. 133–140.

6–7. In this they were remarkably successful, so much so that by the eighteenth century: John Harold Plumb, *England in the Eighteenth Century* (Baltimore: Penguin Books, 1960), pp. 38–41.

7. This compares to a total population of just over five million: E. Anthony Wrigley and Roger S. Schofield, *The Population History of England, 1541–1871. A Reconstruction* (London: Edward Arnold, 1981), p. 533.

7. The same points also underscore the extent to which eighteenth-century England: John Howard Plumb, *The First Four Georges*, third ed. (London: Hamlyn, 1974), pp. 23–24.

8–9. Alcohol—be it beer, gin, wine, port, or rum: Roy Porter, "The Drinking Man's Disease: the 'Pre-History' of Alcoholism in Georgian Britain," *British Journal of Addiction* 80, no. 4 (1985), pp. 385–387.

9. Thomas Turner . . . was a habitual drunkard: David Vaisey, ed., *The Diary of Thomas Turner 1754–1765* (Oxford: Oxford University Press, 1984).

9. Samuel Johnson was also a notorious drunkard: Pat Rogers, ed., *Johnson and Boswell in Scotland. A Journey to the Hebrides* (New Haven: Yale University Press, 1993), p. 150.

9. "The common People . . . are highly obliged to those": *The Country Journal: or, the Craftsman*, 14 August 1736, p. 1.

10. Even the most ardent enemies of gin encouraged workers to drink beer: Jessica F. Warner, "Good Help Is Hard to Find. A Few Comments about Alcohol and Work in Preindustrial England," *Addiction Research* 2, no. 3 (1995), pp. 259–269.

10. "When laboring People use these Liquors in moderate Degree": Josiah Tucker, *An Impartial Enquiry into the Benefits and Damages Arising from the Present Very Great Use of Low-priced Spirituous Liquors* (London: Printed for T. Trye, 1751), p. 29.

10. The industry was well represented in Parliament: Peter Mathias, *The Brewing Industry in England 1700–1830* (Cambridge: Cambridge University Press, 1959), p. 333.

10. Two anonymous letters: *The London Magazine*, March 1751, p. 126; *The Gentleman's Magazine*, April 1751, p. 165.

10. "Would put a stop to the manufacture": Historical Manuscripts Commission, *The Manuscripts of the Marquess Townshend* (London: Her Majesty's Stationery Office, 1887), p. 373.

10. It was not until the early nineteenth century: Brian S. Katcher, "Benjamin Rush's Educational Campaign against Hard Drinking," *American Journal of Public Health* 83, no. 2 (1993), pp. 273–281.

10–11. When temperance emerged as one of the major social movements: James S. Roberts, *Drink, Temperance and the Working Class in Nineteenth-Century Germany* (Boston: George Allen & Unwin, 1984), p. 19.

11. Howard Becker coined the phrase back in 1963: Howard S. Becker, *Outsiders: Studies in the Sociology of Deviance* (New York: The Free Press, 1966), p. 122.

12. At the beginning of the century, less than 20 percent: Penelope J. Corfield, *The Impact of English Towns 1700–1800* (Oxford: Oxford University Press, 1982), p. 2; E. Anthony Wrigley, "Urban Growth and Agricultural Change: England and the Continent during the Early Modern Period," *Journal of Interdisciplinary History* 15, no. 4 (1985), pp. 683–728.

12. London was by 1700 the largest city in Europe: E. Anthony Wrigley, "A Simple Model of London's Importance in Changing English Society and Economy 1650–1750," in *Past and Present*, ed. Philip Abrams and E. Anthony Wrigley, *Past and Present Publications* (Cambridge: Cambridge University Press, 1978), pp. 215–216.

12. Accounted for perhaps 13 percent of the city's population: Penelope J. Corfield, *The Impact of English Towns 1700–1800* (Oxford: Oxford University Press, 1982), p. 68.

13. London's immigrants included . . . rich and poor alike: Michael J. Power, "East and West in Early-modern London," in *Wealth and Power in Tudor England: Essays Presented to S.T. Bindoff*, ed. E.W. Ives, R.J. Knecht, and J.J. Scarisbrick (London: 1978); Lawrence Stone, "The Residential Development of the West End of London in the Seventeenth Century," in *After the Reformation: Essays in Honour of J.H. Hexter*, ed. B. Malament (Manchester: 1980).

13. "Whoever shall pass among the streets, will find Wretches": *The Gentleman's Magazine*, November 1743, p. 629.

14. The wealthy few increasingly avoiding direct contact with the poor: Felicity Heal, *Hospitality in Early Modern England* (Oxford: Oxford University Press, 1990).

14. These were the same people who built high fences: Edward P. Thompson, "Patrician Society, Plebian Culture," *Journal of Social History* 8, no. 4 (1974), p. 398; Roy Porter, *London. A Social History* (London: Hamish Hamilton, 1994), pp. 95–96.

14. As the century wore on London became a cleaner: Roy Porter, "Cleaning up the Great Wen: Public Health in Eighteenth-century London," in *Living and Dying in London*, ed. W.F. Bynum and Roy Porter (London: Wellcome Institute for the History of Medicine, 1991), pp. 61–75; John M. Beattie, *Policing and Punishment in London 1660–1750. Urban Crime and the Limits of Terror* (Oxford: Oxford University Press, 2001).

14. Gin was destroying "all voluntary Submission": *The Gentleman's Magazine*, November 1743, p. 567.

15. "Since the drinking of Gin less Milk is sold": C.L.S. Linnell, ed., *The Diaries of Thomas Wilson* (London: The Camelot Press Ltd., 1964), p. 143.

15. "Since the Suppression of Gin, the coarse Pieces of Beef": *The London Daily Post*, 2 November 1736, p. 2; *The Old Whig*, 4 November 1736, p. 3.

15. There were as yet no norms limiting: Hans Medick, "Plebeian Culture in the Transition to Capitalism," in *Culture, Ideology, and Politics. Essays for Eric Hobsbawm*, ed. Raphael Samuel and Gareth Stedman Jones, History Workshop Series (London: Routeledge & Kegan Paul, 1983), pp. 98–99.

15–16. The same effects can be seen in parts of post-colonial Africa: Boris Serebro, "Total Alcohol Consumption as an Index of Anxiety among Urbanized Africans," *The British Journal of Addiction* 67, no. 4 (1972), pp. 251–254; Elizabeth Colson and Thayer Scudder, *For Prayer and Profit. The Ritual, Economic, and Social Importance of Beer in Gwembe District, Zambia, 1950–1982* (Stanford: Stanford University Press, 1988), p. 129.

16. Heavy drinking would almost certainly have contributed: David A. Leon et al., "Huge Variation in Russian Mortality Rates 1984–94: Artefact, Alcohol, or What?," *Lancet* 350 (1997), pp. 383–388; Francis C. Notzon et al., "Causes of Declining Life Expectancy in Russia," *Journal of the American Medical Association* 279, no. 10 (1998), pp. 793–800; references courtesy of Dr. Robin Room.

16. "When . . . not drunk in such large Quantities as to kill immediately": Thomas Wilson, *Distilled Spirituous Liquors the Bane of the Nation* (London: Printed for J. Roberts, 1736), p. 33.

16. Stephen Hales had made very similar claims: Stephen Hales, *A Friendly Admonition to the Drinkers of Brandy, and other Distilled Spirituous Liquors*, second ed. (London: Printed for Joseph Downing, 1734), p. 3.

16. Like Wilson he was simply repeating: Roy Porter, "The Drinking Man's Disease: the 'Pre-History' of Alcoholism in Georgian Britain," *British Journal of Addiction* 80, no. 4 (1985), pp. 385–396.

16. The real problem was one of poor nutrition coupled with backbreaking work: Michael Mitterauer, *A History of Youth*, ed. Peter Laslett and Michael Anderson, trans. Graeme Dunphy, Family, Sexuality and Social Relations in Past Times (Oxford: Blackwell, 1992), pp. 2–5.

16. That new hires "be full five feet high and fifteen years old": Daniel A. Baugh, ed., *Naval Administration 1715–1750*, vol. 120, Publications of the Navy Record Society (London: The Navy Records Society, 1977), p. 310.

17. The number of barrels brewed in and around London: Peter Mathias, *The Brewing Industry in England 1700–1830* (Cambridge: Cambridge University Press, 1959), p. 544.

17. They were . . . laughably low when compared to the amounts consumed: W. J. Rorabaugh, *The Alcoholic Republic. An American Tradition* (New York: Oxford, 1979).

CHAPTER ONE
PAGE

21. Ames epigraph: Richard Ames, *The Bacchanalian Sessions* (London: Printed for E. Hawkins, 1693), p. 1.

21. Vulnerable to being invaded by the French: Gilbert Burnet, *History of his Own Time* (London: Chatto and Windus, 1875), pp. 498–499.

22. England would fight a total of six wars: John Brewer, *The Sinews of Power. War, Money, and the English State, 1688–1783* (London: Unwin Hyman, 1989), p. 27.

23. Spirits were first distilled from wine: R.J. Forbes, *Short History of the Art of Distillation from the Beginnings up to the Death of Cellier Blumenthal* (Leiden: E.J. Brill, 1948), p. 57; Gregory

A. Austin, *Alcohol in Western Society from Antiquity to 1800. A Chronological History* (Santa Barbara: ABC-Clio Information Services, 1985), p. 80.

23. Commonly known as brandy, or burnt wine: C. Anne Wilson, "Burnt Wine and Cordial Waters: the Early Days of Distilling," *Folk Life* 13 (1975), pp. 54–65.

23. "Serious misconduct and disorder": Gregory A. Austin, *Alcohol in Western Society from Antiquity to 1800. A Chronological History* (Santa Barbara: ABC-Clio Information Services, 1985), p. xxi.

23. A series of other German cities: Lyndal Roper, *The Holy Household. Women and Morals, in Reformation Augsburg* (Oxford: Oxford University Press, 1989), p. 185.

23. "Was taken with a violent Fit of the Cholick": *The London Daily Post*, 5 August 1738, p. 1.

23. A pauper woman was found naked in a ditch: *Sessions Papers of the Old Bailey*, 20–23 April 1737, p. 117.

24. By the second half of the century: Andrzej Wyczanski, "La consommation alimentaire en Pologne au XVIe siècle," in *Pour une histoire de l'alimentation*, ed. Jean-Jacques Hémardinquer (Paris: Libraire Armand Colin, 1970), p. 45.

24. Production had to be temporarily banned: Michael S. Moss and John R. Hume, *The Making of Scotch Whisky. A History of the Scotch Whisky Distilling Industry* (Edinburgh: James & James, 1981), p. 34.

24–25. "Three young men meeting to drinke strong waters" in Essex: Samuel Ward, *Woe to Drunkards. A Sermon* (London: A. Matthewes, 1624), p. 22.

25. "Till two of them decease": Thomas Heywood, *Philosothonista, or the Drunkard Opened, Dissected, and Anatomized* (London: Robert Raworth, 1635), p. 68.

25. "We have strong waters": John Taylor, *Drinke and Welcome* (London: Anne Griffin, 1637), no pagination.

25. Taxed at the rate of eightpence per gallon: C.H. Firth and R.S. Rait, eds., *Acts and Ordinances of the Interregnum, 1642–1660*, vol. 1 (London: His Majesty's Stationery Office, 1911), p. 275.

25. The rate was reduced to just twopence per gallon: C.H. Firth and R.S. Rait, eds., *Acts and Ordinances of the Interregnum, 1642–1660*, vol. 2 (London: His Majesty's Stationery Office, 1911), pp. 846–848.

25. An act of Parliament mentioned... "strongwater houses": C.H. Firth and R.S. Rait, eds., *Acts and Ordinances of the Interregnum, 1642–1660*, vol. 2 (London: His Majesty's Stationery Office, 1911), p. 1163.

25. The nation... "began to abound in strong Water-Shops": Daniel Defoe, *A Brief Case of the Distillers, and of the Distilling Trade in England* (London: Printed for T. Warner, 1726), p. 18.

26. A man by the nature of Richard Drake: George Unwin, *The Gilds and Companies of London*, fourth ed. (London: Frank Cass & Company Ltd, 1963), p. 297.

26. As late as 1668 members of the London Company of Distillers: W. Carew Hazlitt, *The Livery Companies of the City of London. Their Origin, Character, Development, and Social and Political Importance* (London: Swan Sonnenschein & Co., 1982), p. 470.

26. Started to use marginally better ingredients: John A. Chartres, "No English Calvados? English Distillers and the Cider Industry in the Seventeenth and Eighteenth Centuries," in *English Rural Society, 1500–1800: Essays in Honour of Joan Thirsk*, ed. John Chartres and David Hey (New York: Cambridge University Press, 1990), p. 328.

26. Used only "the worst of our Grain": Joseph Jekyll, *The Trial of the Spirits*, second ed. (London: Printed for T. Cooper, 1736), p. 8.

26. Still using "the worst of grain": T.S., *A Proper Reply to a Scandalous Libel, Intituled, The Trial of the Spirits* (London: Printed for J. Roberts, 1736), p. 17.

26. "Coarse foul damaged Grain": *The London Daily Post*, 3 April 1736, p. 1.

26–27. To mask the product's awful taste: "The Natural History of Coffee, Thee, Chocolate, and Tobacco," in *Harleian Miscellany; or, a Collection of Scarce, Curious, and Entertaining Pamphlets and Tracts, as well in Manuscript as in Print, Found in the Late Earl of Oxford's Library* (London: Printed for Robert Dutton, 1811), pp. 32–34; Daniel Defoe, *A Brief Case of the Distillers* (London: Printed for T. Warner, 1726), p. 21; R. Campbell, *The London Tradesman* (New York: Augustus M. Kelley, Publishers, 1969), p. 266; John A. Chartres, "Leeds: Regional Distributive Centre of Luxuries in the Later Eighteenth Century," *Northern History* 37 (2000), pp. 125–127.

27. "Found out a way to hit the palate of the poor": Daniel Defoe, *The Complete English Tradesman*, 2 vols., vol. 2 (New York: Burt Franklin, 1970), p. 220.

27. They were easily monitored by local excisemen: Peter Mathias, "Agriculture and the Brewing and Distilling Industries in the Eighteenth Century," *Economic History Review* 5, no. 2 (1952), p. 251.

27. They diluted the mix with water: R. Campbell, *The London Tradesman* (New York: Augustus M. Kelley, Publishers, 1969), pp. 265–266.

27–28. A ready and seemingly inexhaustible market: Peter Clark, *The English Alehouse: A Social History 1200–1830* (New York: Longman, 1983), p. 242.

28. "The ordinary people are now so very well satisfied": Daniel Defoe, *The Complete English Tradesman*, 2 vols., vol. 2 (New York: Burt Franklin, 1970), p. 219.

28. The London Evening-Post reported that a patent had been issued: *The London Evening-Post*, 7–9 November 1728, p. 2.

28. "BRANDY, universally confessed as fine as any foreign": *The Daily Journal*, 2 January 1736, p. 1.

28–29. The industry was in many ways still struggling: R. Campbell, *The London Tradesman* (New York: Augustus M. Kelley, Publishers, 1969), p. 265.

29. "The Spirits and Geneva distilled and made at Islington and Maidstone: Public Record Office, CUST 43/3, 1718–1787, p. 50.

29. The word geneva . . . was already in use by 1706: *The Whole Tryal Indictment, Arraignment and Examination of Madam Geneva* (London: "Printed for William Toss-Pot", 1711).

29. A prostitute by the name of Martha Dobson: *Sessions Papers of the Old Bailey*, 3–4 March 1719, p. 8.

29. The justices of Middlesex singled out: London Metropolitan Archives, General Orders of Court, Middlesex, MJ/OC 1, 1716–1721, folio 126 recto; *The Weekly Journal: or, British Gazetteer. Being the Freshest Advices Foreign and Domestick*, 4 November 1721, p. 273.

29. "The Bill for laying a Duty upon Compound Waters": Corporation of London Guildhall Library, Journal of the Court of the London Company of Distillers, 6207/1, 1714–1730, no pagination; *The Case of the Master, Wardens and Company of Distillers of London: Humbly Offered to the Honourable the House of Commons* (1729), p. 1.

30. The demand for their grain was stagnant: E. Anthony Wrigley and Roger S. Schofield, *The Population History of England, 1541–1871. A Reconstruction* (London: Edward Arnold, 1981), p. 533; T.S. Ashton, *An Economic History of England: the 18th Century* (London: Methuen & Co., 1961), p. 57.

30. Helped keep wages high: E.H. Phelps Brown and Sheila V. Hopkins, "Seven Centuries of the Price of Consumables, Compared with Builders' Wage-rates," in *Essays in Economic History, ed. E.M. Carus-Wilson* (London: Edward Arnold (Publishers) Ltd., 1962), pp. 179–196; E.H. Phelps Brown and Sheila V. Hopkins, "Seven Centuries of Building Wages," in *Essays in Economic History, ed. E.M. Carus-Wilson* (London: Edward Arnold (Publishers) Ltd., 1962), pp. 168–178; L. D. Schwarz, "The Standard of Living in the Long Run: London, 1700–1860," *Economic History Review* 38, no. 1 (1985), pp. 24–41.

30. The combined effect was to drive down the price: G.E. Mingay, "The Agricultural Depression, 1730–1750," *Economic History Review* 8, no. 3 (1956), pp. 326–327.

30–31. "There is nothing that ever more required": "Reasons for Promoting the British Distillery," in *A Collection of Political Tracts* (London: Printed for T. Cooper, 1736), p. 36.

31. "Not for totally destroying the distillers": Historical Manuscripts Commission, *Diary of the First Earl of Egmont (Viscount Percival)*, vol. 2, Manuscripts of the Earl of Egmont (London: His Majesty's Stationery Office, 1923), p. 257.

32. It was only natural that he should want to deprive his old enemy: J.D. Marshall, ed., *Autobiography of William Stout of Lancaster 1665–1752* (New York: Barnes & Noble, Inc., 1967), p. 94; Henry Horwitz, ed., *The Parliamentary Diary of Narcissus Luttrell 1691–1693* (Oxford: Clarendon Press, 1972), pp. 334; 388.

32. Faced with the escalating costs of waging war: Michael J. Jubb, "Economic Policy and Economic Development," in *Britain in the Age of Walpole*, ed. Jeremy Black (London: Macmillan, 1984), p. 134; John Brewer, *The Sinews of Power. War, Money, and the English State*, 1688–1783 (London: Unwin Hyman, 1989).

32. Banned imports of all distilled spirits: 1 W. & M. c.34, in *The Statutes of the Realm*, vol. 6 (London: Dawsons of Pall Mall, 1963).32. This particular clause was intended to increase output: 2 W. & M. Sess.2. c.9, in *The Statutes of the Realm*, vol. 6 (London: Dawsons of Pall Mall, 1963).

32. "Encourage our own manufacture of sprits made of corn": Henry Horwitz, ed., *The Parliamentary Diary of Narcissus Luttrell 1691–1693* (Oxford: Clarendon Press, 1972), p. 333.

32. Parliament again raised duties on all French imports: 7 & 8 W.3.c.20, in *The Statutes of the Realm*, vol. 7 (London: Dawsons of Pall Mall, 1963).

32. Raised duties on domestically produced spirits: Public Record Office, Excise Rates and Allowances, 1660–1811.

33. Approximately 10 percent of all public revenues: *The Norwich Mercury*, 23 February–2 March 1751, p. 1; B.R. Mitchell and Phyllis Deane, *Abstract of British Historical Statistics* (Cambridge: Cambridge University Press, 1962), p. 387.

33. The net effect was to drive up the going price of domestic spirits: Daniel Defoe, *A Brief Case of the Distillers* (London: Printed for T. Warner, 1726), p. 23.

33. "Ever since the Former and Latter War with France": *The Case of the Distillers of London* (1710), no pagination.

34. Parliament required all individuals retailing distilled spirits: 12 & 13 Wil. 3. c.3, in *The Statutes of the Realm*, vol. 7 (London: Dawsons of Pall Mall, 1963).

34. This modest requirement was repealed just one year later: 1 Anne. Stat. 2. c.14, in Danby Pickering, ed., *The Statutes at Large*, vol. 10 (Cambridge: Joseph Bentham, 1764).

34. The offending clause . . . had proven "a great hindrance": Sidney Webb and Beatrice Webb, *The History of Liquor Licensing in England Principally from 1700 to 1830* (London: Longmans, Green and Co., 1903), p. 21.

34. Evidence suggesting that distillers deliberately kept prices low: John A. Chartres, "No English Calvados? English Distillers and the Cider Industry in the Seventeenth and Eighteenth Centuries," in *English Rural Society, 1500–1800: Essays in Honour of Joan Thirsk*, ed. John Chartres and David Hey (New York: Cambridge University Press, 1990), p. 328.

34. So many distillers went bankrupt in the 1730s: Julian Hoppit, *Risk and Failure in English Business 1700–1800* (Cambridge: Cambridge University Press, 1987), p. 91.

34. "The several Classes of Distillers . . . have a Secret of making large Profits": R. Campbell, *The London Tradesman* (New York: Augustus M. Kelley, Publishers, 1969), p. 267.

35. "Practice . . . to give their Spirits thrice the Degree of Strength required": *Supplement to the Gentleman's Magazine*, December 1743, p. 620.

35. As many as 120,000 such establishments in England: *The Daily Gazetteer*, 18 September 1736, p. 2.

35. The ratio of gin shops to houses: M. Dorothy George, *London Life in the Eighteenth Century*, second ed. (New York: Harper Torchbooks, 1964), p. 41.

35. Publicans in London raised the price: Peter Mathias, *The Brewing Industry in England 1700–1830* (Cambridge: Cambridge University Press, 1959), p. 359.

36. This price had been in effect since 1710: Daniel Defoe, *A Brief Case of the Distillers* (London: Printed for T. Warner, 1726), pp. 22–23.

36. "Damn your Blood": *Sessions Papers of the Old Bailey*, 5–7 December 1734, pp. 19–20.

37. Consumers of all classes had not only the means: Neil McKendrick, "The Consumer Revolution of Eighteenth-century England," in *The Birth of a Consumer Society. The Commercialization of Eighteenth-century England*, ed. Neil McKendrick, John Brewer, and John Harold Plumb (London: Europa Publications Limited, 1982), pp. 9–33; Fernand Braudel, "Alimentation et catégories de l'histoire," *Annales, économies, sociétés, civilisations* 16, no. 4 (1961), p. 725; Fernand Braudel, *Civilization and Capitalism*, trans. Siân Reynolds, vol. 1, *The Structures of Everyday Life* (New York: Harper & Row, 1981), p. 227; John E. Wills, "European Consumption and Asian Production in the Seventeenth and Eighteenth Centuries," in *Consumption and the World of Goods*, ed. John Brewer and Roy Porter (London: Routledge, 1993), pp. 133–147; Sidney W. Mintz, "The Changing Roles of Food in the Study of Consumption," in *Consumption and the World of Goods*, ed. John Brewer and Roy Porter (London: Routledge, 1993), pp. 261–273.

37. "A national Gust or Inclination": Daniel Defoe, *A Brief Case of the Distillers* (London: Printed for T. Warner, 1726), p. 46.

37. "Our very Plough-Fellows drink Wine now a-days: Daniel Defoe, *Augusta triumphans: or, the Way to Make London the Most Flourishing City in the Universe* (London: Printed for J. Roberts, 1728), p. 43.

37. "Even the meanest part of Mankind": Thomas Wilson, *Distilled Spirituous Liquors the Bane of the Nation* (London: Printed for J. Roberts, 1736), p. 7.

37. "Wear Silks and Topknots, drink Tea, and lie on Down Beds": *A Collection of Letters Published in the Daily Papers Relating to the British Distillery* (London: Printed for J. Roberts, 1736), p. 24.

37–38. Farmers "have of late relaxed their frugality": *The Gentleman's Magazine*, November 1743, p. 576.

38. The lurking fear that ostentation on the part of the poor: Joyce Oldham Appleby, "The Tension between Political and Economic Liberalism in Seventeenth-century England," *American Historical Review* 81, no. 3 (1976), pp. 499–515.

38. "Each man is desirous of appearing to be what he is not": Robert Drew, *A Sermon Preached to the Societies for the Reformation of Manners, at St. Mary-le-Bow, on Monday, January 27th, 1734* (London: Printed for M. Downing, 1735), p. 16.

38. "Her Neats-Leathern Shoes are now transform'd": *A Trip from St. James's to the Royal Exchange* (London: Printed for Edward Withers, 1744), p. 60.

38. London, where wages had always been higher than elsewhere in England: E.H. Phelps Brown and Sheila V. Hopkins, "Seven Centuries of Building Wages," in *Essays in Economic History, ed. E.M. Carus-Wilson* (London: Edward Arnold (Publishers) Ltd., 1962), p. 171; L. D. Schwarz, "The Standard of Living in the Long Run: London, 1700–1860," *Economic History Review* 38, no. 1 (1985), p. 24.

38. High wages helped create an enormous market for products: John A. Chartres, "Food

Consumption and Internal Trade," in *London 1500–1700: the Making of the Metropolis*, ed. A.L. Beier and Roger Finlay (London: Longman, 1986), pp. 168–196.

38–39. London was also the place where social controls were especially lax: E. Anthony Wrigley, "A Simple Model of London's Importance in Changing English Society and Economy 1650–1750," in *Past and Present*, ed. Philip Abrams and E. Anthony Wrigley, *Past and Present Publications* (Cambridge: Cambridge University Press, 1978), pp. 215–243; M.J. Daunton, "Towns and Economic Growth in Eighteenth-century England," in *Past and Present*, ed. Philip Abrams and E. Anthony Wrigley, *Past and Present Publications* (Cambridge: Cambridge University Press, 1978), p. 256.

39. Contemporaries were prepared to tolerate its many vices: Peter Clark, "The 'Mother Gin' Controversy in the Early Eighteenth Century," *Transactions of the Royal Historical Society* 38 (1988), p. 83.

39. Gin was gaining in popularity in the provinces: Portsmouth City Records Office, Sessions Files, S3/90/94, 11 July 1728.

39. "A distilled liquor called Geneva": *The Daily Gazetteer*, 18 September 1736, p. 1.

39. "There was not the remotest Town or Village free from it": John Brown, *An Estimate of the Manners and Principles of the Times*, seventh ed., vol. 1 (1750), p. 190.

39. "A greater quantity of gin is consumed than of ale": *The Country Journal: or, the Craftsman*, 26 February 1737, p. 2.

39. "The Taverns and Publick Houses there are in high Spirits": *The London Evening-Post*, 20–22 April 1738, p. 1.39–40..

40. A local woman by the name of Margaret Hubball was convicted: Portsmouth City Records Office, Sessions Files, S3/108/40, 20–22 June 1738.

40. As a rule, provincial magistrates were loathe to penalize local publicans: Norma Landau, *The Justices of the Peace, 1679–1760* (Berkeley: University of California Press, 1986), p. 223.

40. "This ill Success…will put an End to the Progress of such Rascals": *The Country Journal: or, the Craftsman*, 4 November 1738, p. 2.

40. "Hath got too much Footing amongst us in the Country": *The Country Journal: or, the Craftsman*, 14 August 1736, p. 1.

40. "The assemblymen of Norwich appointed a committee": Norfolk Record Office, Folio Book of Proceedings of the Municipal Assembly, Case 16d 10, 1745–1773, folio 40 recto.

41. The records kept by the commissioners of excise: Public Record Office, CUST, 48/13, 1733–1745, p. 216.

41. "Half of the nation's gin-shops catered to just 10 percent of the population": *The Gentleman's Magazine*, October 1736, p. 594; E. Anthony Wrigley, "A Simple Model of London's Importance in Changing English Society and Economy 1650–1750," in *Past and Present*, ed. Philip Abrams and E. Anthony Wrigley, *Past and Present Publications* (Cambridge: Cambridge University Press, 1978), p. 216.

41. Landowners came to London for the social "season": F.J. Fisher, "The Development of London as a Centre of Conspicuous Consumption in the Sixteenth and Seventeenth Centuries," *Transactions of the Royal Historical Society* 30 (1948), pp. 43–43.

CHAPTER TWO
PAGE
43. *The Gentleman's Magazine* epigraph: *The Gentleman's Magazine*, November 1736, p. 677.

43. A vending machine that was fondly known as "puss and mew": *Read's Weekly Journal*, 18 February 1738; Public Record Office, PC 1/15/5, part 1, 1738.

44. Selling gin was often the difference between poverty and destitution: Robert W. Malcolmson, *Life and Labour in England 1700–1780*, Hutchinson Social History of England (London: Hutchinson, 1981), p. 51; L. D. Schwarz, *London in the Age of Industrialisation. Entrepreneurs, Labour Force and Living Conditions, 1700–1850*, ed. Peter Laslett, et al., vol. 19, Cambridge Studies in Population, Economy and Society in Past Time (Cambridge: Cambridge University Press, 1992), p. 38.

44–45. It was here that rents were cheap...and social controls were notoriously lax: Peter Clark, "Migrants in the City: the Process of Social Adaptation in English Towns, 1500–1800," in *Migration and Society in Early Modern England*, ed. Peter Clark and David Souden (London: Hutchinson, 1987), pp. 267–291.

45. Thanks in large part to the absence of magistrates: Sidney Webb and Beatrice Webb, *The Parish and the County, English Local Government* (London: Frank Cass and Co. Ltd., 1963), pp. 325–326; Norma Landau, *The Justices of the Peace, 1679–1760* (Berkeley: University of California Press, 1986), pp. 200–201.

45. "I am...very much concerned for the Gentlemen": *A View of London and Westminster: or, the Town Spy* (London: Sold by T. Warner, 1728), p. 12.

45. Of the various attempts made to count the people selling gin in the capital, two, one from East London for the years 1735 to 1736, the other from the City of London for the year 1751, survive more or less in toto. A third, for the years 1725 to 1726, appears in summary form in William Maitland's monumental *History and Survey of London*, where it was updated with data from the mid-1730s. The latter list, including as it does known drinking establishments in the City, Westminster, East London, and Southwark, is by far the most geographically complete, but is limited to the extent that it does not include petty hawkers and other occasional retailers. Together the reports underscore the extent to which gin was the beverage of choice in the metropolis' poorest and fastest growing neighborhoods. Maitland counted only 307 "brandy shops" in the City of London itself, which translates to slightly more than two percent of the 11,795 houses then standing. The number is low to the extent that it does not include the more respectable inns, taverns, coffeehouses, and alehouses that also sold distilled spirits. In Westminster, by contrast, the number of houses operating as "brandy shops" exceeded six percent, and in the dockside parishes of East London and Southwark it easily exceeded 12 percent. In the City itself, unlicensed retailers were overwhelmingly concentrated in the poorer outlying wards, with just one ward, Farringdon Without, accounting for 103 of the 274 gin-sellers on record in 1751. By contrast, centrally located wards, such as Aldersgate Within, Aldersgate Without, and Cornhill, reported few or no unlicensed retailers. In Middlesex the distribution of retailers more or less followed that of the population, which is to say that both were concentrated in the parishes just north of the old City or to the east of it along the Thames. If the counts are to be believed, Whitechapel had no fewer than 244 retailers in 1736, followed by Shoreditch with 193, Spitalfields with 165, and Shadwell with 138. The numbers were naturally smaller in areas that were as yet sparsely populated, including Stratford and Poplar. For the City's wards, see Corporation of London Records Office, MSS. 82.17, 1751.

45. These were the areas with the lowest property values: Michael J. Power, "The Social Topography of Restoration London," in *London 1500–1700. The Making of the Metropolis*, ed. A.L. Beier and Roger Finlay (London: Longman, 1986), p. 209.

45. A grand jury singled out several "disorderly Geneva Shops": *The London Evening-Post*, 23–25 July 1728, p. 2.

46. "Geneva or other distilled Liquors": Finsbury Library, Archives Department, St James Clerkenwell Vestry Minutes 1725–1775, 1725–1775, pp. 25–26.

46. Several jailers in London were compensated: Michael Ignatieff, *A Just Measure of Pain. the Penitentiary in the Industrial Revolution, 1750–1850* (New York: Pantheon Books, 1978), p. 37; Corporation of London Records Office, Miscellaneous MSS. 184.6, 6 February 1787; John M. Beattie, *Crime and the Courts in England 1660–1800* (Princeton: Princeton University Press, 1986), p. 290.

46. "Swallow'd in every Part of Newgate": Bernard Mandeville, *An Enquiry into the Causes of the Frequent Executions at Tyburn* (London: J. Roberts, 1725), p. 19.

46. "The Prisoners in the Liberties of the Fleet and King's Bench": *The Daily Journal*, 1 October 1736, p. 2.

46–47. The servant of at least one warden was also implicated: Corporation of London Records Office, Reports and Papers of the Court of Aldermen, 9 November 1736; Corporation of London Records Office, Repertories, 1736–1737, pp. 7–8.

47. "But not knowing his Name, and endeavouring to find out": *The Daily Gazetteer*, 17 August 1737, p. 2.

47. "A Perquisite belonging to their Places": *Read's Weekly Journal*, 8 April 1738, p. 2; *The Norwich Mercury*, 9–16 September 1738, p. 2.

47. "A Cup of Ale and a Dram for the Relief of Travellers": *Read's Weekly Journal*, 4 September 1736, p. 2.

47. "A Moveable Hut or Hovell lately placed and set up": Robert East, ed., *Extracts from Records in the Possession of the Municipal Corporation of the Borough of Portsmouth* (Portsmouth: Henry Lewis, 1891), p. 110.

48. "The very Rubbish of the Creation, the worst of both Sexes": *A Trip from St. James's to the Royal Exchange* (London: Printed for Edward Withers, 1744), p. 48.

49. "At a good Price, being esteem'd very great Curiosities": *The London Daily Post*, 19 May 1736, p. 1.

49. "The Black hangs in a very indecent Manner": *Read's Weekly Journal*, 12 March 1737.

49. "They look dismally, and begin to smell": *The London Evening-Post*, 9–12 April 1737, p. 1.

49. "Three or four, and sometimes half a dozen Times": Bernard Mandeville, *An Enquiry into the Causes of the Frequent Executions at Tyburn* (London: J. Roberts, 1725), p. 23.

50. "Intoxicated with Liquor, and supposing there were three order'd for Execution": *The London Daily Post*, 30 March 1738, p. 1

50. Few would appear to have been destitute: Jessica F. Warner and Frank Ivis, "Gin and Gender in Early Eighteenth-century London," *Eighteenth-century Life* 24, no. 2 (2000), p. 89.

51. She was eventually apprehended and convicted: Public Record Office, PC 1/15/5, part 1, 1738; *The Daily Gazetteer*, 22 April 1738, p. 2.

51. The wife of "a reputable Publican" in Covent Garden was convicted: *Read's Weekly Journal*, 8 April 1738, p. 4.

51. Their suppliers consisted almost entirely of men: Corporation of London Guildhall Library, Register of Freedom Admissions of the London Company of Distillers, 6215A, 1721–1956.

51. Phillips sold gin to a hawker by the name of Mary Bryan: British Library, Hardwicke Papers, Additional MS. 35600, 1733–1741, folio 108 recto; reference courtesy of Professor Norma Landau.

51–52. Of 586 defendants too poor to pay the penalty: Joanna Innes, "Prisons for the Poor: English Bridewells, 1555–1800," in *Labour, Law and Crime: a Historical Perspective*, ed. Francis Snyder and Douglas Hay (London: Tavistock Publications, 1987), p. 100; Robert B. Shoemaker, *Prosecution and Punishment. Petty Crime and the Law in London and Rural Middlesex, c. 1660–1725* (Cambridge: Cambridge University Press, 1991), pp. 185–186.

52. They belonged to the vast population of young single women: "Migrants and the Population Structure of Later Seventeenth-century Provincial Cities and Market Towns," in *The*

Transformation of English Provincial Towns, ed. Peter Clark (1981); Peter Clark, *The English Alehouse: A Social History 1200–1830* (New York: Longman, 1983), pp. 79; 203; Peter Clark, "The 'Mother Gin' Controversy in the Early Eighteenth Century," *Transactions of the Royal Historical Society* 38 (1988), p. 70; Peter Earle, "The Female Labour Market in London in the Late Seventeenth and Early Eighteenth Centuries," *Economic History Review* 42, no. 3 (1989), pp. 331–333.

52. An economy that was both seasonal and subject to sharp fluctuations: John M. Beattie, Crime and the Courts in England 1660–1800 (Princeton: Princeton University Press, 1986), p. 242.

52. "I turn my hand to any thing to get a penny": Elias Bockett, *Blunt to Walpole* (London: Printed for J. Wilford, 1730).

52. Hawking, moreover, had the additional advantage: Bridget Hill, *Women, Work, and Sexual Politics in Eighteenth-century England* (New York: Basil Blackwell, 1989), pp. 168–169.

52. Women in their twenties or even in their teens to be widowed: Peter Earle, "The Female Labour Market in London in the Late Seventeenth and Early Eighteenth Centuries," *Economic History Review* 42, no. 3 (1989), p. 345.

52. Rose Biquall was married at the time she was committed: London Metropolitan Archives, Sessions Rolls, Middlesex Quarter Sessions, MJ/SR 2684, October 1737.

52. While among the defendants profiled: *A Short History of the Gin Act* (London: Published for H. Goreham, 1738), pp. 46; 59.

52. *The Daily Journal* reported that "one Chapman": *The Daily Journal*, 12 January 1737, p. 1.

52–53. Elizabeth Judd of Westminster and Mary Blake of Southwark: Public Record Office, PC 1/15/5, part 2, 1738; Surrey Record Office, Sessions Bundles, General Quarter Sessions, Surrey, QS2/6/1737/Epiphany, 1737.

53. "Very sickly on account of the great number of prisoners there": John M. Beattie, *Crime and the Courts in England 1660–1800* (Princeton: Princeton University Press, 1986), p. 302.

53. It was at this time that the wife of John Saxby: *Read's Weekly Journal*, 10 June 1738, p. 4.

53. It included Mary Goudge, the wife of a distiller: London Metropolitan Archives, Sessions Rolls, Middlesex Quarter Sessions, MJ/SR 2691, February 1737.

53. Catherine Croft, the wife of a prosperous victualler: Public Record Office, KB 1/6, Michaelmas, 13 Geo. 2, bundle 3, 22 November 1739.

53–54. The women who hawked gin stood to lose: Wendy Thwaites, "Women in the Market Place: Oxfordshire c. 1690–1800," *Midland History* 9 (1984), p. 38.

54. These protests typically took the form of attacks on informers: Jessica F. Warner and Frank Ivis, "'Damn you, you informing Bitch.' Vox populi and the Unmaking of the Gin Act of 1736," *Journal of Social History* 33, no. 2 (1999), pp. 299–330.

54. "Thing who refused to tell her Christian name": London Metropolitan Archives, Calendar of Commitments to the Westminster House of Correction, WJ/CC/B 148, 6 January 1738.

54. Judith Wamsley, who in April of 1738 "was Committed": Public Record Office, PC 1/15/5, part 1, 1738; *The Daily Gazetteer*, 17 April 1738, p. 1.

55. John Canfield ... admitted to drinking until four: *Sessions Papers of the Old Bailey*, 23–24 February 1744, p. 78.

55. Elizabeth Bailey and Elizabeth Cooper were also refused service: London Metropolitan Archives, Calendar of Commitments to the Westminster House of Correction, WJ/CC/B 150, 6 October 1739.

55. There was the barman who went too far: The Country Journal: or, the Craftsman, 15 August 1741, p. 2.

56. "The Places where these Liquors were sold": *The Daily Gazetteer*, 7 October 1736, p. 1.

56. "Gin–shops . . . are undoubtedly the Nurseries of all manner of Vice": Henry Fielding, *A Dissertation on Mr. Hogarth's Six Prints Lately Publish'd, viz. Gin-Lane, Beer-Street, and the Four Stages of Cruelty* (London: Printed for B. Dickinson, 1751), p. 18.

56. "He sold Gin, and entertained all Sorts of bad Company": *Sessions Papers of the Old Bailey*, 29 June–1 July 1743, p. 289.

57. Prostitutes often enjoyed a symbiotic relationship with the proprietors: Tony Henderson, *Disorderly Women in Eighteenth-century London: Prostitution and Control in the Metropolis 1730–1830*, ed. Patricia Skinner, Pamela Sharpe, and Penny Summerfield, Women and Men in History (London: Longman, 1999), p. 33.

57. Joseph Reeves remembered that a woman by the name of Elizabeth Howard: *Sessions Papers of the Old Bailey*, 16–19 April 1740, pp. 73–74.

57–58. Daniel Flannigal had high hopes of spending the night: *Sessions Papers of the Old Bailey*, 29 June–1 July 1743, p. 187.

58. James Powell "happen'd to light on" Clare Dickinson: *Sessions Papers of the Old Bailey*, 14–17 January 1736, p. 43.

58. Richard Summer lost his watch under very similar circumstances: *Sessions Papers of the Old Bailey*, 17–19 October 1739, p. 145.

58. John Godday told a jury that he "met with a Woman, who stopp'd me": *Sessions Papers of the Old Bailey*, 17–19 October 1739, pp. 161–162.

58. Charles Dickerson claimed that Elizabeth Jarvis accosted him: *Sessions Papers of the Old Bailey*, 17–19 October 1739, p. 85.

58. There is the story of "a poor Countryman": *The Weekly Register*, 17 April 1731, p. 3.

59. "Two women being very drunk with gin, one struck the other": *The Grub-Street Journal*, 26 February 1736.

59. "Two Women at a Ginshop in Golden Lane having Words": *Read's Weekly Journal*, 28 April 1750, pp. 2–3.

59. Gin also played a role in the death of Elizabeth Lewis: *Sessions Papers of the Old Bailey*, 29 June–1 July 1743, p. 238.

59. "All Sense of Fear and Shame": Henry Fielding, *An Enquiry into the Causes of the Late Increase of Robbers*, ed. Malvin R. Zirker (Middletown: Wesleyan University Press, 1988), p. 89.

60. When a woman by the name of Jane Grew wanted a pint of gin: Ruth Paley, ed., *Justice in Eighteenth-century Hackney: the Justicing Notebook of Henry Norris and the Hackney Petty Sessions Book*, vol. 28, London Record Society Publications (London: London Record Society, 1991), p. 11.

60. Samuel Heep stole four pounds of candles: *Sessions Papers of the Old Bailey*, 16–19 April 1740, p. 117.

60. And when John Purder of Marylebone was indicted: *Sessions Papers of the Old Bailey*, 6–9 July 1737, p. 146.

60. "That every separate Room in some Houses": Thomas Wilson, *Distilled Spirituous Liquors the Bane of the Nation* (London: Printed for J. Roberts, 1736), p. 12.

60. Margaret Tyson was indicted for selling gin: London Metropolitan Archives, Sessions Rolls, Middlesex Quarter Sessions, MJ/SR 2701, September 1738.

60–61. Mary Tidcomb was caught selling gin: Corporation of London Records Office, Sessions Rolls, City of London Quarter Sessions, SF 759, 4 December 1738; *Sessions Papers of the Old Bailey*, 17–20 January 1738, p. 43.

61. An informer by the name of Elizabeth Cull duped: Corporation of London Records Office, Southwark Sessions Files, Box 10, 1733–1739.

61. When Martha Hopkins wanted a glass of liquor: *Sessions Papers of the Old Bailey*, 17–19 October 1739, p. 11.

61. These shops seem to have catered primarily to women: R. Campbell, *The London Tradesman* (New York: Augustus M. Kelley, Publishers, 1969), p. 280.

61. Affording countless "servant maids an opportunity of tippling": *The Grub-Street Journal*, 27 January 1736, p. 1.

61. "Females, Servant-Maids, and the Wives of middling": Henry Fielding, *A Dissertation on Mr. Hogarth's Six Prints Lately Publish'd, viz. Gin-Lane, Beer-Street, and the Four Stages of Cruelty* (London: Printed for B. Dickinson, 1751), p. 9.

61. "Fall once into a Chandler's-Shop-Acquaintance, give Ear": Eliza Fowler Haywood, *A Present for Women Addicted to Drinking. Adapted to All the Different STATIONS of Life, from a Lady of Quality to a Common Servant* (London: Printed for W. Owen, 1750), p. 21.

61. "In an Alley in Chancery-Lane": *Sessions Papers of the Old Bailey*, 5–7 December 1734, p. 5.

61. Lydia Clapp, a notorious informer, entered a chandler's shop: Reay Sabourn, *A Perfect View of the Gin Act* (London: Printed for W. Thorne, 1738), p. 40.

61–62. "Two well-dress'd Women with Capuchins on": *The Westminster Journal*, 5 March 1742–1743, p. 3.

62. "Too common a practice among chandlers and others": London Metropolitan Archives, General Orders of Court, Middlesex, MJ/OC 3, 1724–1733, folios 42 verso–43 recto; *A Dissertation upon Drunkenness* (London: Printed for T. Warner, 1727), p. 14; London Metropolitan Archives, Middlesex Sessions Books & Orders of Court Calendar, 1735–1738, p. 9.

62. "Masters will every Day have greater Reason to complain" Thomas Wilson, *Distilled Spirituous Liquors the Bane of the Nation* (London: Printed for J. Roberts, 1736), p. 8.

62. "Many who sell privately in Garrets, Cellars, back Rooms": Thomas Wilson, *Distilled Spirituous Liquors the Bane of the Nation* (London: Printed for J. Roberts, 1736), p. 15.

62. Thomas Croft . . . simply ceased to sell gin out of his front room: Public Record Office, KB 1/6, Trinity, 13–14 Geo. 2, 1739.

63. "A great many People drinking Gin": *Sessions Papers of the Old Bailey*, 17–19 October 1739, p. 11.

63. "These taverns are almost always full of men and women": von Muyden, ed., *A Foreign View of England in the Reigns of George I. and George II. The Letters of Monsieur César de Saussure to his Family* (London: John Murray, 1902), p. 165.

63. Paris had its taverns, but they catered primarily to men: Thomas Brennan, *Public Drinking and Popular Culture in Eighteenth-century Paris* (Princeton: Princeton University Press, 1988), p. 8.

63. "Agreed to toss up Heads or Tails, who should treat": *Sessions Papers of the Old Bailey*, 8–10 December 1742, p. 25.

63. When Robert Stafford met Elizabeth Jerron in 1720: *Sessions Papers of the Old Bailey*, 7–10 September 1720, p. 2.

CHAPTER THREE
PAGE

65. Mother Gin epigraph: *Mother Gin, a Tragi-comical Eclogue* (London: Printed for L. Giliver, and J. Clarke, 1737), p. 15.

65. Several women, some of them prostitutes and some of them thieves: *The London Evening-Post*, 17–20 July 1742, p. 3; *The London Evening-Post*, 9–11 September 1742, p. 2.

65–66. "The Ladies Delight": *The London Daily Post*, 22 October 1736, p. 2.

66. Mother Gin was "held in the highest Esteem": *The London Magazine*, June 1737, p. 323.

66. It was here that women emerged, for the first time in history, as heroic drinkers: Bridget

Hill, *Women, Work, and Sexual Politics in Eighteenth-century England* (New York: Basil Blackwell, 1989), pp. 163–173; Peter Earle, "The Female Labour Market in London in the Late Seventeenth and Early Eighteenth Centuries," *Economic History Review* 42, no. 3 (1989), pp. 328–53.

66. Working women were largely left to their own devices: John M. Beattie, "The Criminality of Women in Eighteenth-century England," *Journal of Social History* 8 (1975), pp. 98–99, John M. Beattie, *Crime and the Courts in England 1660–1800* (Princeton: Princeton University Press, 1986), p. 242.

67. "Good Wives" discretely "furnish'd their little Fire-side Cupboards": Daniel Defoe, *A Brief Case of the Distillers* (London: Printed for T. Warner, 1726), p. 19.

67. "Whilst the husband and perhaps his wife also are drinking": London Metropolitan Archives, General Orders of Court, Middlesex, MJ/OC 3, 1724–1733, folio 42 recto; London Metropolitan Archives, Middlesex Sessions Books & Orders of Court Calendar, 1735–1738, p. 8.

67. Its author proposed a ban on sales of all distilled spirits: *The Grub-Street Journal*, 27 January 1736, p. 2.

'67–68. The hero, Colonel Jack, marries a woman who dies: Daniel Defoe, *The History and Remarkable Life of the Truly Honourable Col. Jacque*, ed. Samuel Holt Monk, Oxford English Novels (London: Oxford University Press, 1965), p. 240.

68. A wife who "came home so much intoxicated with Geneva" *Read's Weekly Journal*, 13 December 1735, p. 3.

68. "Going home . . . found his wife excessive drunk with Geneva": *The Grub-Street Journal*, 22 April 1736, p. 2.

68. Thomas Bridge, charged with having stabbed his wife to death: *Sessions Papers of the Old Bailey*, 18–20 July 1739, p. 121.

68. "Laid a Wager with a Neighbour that he and his Wife": *The London Morning Penny Post*, 26–29 July 1751, p. 2.

69. Mary Estwick, an elderly woman who came home on Tuesday: *The London Daily Post*, 6 February 1736, p. 2; *The London Magazine*, February 1736, p. 73.

69. The Royal College of Physicians petitioned the House of Commons: Royal College of Physicians of London, Annals, 19 January 1725, folio 72 recto.

69. Gin "murders Infants in the Womb": *The Gentleman's Magazine*, February 1732, p. 603.

69. "Children coming into the World half burnt up": Thomas Wilson, *Distilled Spirituous Liquors the Bane of the Nation* (London: Printed for J. Roberts, 1736), p. 36.

69. "In pregnant Dames gin cou'd Abortion cause": *An Elegy on the Much Lamented Death of the Most Excellent, the Most Truly-beloved, and Universally-admired Lady, Madam Geneva* (London: Printed for T. Cooper, 1736), p. 7.

70. Wet nurses ran the risk of imparting gin to the infants whom they suckled: Eliza Fowler Haywood, *A Present for Women Addicted to Drinking. Adapted to All the Different STATIONS of Life, from a Lady of Quality to a Common Servant* (London: Printed for W. Owen, 1750), pp. 41–42.

70. "How many . . . have unhappily drunk this deadly Poison with their Nurses Milk!": Thomas Wilson, *Distilled Spirituous Liquors the Bane of the Nation* (London: Printed for J. Roberts, 1736), p. 34.

70. Henry Fielding envisioned a dreadful future for the infant: Henry Fielding, *An Enquiry into the Causes of the Late Increase of Robbers*, ed. Malvin R. Zirker (Middletown: Wesleyan University Press, 1988), p. 90.

70. "The sucking Brat declines her shrvil'd Pap": *An Elegy on the Much Lamented Death of the*

Most Excellent, the Most Truly-beloved, and Universally-admired Lady, Madam Gineva (London: Printed for T. Cooper, 1736), p. 7.

70. Even the great philanthropists of the age adopted: Ruth K. McClure, *Coram's Children. The London Foundling Hospital in the Eighteenth Century* (New Haven: Yale University Press, 1981), pp. 244–245.

70. Jonas Hanway... subsidized a hospital for saving London's foundlings: James Stephen Taylor, "Philanthropy and Empire: Jonas Hanway and the Infant Poor of London," *Eighteenth-century Studies* 12, no. 3 (1979), pp. 287–288.

71. Thomas Wilson's enthusiastic support for Henry Fielding's plan: C.L.S. Linnell, ed., *The Diaries of Thomas Wilson* (London: The Camelot Press Ltd., 1964), p. 258.

71. "If the Manufacturers be few, Labour will be dear": *The Gentleman's Magazine*, February 1744, p. 60.

71. This was a core tenet of mercantilism: Joyce Oldham Appleby, "The Tension between Political and Economic Liberalism in Seventeenth-century England," *American Historical Review* 81, no. 3 (1976), pp. 499–515.

71. "These wretched Infants" would even survive: Henry Fielding, *An Enquiry into the Causes of the Late Increase of Robbers*, ed. Malvin R. Zirker (Middletown: Wesleyan University Press, 1988), p. 90.

71. "Natural and inevitable Losses" of war while also supplying "Commerce": *Supplement to the Gentleman's Magazine*, December 1743, p. 629.

71–73. "The working poor constituted "Strength and riches of every Nation": *The Gentleman's Magazine*, November 1743, pp. 565–566.

73. "The Strength and Riches of a National Community consist": Joseph Jekyll, *The Trial of the Spirits*, second ed. (London: Printed for T. Cooper, 1736), p. 3.

73. "Lord! What an outcry there has been": Elias Bockett, *Blunt to Walpole* (London: Printed for J. Wilford, 1730), p. 21.

74. "The good old Lady": "The Downfall of Mother GIN," *The Gentleman's Magazine*, June 1736, p. 310.

74. "The happy Dame, the candid Madam Gin": *Mother Gin, a Tragi-comical Eclogue* (London: Printed for L. Giliver, and J. Clarke, 1737), p. 21.

74. "Was of very mean and obscure Birth": *The Life of Mother Gin; Containing, a True and Faithful Relation of her Conduct and Politicks* (London: Printed for W. Webb, 1736), p. 5.

74. Mary Clues, described as "much addicted to drinking": Bradford Wilmer, "An Account of a Woman Accidentally Burnt to Death in Coventry," in *The Annual Register* (London: Printed for J. Dodsley, 1776), p. 79.

74. "Drunk very plentifully of Gin": "An Extract, by Mr. Paul Rolli, F.R.S. of an Italian Treatise, Written by the Reverend Joseph Bianchini," *Philosophical Transactions* 43, no. 476 (1745), p. 464.

75. "Contracted such a combustible Disposition, that one Night": Thomas Bartholin, *Acta medica et philosophica hafniensia* 1 (1673), p. 211; "An Extract, by Mr. Paul Rolli, F.R.S. of an Italian Treatise, Written by the Reverend Joseph Bianchini," *Philosophical Transactions* 43, no. 476 (1745), pp. 450–453.

75. Bartholin's account next surfaced in 1717: Joannes Henricus Cohausen, *Lumen novum phosphoris accensum, sive exercitatio physico-chymica* (Amsterdam: Joannem Ooterwyk, 1717).

75. "Lady of Quality," later identified as the Countess Cornelia: *The Gentleman's Magazine*, June 1731, p. 263.

75. By now *The Gentleman's Magazine* was a flourishing concern: John Brewer, *The Pleasures of the Imagination. English Culture in the Eighteenth Century* (New York: Farrar Straus Giroux, 1997), pp. 608–609.

75. In 1775 there was a new victim, Mary Clues: Bradford Wilmer, "An Account of a Woman Accidentally Burnt to Death in Coventry," in *The Annual Register* (London: Printed for J. Dodsley, 1776), pp. 76–8.

76. Their stories appear in a variety of sources: "Observation sur un effet singulière de la combustion; par m. Muraire, maître en chirurgie à Aix en Provence," *Journal de médecine, chirurgie, pharmacie* 59, no. 5–6 (1783), pp. 5–6; Pierre-Aimé Lair, *Essai sur les combustions humaines, produites par un long abus des liqueurs spiritueuses* (Paris: Crapelet, 1800).

76. Four years later, in 1804, the English physician: Thomas Trotter, *An Essay, Medical, Philosophical, and Chemical on Drunkenness and its Effects on the Human Body*, ed. Roy Porter (London: Routledge, 1988), pp. 131–132.

77. In Caen, another "woman of the lower classes": Thomas Trotter, *An Essay, Medical, Philosophical, and Chemical on Drunkenness and its Effects on the Human Body*, ed. Roy Porter (London: Routledge, 1988), p. 65.

77. The known ages of the victims range from forty-five years to about eighty: D. De Moulin, "Spontaneous Combustion. An Odd Chapter in the History of Burns," *Archivum chirugicum neerlandicum* 24, no. 4 (1975), pp. 223–227.

77. The victims were either very fat . . . or very thin: Pierre-Aimé Lair, *Essai sur les combustions humaines, produites par un long abus des liqueurs spiritueuses* (Paris: Crapelet, 1800), pp. 37–39.

78. Cremation, even at the most intense temperatures: Larry E. Arnold, "Human Fireballs," *Science Digest* 89, no. 9 (1981), pp. 88–91; 115.

78. The stories also played on contemporary beliefs: C. Anne Wilson, "Burnt Wine and Cordial Waters: the Early Days of Distilling," *Folk Life* 13 (1975), pp. 54–65.

78. "Maudlen Moonface, a merry gentlewoman of Dublin": *Philip Foulface, Bacchus Bountie* (London: Henry Krykham, 1593), no pagination.

78. These prejudices were already several centuries old: Peter Clark, *The English Alehouse: A Social History 1200–1830* (New York: Longman, 1983), pp. 31–32; Judith M. Bennett, "Misogyny, Popular Culture, and Women's Work," *History Workshop* 31 (1991), pp. 166–187.

78. Elinor Rumming is a brewster "well worn in age": John Skelton, "Elinor Rumming," in *The Complete Poems of John Skelton*, ed. Philip Henderson (London: J.M. Dent and Sons, Ltd., 1931).

79. Dell was almost certainly a widow: "The Most Cruell and Bloody Murther Committed by an Innkeepers Wife, Called Annis Dell, and her Sonne George Dell," in *Witchcraft in England, 1558–1618*, ed. Barbara Rosen (Amherst: The University of Massachusetts Press, 1991), pp. 323–328.

79. A widow . . . "is frequently a Sovereign": Eliza Fowler Haywood, *A Present for Women Addicted to Drinking. Adapted to All the Different STATIONS of Life, from a Lady of Quality to a Common Servant* (London: Printed for W. Owen, 1750), pp. 48–49.

79. "Poor melancholike women": Reginald Scott, *The Discoverie of Witchcraft* (Carbondale: Southern Illinois University Press, 1964), book 3, chapter 10.

80. Old and in the way, widows lived in a world no longer willing: Keith Thomas, *Religion and the Decline of Magic* (New York: Charles Sribner's Sons, 1971).

80. The witches of earlier generations . . . post-menopausal women of their property: Carol F. Karlsen, *The Devil in the Shape of a Woman. Witchcraft in Colonial New England* (New York: W.W. Norton & Company, 1987).

80. It was in the cities . . . tiresome old woman next door as a witch: Brian P. Levack, *The Witch-hunt in Early Modern Europe* (London: Longman, 1987), pp. 121–123.

81. Drunken women all but drop from literature: Harry Gene Levine, "Temperance and Women in 19th-century United States," in *Alcohol and Drug Problems in Women*, ed. Oriana Josseau

Kalant, *Research Advances in Alcohol and Drug Problems* (New York: Plenum Press, 1980), pp. 25–67.

81. Zola's Docteur Pascal in 1893: Aida Farrag, "Zola, Dickens, and Spontaneous Combustion," *Romance Notes* 19, no. 2 (1978), pp. 190–195.

81–82. The other victims include, in chronological order, the narrator's father: William F. Long, "William Edmonstoune Aytoun and Another Case of Spontaneous Combustion," *The Dickensian* 87 (1991), pp. 85–92.

82. Mr. Krook of Dickens' Bleak House . . . flames for no apparent reason: Warren S. Walker, "Lost Liquor Lore: the Blue Flame of Intemperance," *Journal of Popular Culture* 16, no. 2 (1982), p. 19.

82. Dickens' most assiduous critic on this point was George Henry Lewes: Peter Denman, "Krook's Death and Dickens's Authorities," *The Dickensian* 82, no. 410 (1986), pp. 131–141.

82. Here women ruled, but at the price of being barred: Harry Gene Levine, "Temperance and Women in 19th-century United States," in *Alcohol and Drug Problems in Women*, ed. Oriana Josseau Kalant, *Research Advances in Alcohol and Drug Problems* (New York: Plenum Press, 1980), pp. 25–67.

CHAPTER FOUR
PAGE

85. Bockett epigraph: *Elias Bockett, Blunt to Walpole* (London: Printed for J. Wilford, 1730), p. 24.

86. "More anxious to keep his power than to raise": Romney Sedgwick, ed., *The History of Parliament. The House of Commons 1715–1745*, 2 vols., vol. 2 (New York: Oxford University Press, 1970), p. 516.

87. In 1732 Walpole refused to raise the land tax: William J. Hausman and John L. Neufeld, "Excise Anatomized: the Political Economy of Walpole's 1733 Tax Scheme," *Journal of European Economic History* 10, no. 1 (1981), p. 136.

87. The net effect of Walpole's fiscal policies: Michael J. Jubb, "Economic Policy and Economic Development," in *Britain in the Age of Walpole*, ed. Jeremy Black, Problems in Focus (London: Macmillan, 1984), p. 137.

87. Excises, in turn, were to grow by leaps and bounds: John Brewer, *The Sinews of Power. War, Money, and the English State, 1688–1783* (London: Unwin Hyman, 1989).

87. Excises on gin would grow by more than 1,200 percent: Jessica F. Warner et al., "Can Legislation Prevent Debauchery? Mother Gin and Public Health in Eighteenth-century England," *American Journal of Public Health* 91, no. 3 (2001), pp. 375–384.

87–89. The City Elections Act also greatly expanded the powers: Lucy Sutherland, "The City of London in Eighteenth-century Politics," in *Essays Presented to Sir Lewis Namier*, ed. Richard Pares and A.J.P. Taylor (London: Macmillan & Co Ltd, 1956), pp. 49–74; Nicholas Rogers, *Whigs and Cities. Popular Politics in the Age of Walpole and Pitt* (Oxford: Oxford University Press, 1989), pp. 37–40.

89. The Court of Aldermen proved to be far less compliant than Walpole hoped: Nicholas Rogers, *Whigs and Cities. Popular Politics in the Age of Walpole and Pitt* (Oxford: Oxford University Press, 1989), pp. 67–70.

89. Pulteney had been passed over for office . . . he was prepared to tolerate gin up to a point: *The Gentleman's Magazine*, October 1736, pp. 575–578; William Cobbett, ed., *The Parliamentary History of England*, vol. 9 (London: T.C. Hansard, 1811), columns 137–141; Peter Clark, "The 'Mother Gin' Controversy in the Early Eighteenth Century," *Transactions of the Royal Historical Society* 38 (1988), p. 78.

90. Political arithmetic had its origins ... and with them the cost of English exports: T.S. Ashton, *An Economic History of England: the 18th Century* (London: Methuen & Co., 1961), p. 1; Peter Gay, *The Enlightenment*, 2 vols., vol. 2 (New York: W.W. Norton & Company, 1996), pp. 344–347.

92. The justices of Westminster ordered their constables to count: London Metropolitan Archives, General Orders of Court, Westminster, WJ/OC 2, 1724–1731, folio 12 verso.

92. "Houses & shops wherein geneva": London Metropolitan Archives, General Orders of Court, Middlesex, MJ/OC 3, 1724–1733, folio 41 recto.

93. "Specifick to cure all Maladies of Life": Daniel Defoe, "Self Murder. Royal Gin Recommended. A Satire," in *Daniel Defoe. His Life, and Recently Discovered Writings, ed. William Lee* (New York: Burt Franklin, 1969), p. 452.

93. He blamed gin for the lack of fear shown by felons: Bernard Mandeville, *An Enquiry into the Causes of the Frequent Executions at Tyburn* (London: J. Roberts, 1725).

93. Defoe would write a pamphlet on behalf of the London Company of Distillers: Daniel Defoe, *A Brief Case of the Distillers* (London: Printed for T. Warner, 1726).

93–94. While Mandeville, true to the radical spirit: Bernard Mandeville, *The Fable of the Bees: or, Private Vices, Publick Benefits*, ed. F.B. Kaye, 2 vols., vol. 1 (Oxford: Clarendon Press, 1924), I.92.

94. George Cheyne. ... was the author of *An Essay of Health and Long Life*: Roy Porter, "The Drinking Man's Disease: the 'Pre-History' of Alcoholism in Georgian Britain," *British Journal of Addiction* 80, no. 4 (1985), pp. 385–396.

94. "Gout, Stone, and Rheumatism": George Cheyne, *An Essay of Health and Long Life*, fourth ed. (London: Printed for George Strahan, 1725), p. 44; Roy Porter, "The Drinking Man's Disease: the 'Pre-History' of Alcoholism in Georgian Britain," *British Journal of Addiction* 80, no. 4 (1985), pp. 385–396.

95. He was, however, a staunch Tory: William Munk, *The Roll of the Royal College of Physicians of London; Compiled from the Annals of the College and from Other Authentic Sources*, 2 vols., vol. 2 (London: Longman, Green, Longman, and Roberts, 1861), p. 47.

95. As were most of his patients: Romney Sedgwick, ed., *The History of Parliament. The House of Commons 1715–1745*, 2 vols., vol. 2 (New York: Oxford University Press, 1970), p. 53.

95. "Without any Detriment": *The London Evening-Post*, 2–5 February 1740, p. 2.

95. "Great numbers of both Sexes " for work: Royal College of Physicians of London, Annals, 19 January 1725, folio 72 recto.

96. "Several of his Majesty's Justices of the Peace for the Liberty": *The London Evening-Post*, 26–29 October 1728, p. 3.

96. Gonson was an ardent supporter of both the Societies: Peter Clark, "The 'Mother Gin' Controversy in the Early Eighteenth Century," *Transactions of the Royal Historical Society* 38 (1988), p. 74; Robert B. Shoemaker, *Prosecution and Punishment. Petty Crime and the Law in London and Rural Middlesex, c. 1660–1725*, ed. Anthony Fletcher, John Guy, and John Morrill, Cambridge Studies in Early Modern British History (Cambridge: Cambridge University Press, 1991), p. 86.

96. And from 1728 on he put their agendas into action: John Gonson, *Five Charges to Several Grand Juries*, fourth ed. (London: Printed for W. Meadows, 1740), p. 13.

96. Among the vices that Gonson singled out was drunkenness: T. C. Curtis and William A. Speck, "The Societies for the Reformation of Manners: a Case Study in the Theory and Practice of Moral Reform," *Literature and History* 3 (1976), pp. 56–57.

97. "The frequent Robberies of late committed in the Streets of London": *The London Evening-Post*, 10–12 October 1728, p. 1.

98. "The great Mischiefs occasion'd among the meaner Sort of People": *The Historical Register* (London: Printed and sold by R. Nutt, 1729), p. 179.

98. The London Company of Distillers asked only that its members be allowed: *The Case of the Master, Wardens and Company of Distillers of London: Humbly Offered to the Honourable the House of Commons* (1729).

98. "A Representation to be made Publick & Incerted": Corporation of London Guildhall Library, Journal of the Court of the London Company of Distillers, 6207/1, 1714–1730, no pagination.

98. The company's members seem to have welcomed the prospect: Corporation of London Records Office, Repertories, 1728–1729, pp. 479; 538–539.

99. Only 453 licenses were purchased over the lifetime: Public Record Office, An Account of the Quantities of the Several Articles which Have Been Charged with Excise Duties in Each Year, and their Amounts of Duty According to the Respective Rates; from the Earliest Period the Same Can be Obtained from the Records in the Excise Office. Also Tables of the Rates of Duty Imposed on Each Article with their Variations from Time to Time, from the Commencement of Each Duty, no accession number, p. 233.

99. Had he not also gone out of his way to insult the justice: *The Grub-Street Journal*, 2 April 1730, p. 2.

99. Excisemen seized some 250 gallons of untaxed spirits: *The Weekly News and Register*, 14 August 1730, p. 3.

100. "Concerting in order to intoxicate the Mob" *The London Evening-Post*, 26–28 June 1729, p. 3.

100. They were, according to Pulteney, as widely drunk as compound spirits: William Cobbett, ed., *The Parliamentary History of England*, vol. 9 (London: T.C. Hansard, 1811), column 1040.

100. "Had been a Discouragement to the distilling of Spirits": *The Historical Register* (London: Printed and Sold by S. Nevill, 1733), p. 257.

100. "Their Great Services done for the Company in Parliament": Corporation of London Guildhall Library, Journal of the Court of the London Company of Distillers, 6207/1, 1714–1730, no pagination.

100. An alderman for thirty years, he led the City's tradesmen: Lucy Sutherland, "The City of London in Eighteenth-century Politics," in *Essays Presented to Sir Lewis Namier*, ed. Richard Pares and A.J.P. Taylor (London: Macmillan & Co Ltd, 1956), p. 62; Nicholas Rogers, "The Urban Opposition to Whig Oligarchy, 1720–60," in *The Origins of Anglo-American Radicalism*, ed. Margaret Jacob and James Jacob (London: George Allen & Unwin, 1984), p. 146; Henry Horwitz, "Party in a Civic Context: London from the Exclusion Crisis to the Fall of Walpole," in *Britain in the First Age of Party 1680–1750: Essays Presented to Geoffrey Holmes*, ed. Clyve Jones (London: 1987), p. 188.

101. In March of 1733, Barnard and Perry joined with Walpole: *Journals of the House of Commons*, vol. 22 (London: 1803), p. 84.

101. "Great alarum to the clandestine dealers in wine and tobacco": J.D. Marshall, ed., *Autobiography of William Stout of Lancaster 1665–1752* (New York: Barnes & Noble, Inc., 1967), p. 212.

102. By resorting to informers, the reformers repeated the mistakes: T. C. Curtis and William A. Speck, "The Societies for the Reformation of Manners: a Case Study in the Theory and Practice of Moral Reform," *Literature and History* 3 (1976), p. 53; Robert B. Shoemaker, *Prosecution and Punishment. Petty Crime and the Law in London and Rural Middlesex, c. 1660–1725*, ed. Anthony Fletcher, John Guy, and John Morrill, Cambridge Studies in Early Modern British History (Cambridge: Cambridge University Press, 1991), p. 243.

CHAPTER FIVE
PAGE

105. "A very exact man in his family": C.L.S. Linnell, ed., *The Diaries of Thomas Wilson* (London: The Camelot Press Ltd., 1964), pp. 170–171.

105. "Left his next immediate heir...out of his will": Historical Manuscripts Commission, *Diary of the First Earl of Egmont (Viscount Percival)*, vol. 2, Manuscripts of the Earl of Egmont (London: His Majesty's Stationery Office, 1923), p. 507.

107. He lived a long life and died a very wealthy man: *The London Daily Post*, 23 August 1738, p. 1.

107. Young, ambitious, and impatient at Walpole's seemingly endless tenure: H.T. Dickinson, "Walpole and His Critics," *History Today* 22, no. 6 (1972), pp. 411–413.

107. "Though no individual in the House ever spoke of him with esteem": John Wilson Croker, ed., *Memoirs of the Reign of King George the Second, from His Accession to the Death of Queen Caroline. By John, Lord Hervey*, 3 vols., vol. 1 (London: John Murray, 1848), p. 374.

109. "His Face was like a Winter's Day": Charles Hanbury Williams, *S–S and J–L. A New Ballad*, second ed. (London: Printed for W. Webb, 1743), p. 3.

109. One of these was Lord Hardwicke, to whom he was related: Peter Clark, "The 'Mother Gin' Controversy in the Early Eighteenth Century," *Transactions of the Royal Historical Society* 38 (1988), p. 76.

109. As Lord Chancellor and Lord Chief Justice, Hardwicke would: British Library, Hardwicke Papers, Additional MS. 35600, 1733–1741, folios 26 recto; 27 recto.

109. "Growing Evil threatening his Country": Joseph Jekyll, *The Trial of the Spirits*, second ed. (London: Printed for T. Cooper, 1736), p. 26.

109. The queen, having witnessed "a great deal of Bestialities": C.L.S. Linnell, ed., *The Diaries of Thomas Wilson* (London: The Camelot Press Ltd., 1964), p. 143.

111. In January of 1736, Wilson completed a draft of his own opus: Peter Clark, "The 'Mother Gin' Controversy in the Early Eighteenth Century," *Transactions of the Royal Historical Society* 38 (1988), p. 74.

111. Jekyll, however, was already at the limit of his influence: Public Record Office, Hanoverian State Papers Domestic 1714–1782, SP 36/39, 1736, folio 353 recto.

111. And then again in 1737: Public Record Office, Hanoverian State Papers Domestic 1714–1782, SP 36/42, 1737, folios 112 recto; 120 recto.

111. This was especially true of the Societies for the Reformation of Manners: T. C. Curtis and William A. Speck, "The Societies for the Reformation of Manners: A Case Study in the Theory and Practice of Moral Reform," *Literature and History* 3 (1976), p. 59; Robert B. Shoemaker, *Prosecution and Punishment. Petty Crime and the Law in London and Rural Middlesex, c. 1660–1725* (Cambridge: Cambridge University Press, 1991), p. 242.

112. The bill that Jekyll proposed was..."as if intended to try the submission": William Cobbett, ed., *The Parliamentary History of England*, vol. 9 (London: T.C. Hansard, 1811), column 1110.

112. Both Jekyll and Wilson had an essentially conservative vision: A.W. Coats, "Changing Attitudes to Labour in the Mid-Eighteenth Century," *Economic History Review* 11, no. 1 (1958), pp. 35–51.

112. Hard work at low wages, in turn, served two goals: Daniel A. Baugh, "Poverty, Protestantism, and Political Economy: English Attitudes toward the Poor, 1660–1800," in *England's Rise to Greatness, 1660–1763*, ed. Stephen B. Baxter (Berkeley: University of California Press, 1983), p. 72.

112. "Instead of being contented with Beer and Ale brewed at home": Thomas Wilson, *Distilled Spirituous Liquors the Bane of the Nation* (London: Printed for J. Roberts, 1736), p. 7.

113. "Why, the miserable Creatures, in such a Situation": Joseph Jekyll, *The Trial of the Spirits*, second ed. (London: Printed for T. Cooper, 1736), p. 12.

113. Jekyll and Wilson frowned on high wages and consumerism: Joyce Oldham Appleby, "The Tension between Political and Economic Liberalism in Seventeenth-Century England," *American Historical Review* 81, no. 3 (1976), pp. 499–515.

114. "Having represented to the Queen the pernicious Consequences": *The Gentleman's Magazine*, June 1735, p. 331.

114. "Memorials of Proposals which they may think adviseable": Corporation of London Guildhall Library, Journal of the Court of the London Company of Distillers, 6207/1A, 1730–1756, no pagination.

114. In October of 1735, the justices of both Westminster and East London: London Metropolitan Archives, General Orders of Court, Middlesex, MJ/OC 4, 1733–1743, folios 47 recto-verso.

114. The report's key findings were published in London's leading newspapers: *The Daily Gazetteer*, 24 January 1736, p. 2.

115. "There is . . . hardly a Week, I may say a Day, that we don't hear": *The London Magazine*, February 1736, p. 73.

116. In 1751, Hogarth incorporated it into *Gin Lane*: Tobias George Smollett, *The History of England, from the Revolution in 1688, to the Death of George the Second* (Philadelphia: M'Carty & Davis, 1840), p. 452.

116. In 1725, Defoe had claimed that in just one month: Daniel Defoe, "Self Murder. Royal Gin Recommended. A Satire," in *Daniel Defoe. His Life, and Recently Discovered Writings, ed. William Lee* (New York: Burt Franklin, 1969), p. 451.

116. "A Journeyman Pewterer, after drinking largely at a Brandy Shop": *The London Evening-Post*, 9–11 April 1728, p. 3.

116. "The Wife of a Shoe-Blacker . . . came home so much intoxicated": *Read's Weekly Journal*, 13 December 1735, p. 3.

117. Up until 1736, however, stories implicating gin: Jessica F. Warner, Carol Birchmore-Timney, and Frank Ivis, "On the Vanguard of the First Drug Scare. Newspapers and Gin in London, 1736–1751," *Journalism History* 27, no. 4 (2001–2002), pp. 178–187.

117. "A young Woman died in Isleworth Church-Yard": *Read's Weekly Journal*, 6 March 1736, p. 3.

117. "One William Thomas having drank nine Quarterns of Geneva": *The Daily Gazetteer*, 24 January 1736, p. 2.

117. "Two Glaziers and a bricklayer came to a shop in Field-Lane": *The Grub-Street Journal*, 1 April 1736, p. 2.

117. "Excessive Drinking": *Read's Weekly Journal*, 3 April 1736, p. 2.

117. "Four Men drank Gin to such an Excess, in an Alley": *The Norwich Mercury*, 13–20 March 1736, p. 2.

118. It would not only fail to achieve its goals but would also lead to riots: "Letter of Sir Robert Walpole to Horace Walpole on the Riots Occasioned by the Gin Act," in *Memoirs of the Life and Administration of Sir Robert Walpole, Earl of Orford*, ed. William Coxe (London: Printed for T. Cadell, 1798), pp. 359–360.

118. "Raise great Disaffection to the present Government": *The Gentleman's Magazine*, October 1736, p. 577.

118. The new fee, having originally been proposed at £40 a year: *Read's Weekly Journal*, 21 February 1736, p. 2.

118. Was almost immediately raised to £50: *The London Daily Post*, 25 February 1736, p. 1.

119. Jekyll wanted a minimum of five gallons: Eveline Cruickshanks, "The Political

Management of Sir Robert Walpole, 1720–42," in *Britain in the Age of Walpole*, ed. Jeremy Black, Problems in Focus (London: Macmillan, 1984), p. 26.

119. A final agreement...was not reached until the first week in April: *The Norwich Mercury*, 13–20 March 1736, p. 1.

119. Early in May the lords passed the bill without amendment: *Journals of the House of Lords*, vol. 24 , pp. 658–659.

120. "Your little peddling Retailers" as people: *The London Daily Post*, 25 February 1736, p. 1.

120. "The interest of every particular man must give way to the general interest": William Cobbett, ed., *The Parliamentary History of England*, vol. 9 (London: T.C. Hansard, 1811), column 1042.

120–121. The London Company of Distillers...commissioned hacks to write on its behalf: *The Case of the Distillers Company, and Proposals for the Better Regulating the Trade* (1736); *The Case of the Malt Distillers, &c.* (1736); *The Case of Such of the Distillers as Are the Younger Branch of the Trade* (1736); "Reasons for Promoting the British Distillery," in *A Collection of Political Tracts* (London: Printed for T. Cooper, 1736).

121. One of these hacks was a Mr. Crawford, who was probably responsible: *The Norwich Mercury*, 13–20 March 1736, p. 2.

121. "By reason of the great Sums which the Company have already Expended": Corporation of London Guildhall Library, Journal of the Court of the London Company of Distillers, 6207/1A, 1730–1756, no pagination.

121. "Not like to be of any particular Service": Corporation of London Guildhall Library, Journal of the Court of the London Company of Distillers, 6207/1A, 1730–1756, no pagination.

121. "Since the Rising of Parliament, applied to some in the Administration": *The Norwich Mercury*, 26 June–3 July 1736, p. 2.

122. *The London Daily Post* reported that several distillers: *The London Daily* Post, 16 September 1736, p. 1; *The London Daily Post*, 15 October 1736, p. 2; *The Daily Gazetteer*, 9 October 1736, p. 1.

122. Their lobby was by far the most powerful of the colonial lobbies: Richard B. Sheridan, "The Molasses Act and the Market Strategy of the British Sugar Planters," *Journal of Economic History* 17, no. 1 (1957), pp. 70–71; Michael J. Jubb, "Economic Policy and Economic Development," in *Britain in the Age of Walpole*, ed. Jeremy Black, Problems in Focus (London: Macmillan, 1984), pp. 128–129.

122. They asked only that rum be exempted from any restrictions on spirits: *The Case of the Sugar-Trade, with Regard to the Duties Intended to Be Laid on All Spirituous Liquors, Sold by Retail* (1736), p. 2.

123. The newspaper received generous subsidies from the ministry: Robert Louis Haig, *The Gazetteer 1735–1797. A Study in the Eighteenth-Century English Newspaper* (Carbondale: Southern Illinois University Press, 1960), p. 4.

123–124. Informers served an important function at a time: Maurice W. Beresford, "The Common Informer, the Penal Statutes and Economic Regulation," *Economic History Review* 10, no. 2 (1958), pp. 221–237.

124. The Societies for the Reformation of Manners had employed them: Robert B. Shoemaker, Prosecution and Punishment. *Petty Crime and the Law in London and Rural Middlesex, c. 1660–1725* (Cambridge: Cambridge University Press, 1991), p. 193.

124. "Upwards of twenty Informers about Town": *The London Evening-Post*, 25–28 September 1736, p. 2.

124. "A generall disorder": "Letter of Sir Robert Walpole to Horace Walpole," in *Memoirs of the Life and Administration of Sir Robert Walpole, Earl of Orford*, ed. William Coxe (London: Printed for T. Cadell, 1798).

125. "Seem'd very cool, of giving any Assistance in the Affair": British Library, Hardwicke Papers, Additional MS. 35600, 1733–1741, folio 27 recto. Reference courtesy of Professor Norma Landau.

125. "I will . . . be watchful at this Criticall time in which": Public Record Office, Hanoverian State Papers Domestic 1714–1782, SP 36/39, 1736, folio 152 recto.

125. Walpole's spies had intercepted four letters showing that publicans: "Letter of Sir Robert Walpole to Horace Walpole on the Riots Occasioned by the Gin Act," in *Memoirs of the Life and Administration of Sir Robert Walpole, Earl of Orford*, ed. William Coxe (London: Printed for T. Cadell, 1798), p. 359; George F.E. Rudé, "'Mother Gin' and the London Riots of 1736," *Guildhall Miscellany* 10 (1959), pp. 59–60.

125. He had already received several threatening letters: *The Norwich Mercury*, 25 September–2 October 1736, p. 3.

125–126. And on the night before the act took effect sixty foot soldiers: *The Daily Journal*, 29 September 1736, p. 2.

126. Guards, their bayonets fixed, remained posted: *The Grub-Street Journal*, 1 April 1736, p. 2; *The London Daily Post*, 15 October 1736, p. 2.

126. Newcastle, a born survivor, wisely decided to abandon the prime minister: Public Record Office, SP 43/20, 1 October 1736, folio 123 recto.

126. "At the Gin-shops, Distillers, and Publick-houses about the Town": *The Daily Journal*, 29 September 1736, p. 2.

126. "Lay in the Streets dead drunk, with their taking Leave of that Liquor": *The Daily Journal*, 30 September 1736, p. 2.

127–129. "The Exit of Mother Gin in Bristol . . . by sipping too large a Draught": *The Daily Gazetteer*, 5 October 1736, pp. 1–2.

129. "The ill Consequences from such a Funeral": *The London Evening-Post*, 25–28 September 1736, p. 2.

129. "A few rascally Fellows" who upon getting drunk: *The Norwich Mercury*, 25 September–2 October 1736, p. 3.

129–130. Newcastle returned to London just in time to take some of the credit: British Library, Additional MS. 33033, 1737?, folio 327 verso.

130. "All remains very quiet": *The London Daily Post*, 25 February 1736, p. 2.

130. "To prevent their acting contrary to the Tenour": *The London Evening-Post*, 25–28 September 1736, p. 2.

130. Only twenty licenses, each good for only one year: Public Record Office, Treasury Papers, T 1/309, October–December 1742, entry 126.

130. Some publicans made little or no attempt to conceal: *The Grub-Street Journal*, 1 April 1736, p. 2.

130–131. "Tho' the Common People are deprived of Gin": *The London Daily Post*, 15 October 1736, p. 2.

131. These included a variety of hasty wines concocted from berries and other fruits: *The London Evening-Post*, 21–23 October 1736, p. 2.

131. "Gripe and Cholick Water, &c": *The London Evening-Post*, 25–28 September 1736, p. 2.

131. "A certain Person near St. James's-Market": *Read's Weekly Journal*, 9 October 1736, p. 2.

131. "The Pretence of Medicine, Cordials, and such": *The London Daily Post*, 15 October 1736, p. 2.

131. It was at this point that the Society of Apothecaries also intervened: *The Norwich Mercury*, 25 September–2 October 1736, p. 1.

132. "Generally amended in their conduct; that whereas there us'd to be frequent": *The Daily Gazetteer*, 5 October 1736, p. 2.

132. The "lower Sort of People" had already regained: *The Old Whig*, 14 October 1736, p. 4.

132. "In all the Towns round London as much as ever": *The London Evening-Post*, 9–12 April 1737, p.1; *The London Evening-Post*, 1–4 October 1737, p. 2.

133. The editors of the pro-ministerial *Daily Gazetteer* increasingly chose: Jessica F. Warner, Carol Birchmore-Timney, and Frank Ivis, "On the Vanguard of the First Drug Scare. Newspapers and Gin in London, 1736–1751," *Journalism History* 27, no. 4 (2001–2002), pp. 178–187.

133. "Well intended, but . . . dictated by Anger": *Supplement to the Gentleman's Magazine*, December 1743, p. 695.

CHAPTER SIX
PAGE

135. De Veil epigraph: Thomas De Veil, *Memoirs of the Life and Times, of Sir Thomas Deveil, Knight* (London: M. Cooper, 1748), p. 39.

135. "Under Pretence of a Horse's being ill": *The London Evening-Post*, 26–28 April 1737, p. 2; *The Daily Post*, 27 April 1737, p. 2; Henry Stonecastle, *The Universal Spectator, and Weekly Journal*, 30 April 1737, p. 3.

136. "Told three or four of his acquaintance": *The London Evening-Post*, 26–28 April 1737, p. 2; *The Grub-Street Journal*, 18 August 1737, p. 3.

136. "Brought a Pitch-Kettle, pitch'd him all over": *Read's Weekly Journal*, 1 October 1737.

137. "The rough Discipline of the Rabble": *Read's Weekly Journal*, 18 February 1738.

137. She could work for a year as a maid and earn £5: David A. Kent, "Ubiquitous but Invisible: Female Domestic Servants in Mid-eighteenth Century London," *History Workshop Journal* 28 (1989), p. 118.

137. Most did so only once, collecting their reward: Jessica F. Warner, Frank Ivis, and Andrée Demers, "A Predatory Social Structure: Informers in Westminster, 1737–1741," *Journal of Interdisciplinary History* 33, no. 4 (2000), p. 625.

137–138. "Having given Information . . . guilty of the like again": *Read's Weekly Journal*, 1 October 1737.

138–139. The distinction was frequently blurred, with the result: Reay Sabourn, *A Perfect View of the Gin Act* (London: Printed for W. Thorne, 1738), p. 22.

139–140. Petty hawkers had been convicted and incarcerated in greater London: *The Old Whig*, 25 August 1737, p. 2.

140. Two months later the number had jumped had jumped to 432: *Read's Weekly Journal*, 1 October 1737.

140. The commissioners' own records list only about 900 convictions: Lee Davison, "Experiments in the Social Regulation of Industry: Gin Legislation, 1729–1751," in *Stilling the Grumbling Hive. The Response to Social and Economic Problems in England, 1689–1750*, ed. Lee Davison, et al. (New York: St. Martin's Press, 1992), pp. 36–37; Public Record Office, CUST, 48/13, 1733–1745, p. 397; Public Record Office, Treasury Papers, T 1/309, October–December 1742, entry 128.

140. Another 3,000 or so had reportedly paid £10: *The London Daily Post*, 9 May 1738, p. 1; Richard Hooker, *The Weekly Miscellany*, 28 July 1738, pp. 2–3; *Read's Weekly Journal*, 1 April 1738, p. 4; *The Gentleman's Magazine*, July 1738, p. 379; *The London Magazine*, August 1738, p. 411.

141. The "wicked Design" of an informer in Southwark: *The London Evening-Post*, 22–24 December 1737, p. 1.

141. Another woman "fail'd in the Proof of her Informations": *The London Evening-Post*, 16–18 March 1738, p. 2.

141. By 1750, the capital had a population of about 675,000: E.Anthony Wrigley, "Urban Growth and Agricultural Change: England and the Continent during the Early Modern Period," *Journal of Interdisciplinary History* 15, no. 4 (1985), p. 686.

141. Two women, described as "very expert in their Business": *The London Daily Post*, 24 January 1738, p. 2.

141. Two other female informers, described as strangers belonging to a gang: *The London Daily Post*, 9 May 1738, p. 2.

142. "There were not five Publick Houses in both Parishes": *Read's Weekly Journal*, 5 August 1738, p. 3.

142. In order to exchange information many informers entered: Reay Sabourn, *A Perfect View of the Gin Act* (London: Printed for W. Thorne, 1738), pp. 36–38; *The Old Whig*, 9 March 1738, p. 4; *Read's Weekly Journal*, 1 April 1738, p. 2; *The London Daily Post*, 9 May 1738 p. 2; *A Short History of the Gin Act* (London: Published for H. Goreham, 1738), p. 64.

143. Several of their leaders were under indictment: Jessica F. Warner, Frank Ivis, and Andrée Demers, "A Predatory Social Structure: Informers in Westminster, 1737–1741," *Journal of Interdisciplinary History* 33, no. 4 (2000), p. 624.

143. "Are you one of our clan, and will you": Reay Sabourn, *A Perfect View of the Gin Act* (London: Printed for W. Thorne, 1738), pp. 34–35.

144. Charles Darley asked Elizabeth Gardiner: Reay Sabourn, *A Perfect View of the Gin Act* (London: Printed for W. Thorne, 1738), p. 33; London Metropolitan Archives, Sessions Rolls, Middlesex Quarter Sessions, MJ/SR 2701, September 1738.

144. Luke Burgis and Henry Devon testified together: London Metropolitan Archives, Sessions Papers, Middlesex Sessions, MJ/SP/1737/10/108, 1737.

144. And Sarah Jones and Elizabeth Armstrong testified: London Metropolitan Archives, Sessions Rolls, Middlesex Quarter Sessions, MJ/SR 2701, September 1738.

144. Most eighteenth-century Londoners rarely ventured outside: M. Dorothy George, *London Life in the Eighteenth Century*, second ed. (New York: Harper Torchbooks, 1964), pp. 67–68; Jeremy Boulton, "Neighbourhood Migration in Early Modern London," in *Migration and Society in Early Modern England*, ed. Peter Clark and David Souden (London: Hutchinson, 1987), p. 134.

144. Their existing jurisdictions covered large geographical areas: John Brewer, *The Sinews of Power. War, Money, and the English State, 1688–1783* (London: Unwin Hyman, 1989), pp. 105–108.

144. "To detect and inform against all persons that retail Spirituous Liquors": *The Old Whig*, 16 June 1737, p. 2.

144. John James, who ordinarily collected duties from barbers: Public Record Office, PC 1/15/5, part 3, 3 April–7 June 1738.

145. Gardiner and Darley, who were subsequently convicted of perjury: London Metropolitan Archives, Calendar of Prisoners, Middlesex, MJ/CP/P 58, 7 September 1738; London Metropolitan Archives, Calendar of Prisoners, Middlesex, MJ/CP/P 59, 7 September 1738.

145. Two men were sent to prison for having assaulted him: *The London Evening-Post*, 15–17 November 1737, p. 1.

145. While two months later, in January of 1738: Public Record Office, Court of King's Bench Crown Side. Indictment Files for London and Middlesex, KB 10/23, part 2, Hilary, 11 Geo. 2, 1737; *The London Daily Post*, 24 January 1738, p. 2.

145. "Instrumental in giving Informations against upwards of 1500 Persons": *Read's Weekly Journal*, 6 January 1739, p. 2.

145. "Upwards of 1000£ by swearing against People": *The London Daily Post*, 28 December 1738, p. 1.

145. "The Excise Officer who has constantly attended the Justices": Public Record Office, PC 1/15/5, part 1, 1738.

146. "Notwithstanding the Difficulties which have of late arisen": Public Record Office, PC 1/15/5, part 2, 1738.

146. "Obstinately and contemptuously": London Metropolitan Archives, Sessions Rolls, Middlesex Quarter Sessions, MJ/SR 2684, October 1737; The Daily Gazetteer, 17 October 1737, p. 2; *The Old Whig*, 20 October 1737, p. 3.

146–147. He had, it was alleged, asked John Smith: Corporation of London Records Office, Sessions Rolls, City of London Quarter Sessions, SF 758, October 1738.

147. Bail was set at £100—an unusually high amount: Corporation of London Records Office, Sessions Rolls, City of London Quarter Sessions, SF 759, 4 December 1738; Corporation of London Records Office, Quarter Sessions Minutes, City of London, SM 106, 1738–1739.

147. The jury had deliberated for seven hours: *The London Evening-Post*, 16–18 March 1738, p. 2.

147. "Almost immediately pronounced the Prisoner, Guilty": Joseph Gurney, *The Trial (at Large) of James Hill; Otherwise James Hind; Otherwise, James Actzen* (London: G. Kearsly, 1777), col. 1363.

149. "The Informers were in jail for several notorious crimes": *Read's Weekly Journal*, 22 July 1738, p. 3.

149. "Been very diligent in detecting the Retailers": *The London Evening-Post*, 16–18 March 1738, p. 2.

149. Robert Smith and Daniel Bartlett were dismissed for perjury: Public Record Office, Excise Board's Minutes, 7 November 1738 to 16 April 1739, CUST 47/170, 1738–1739, p. 94.

149. And in 1741, three more excisemen were dismissed: *The London Evening-Post*, 14–17 November 1741, p. 2.

149. Excisemen had never been popular among justices: Norma Landau, *The Justices of the Peace, 1679–1760* (Berkeley: University of California Press, 1986), p. 223.

150. "There was scarce one day passed": Thomas De Veil, *Memoirs of the Life and Times, of Sir Thomas Deveil, Knight* (London: M. Cooper, 1748), p. 40.

150. He was also knighted: Sidney Webb and Beatrice Webb, *The Parish and the County, English Local Government* (London: Frank Cass and Co., 1963), p. 338.

150–151. Their reputation was—and remains—very poor: Sidney Webb and Beatrice Webb, *The Parish and the County, English Local Government* (London: Frank Cass and Co. Ltd., 1963), pp. 325–331; Norma Landau, *The Justices of the Peace, 1679–1760* (Berkeley: University of California Press, 1986), pp. 184–187.

151. "Were generally the scum of the earth": Sidney Webb and Beatrice Webb, *The Parish and the County, English Local Government* (London: Frank Cass and Co. Ltd., 1963), p. 325.

151. "A vast Concourse of People" who "began to Murmur": British Library, Hardwicke Papers, Additional MS. 35600, 1733–1741, folio 95 recto; reference courtesy of Professor Norma Landau.

151. Farmer ruled on behalf of the two excisemen: *The London Evening-Post*, 15–17 November 1737, p. 1; *The London Evening-Post*, 26–28 April 1737, p. 2.

152. "The Officers of Excise made Complaint": *The Norwich Mercury*, 30 October–6 November 1736, p. 2.

153. "Being left out of a Commission when once in leaves an Odium": British Library, Hardwicke Papers, Additional MS. 35601, 1742–1744, folio 236 verso.

153. He also sued Farmer for libel: Public Record Office, KB 1/5 Easter, 11 Geo. 2, bundle 1, 1736–1738; Public Record Office, KB 1/5 Hilary, 11 Geo. 2, bundle 2, 1736–1738.

153. Bryan took the unusual step of appealing her newest conviction: Public Record Office, Court of King's Bench Crown Side. Indictment Files for London and Middlesex, KB 10/23, part 2, Hilary, 11 Geo. 2, 1737.

153. In a census dating from 1736 she is listed simply as "Retailer": London Metropolitan Archives, MR/LV/6/44, 3 January 1736.

153. Like most working women of the time, she was illiterate: London Metropolitan Archives, MR/LV/6/44, 3 January 1736, folio 115 verso.

153. Catherine Croft sold them gin: London Metropolitan Archives, Sessions Rolls, Middlesex Quarter Sessions, MJ/SR 2714, May 1739.

154. Croft "begged of the Justices to take Notice how they": Public Record Office, KB 1/6, Michaelmas, 13 Geo. 2, bundle 3, 22 November 1739.

154. Croft, however, was determined, and a week later: London Metropolitan Archives, Middlesex Sessions, Process Register of Indictments, MJ/SBP/14, 1734–1741.

154–155. Croft also put himself to the trouble and expense of suing: Public Record Office, Court of King's Bench Crown Side. Indictment Files for London and Middlesex, KB 10/24, part 2, Trinity, 13 Geo. 2, 1739; Public Record Office, Process Book. London and Middlesex, KB 15/22, 1736–1745; Public Record Office, Court of King's Bench Crown Side Rule Books, KB 21/35, 1739–1745.

155. "Recommending an exact and vigorous Execution of the Laws": *Read's Weekly Journal*, 1 April 1738, p. 2.

155. Westminster's justices responded by holding special sessions: Public Record Office, PC 1/15/5, part 3, 3 April–7 June 1738; Public Record Office, PC 1/15/5, part 4, 3 April–12 June 1738.

156. Southwark's justices convicted 236 individuals: Jessica F. Warner and Frank Ivis, "'Damn you, you informing Bitch.' Vox populi and the Unmaking of the Gin Act of 1736," *Journal of Social History* 33, no. 2 (1999), p. 302.

156. In February of 1738 he convicted a publican: *The Daily Gazetteer*, 11 February 1738, p. 2.

156. A mob gathered outside Lade's house while he tried an informer: *The Daily Gazetteer*, 20 May 1738, p. 1.

157. "Committed to the New Gaol [jail] in Southwark": *The Country Journal: or, the Craftsman*, 13 May 1738, p. 2.

157. "One very vigilant Superior Officer of Excise in Southwark": *The London Evening-Post*, 3–5 January 1738, p. 1.

157. "Under the Notion of his being an Informer": *The Norwich Mercury*, 4–11 March 1738, p. 1.

157. Sarah Clewly... belonged to a gang of counterfeiters: *The London Evening-Post*, 16–18 March 1738, p. 2.

157. By 1737 the Excise Office had assigned up to thirty of its men: *The Grub-Street Journal*, 16 June 1737, p. 2.

158. In East London... at least six informers were employed: Jessica F. Warner and Frank Ivis, "Informers and their Social Networks in Eighteenth-century London. A Comparison of Two Communities," *Social Science History* 25, no. 4 (2001), pp. 563–587.

158. Both trades were subject to sharp seasonal: John G. Rule, *The Experience of Labour in Eighteenth-century Industry* (London: Croon Helm, 1981), p. 51.

158. The same trades are also heavily represented in the census: London Metropolitan Archives, Middlesex Sessions Books & Orders of Court Calendar, 1735–1738, p. 6.

159. "Come Brother Joe, my sturdy Lad": *The London Daily Post*, 24 January 1738, p. 2.

CHAPTER SEVEN
PAGE

161. "The summary Power" epigraph: *A Letter to a Friend in the Country in Relation to the New Law Concerning Spirituous Liquors* (London: Printed for M. Cooper, 1743), p. 13.

161. "An Informer against Persons for retailing Spirituous Liquors": *The London Evening-Post*, 11–14 February 1738, p. 2.

161. Four months later, in August, Sir Joseph Jekyll died: *The London Daily Post*, 24 January 1738, p. 2.

162–163. "I am," Walpole wrote in October of 1736: "Letter of Sir Robert Walpole to Horace Walpole on the Riots Occasioned by the Gin Act," in *Memoirs of the Life and Administration of Sir Robert Walpole, Earl of Orford*, ed. William Coxe (London: Printed for T. Cadell, 1798), pp. 359–360.

163. Four months into the act, riots, including those against the informers: British Library, Additional MS. 33033, 1737?, folios 327 recto–328 recto; William Cobbett, ed., *The Parliamentary History of England*, vol. 9 (London: T.C. Hansard, 1811), columns 1278, 1281 ff.

163. "Several Mobs have of late assembled themselves in riotous manner": Public Record Office, CUST, 48/13, 1733–1745, p. 179.

163. "For discovering the Persons, who have been or shall hereafter be guilty": Public Record Office, Treasury Minute Book, T 29/28, 1736–1741, p. 44; Public Record Office, General Out-letters of the Treasury, T 27/25, 1730–1741, p. 449.

164. A woman in the Strand "cry'd out Informers": *Read's Weekly Journal*, 30 July 1737.

164. Mary Brown and Susanna Fritter routinely harassed Anne Furth: London Metropolitan Archives, Calendar of Commitments to the Westminster House of Correction, WJ/CC/R 10, 1 April 1739.

164. Mary Burt was sentenced to twelve months' hard labor: *The Daily Gazetteer*, 10 April 1738, p. 1.

164. Elizabeth Burt was committed: London Metropolitan Archives, Calendar of Commitments to the Westminster House of Correction, WJ/CC/R 9, 4 October 1738.

164–165. Sarah Miller . . . stationed herself: Corporation of London Records Office, Sessions Rolls, City of London Quarter Sessions, SF 758, October 1738; Corporation of London Records Office, Quarter Sessions Minutes, City of London, SM 106, 1738–1739.

165. Anne Bray, Margaret Reilly, a man by the name of Plant, and his wife: Public Record Office, PC 1/15/5, part 4, 3 April–12 June 1738.

165. Susanna Harold, wife of John Harold, and Henrietta Wells, a spinster: Public Record Office, Process Book. London and Middlesex, KB 15/22, 1736–1745; Public Record Office, Court of King's Bench Crown Side. Indictment Files for London and Middlesex, KB 10/24, part 2, Easter, 11 Geo. 2, 1738.

165. "An elderly Woman having inform'd against a Retailer": *Read's Weekly Journal*, 18 February 1738.

165. Another woman . . . "fell into the Hands of the Mob": *The London Daily Post*, 9 February 1738, p. 1.

165–166. Letitia Heathcoate, the especially notorious informer: Public Record Office, KB 1/6, Trinity, 13–14 Geo. 2, 1739.

166. "Rough music": Martin Ingram, "Ridings, Rough Music and the 'Reform of Popular Culture' in Early Modern England," *Past and Present* 105 (1984), p. 92.

166. "Set upon an Ass . . . whilst others beat and pelted him": *The London Daily Post*, 9 February 1738, p. 1.

166. "Carry'd in Effigy about the several Streets, Squares, &c": *The London Evening-Post*, 15–18 January 1737, p. 2.

167. "The prisoner cry'd out Informers," upon which "the Mob": *The London Daily Post*, 9 February 1738, p. 1.

167. "Cry'd out Informers, on which the Mob secur'd": *Read's Weekly Journal*, 30 July 1737.

167. When two gin-sellers in Southwark cried out, "Informers!": *Read's Weekly Journal*, 18 February 1738.

167. Abraham Maudley "rais'd a very great Mob on the Constables": Public Record Office, PC 1/15/5, part 1, 1738; *Read's Weekly Journal*, 20 May 1738, p. 3; *Read's Weekly Journal*, 27 May 1738, p. 3.

167–168. Constables were reluctant to arrest gin-sellers: Joan R. Kent, "The English Village Constable, 1580–1642: the Nature and Dilemmas of the Office," *Journal of British Studies* 20, no. 2 (1981), pp. 26–49.

168. A constable was actually called on to serve a warrant: *The Norwich Mercury*, 13–20 May 1738, p. 3.

168–169. Two informers, James Dover and William MacCullock: *The London Daily Post*, 24 January 1738, p. 2.

169. Westminster was ground zero. There were more riots here: Nicholas Rogers, *Whigs and Cities. Popular Politics in the Age of Walpole and Pitt* (Oxford: Oxford University Press, 1989), pp. 161, 180.

169–170. The worst of these riots occurred: Thomas De Veil, *Memoirs of the Life and Times, of Sir Thomas Deveil, Knight* (London: M. Cooper, 1748), p. 40.

170. His only option was to read the Riot Act: *The London Daily Post*, 24 January 1738, p. 2; Public Record Office, Court of King's Bench Crown Side. Indictment Files for London and Middlesex, KB 10/23, part 2, Hilary, 11 Geo. 2, 1737.

170. In February, Allen was charged with violating the Riot Act: *The London Daily Post*, 9 February 1738, p. 1.

170. Prosecutions under the Riot Act: Nicholas Rogers, "Popular Protest in Early Hanoverian London," in *Rebellion, Popular Protest and the Social Order in Early Modern England*, ed. Paul Slack, *Past and Present Publications* (Cambridge: Cambridge University Press, 1984), p. 281; Robert B. Shoemaker, "The London "Mob" in the Early Eighteenth Century," *Journal of British Studies* 26, no. 3 (1987), pp. 273–304.

170. "So full you might have walk'd on the People's Heads": *The London Daily Post*, 24 January 1738, p. 2.

170. "My own life had certainly been lost": Thomas De Veil, *Memoirs of the Life and Times, of Sir Thomas Deveil, Knight* (London: M. Cooper, 1748), p. 42.

170. Allen's mother was in on the act: *The London Daily Post*, 24 January 1738, p. 2.

171. "Witnesses were so terrified on Allens Acquittal": Public Record Office, PC 1/15/5, part 1, 1738.

171. Allen . . . became a local hero, receiving gifts: *The London Daily Post*, 9 February 1738, p. 1.

171. Back in February, while Allen was in Newgate: *The London Evening-Post*, 11–14 February 1738, p. 2.

171. "Herself in a forcible and Contemptuous manner before the bench": Public Record Office, PC 1/15/5, part 1, 1738; *The London Daily Post*, 24 January 1738, p. 2.

171. "In a very audacious insolent Manner": *Read's Weekly Journal*, 30 July 1737.

172. "Every Tuesday and Thursday, for trying all Offenses": *Read's Weekly Journal*, 30 July 1737.

172. In March of 1738, the justices in the capital: Corporation of London Records Office, Repertories, 1737–1738, p. 267.

172. In Westminster, the average number of justices: Jessica F. Warner and Frank Ivis, "'Damn you, you informing Bitch.' Vox populi and the Unmaking of the Gin Act of 1736," *Journal of Social History* 33, no. 2 (1999), p. 319.

172. "The Trade of informing against Persons": *The London Evening-Post*, 22–24 March 1739, p. 2.

173. "That it appears to them that the selling": Public Record Office, PC 1/15/5, part 1, 1738.

173. "Their Hounours," it was reported at the time: *The London Evening-Post*, 6–9 November 1736, p. 2; *The Daily Post*, 12 November 1736, p. 1.

173. Six months later . . . the commissioners chose to reduce the fines: Public Record Office, Excise Board's Minutes, 25 February 1736 to 12 July 1737, CUST 47/166, 1736–1737, pp. 116–117, 156–158.

173. "All the Persons before them, who had paid in their Fines": *The Old Whig*, 24 June 1737, p. 3.

173. The commissioners continued to commute fines over the next two years: Public Record Office, Excise Board's Minutes, 13 July 1737 to 13 January 1737, CUST 47/167, 1737, pp. 47–48, 128; Public Record Office, Excise Board's Minutes, 7 November 1738 to 16 April 1739, CUST 47/170, 1738–1739, p. 18; *The London Evening-Post*, 15–18 January 1737, p. 2; *Read's Weekly Journal*, 30 July 1737; *The Grub-Street Journal*, 10 February 1737, p. 2; *The Norwich Mercury*, 30 July–6 August 1737, p. 1; *The Old Whig*, 15 December 1737, p. 2; *The Country Journal: or, the Craftsman*, 8 July 1738, p. 2; *Read's Weekly Journal*, 7 July 1739, p. 3; *The London Evening-Post*, 22–24 March 1739, p. 2.

174. "Without the Matter of Complaint first being exhibited to them": *The Grub-Street Journal*, 10 February 1737, p. 2.

174. "Not to receive any more Informations against persons": *Read's Weekly Journal*, 7 July 1739, p. 3.

174. They had not been consulted in drafting the act: Peter Clark, "The 'Mother Gin' Controversy in the Early Eighteenth Century," *Transactions of the Royal Historical Society* 38 (1988), p. 77.

174. The revolt of the vestries was highly significant: City of Westminster Archives Centre, Vestry Minute Book, Parish of St. James, Piccadilly, D1759, 1712–1736, p. 420; Finsbury Library, Archives Department, St James Clerkenwell Vestry Minutes 1725–1775, 1725–1775, pp. 25–26; Sidney Webb and Beatrice Webb, *The History of Liquor Licensing in England Principally from 1700 to 1830* (London: Longmans, Green and Co., 1903), pp. 62–64, 74–76.

174–175. In August of 1738, the vestry of St. Giles-in-the-Fields: *Read's Weekly Journal*, 20 May 1738, p. 3.

175. Several parishes in greater London had returned most of the fines: Richard Hooker, *The Weekly Miscellany*, 18 August 1738, p. 3.

175. "Some church wardens or overseers of the poor": London Metropolitan Archives, Middlesex Sessions Books & Orders of Court Calendar, 1735–1738, p. 106.

175. "A great many Poor Familys from honestly getting their Bread": British Library, Hardwicke Papers, Additional MS. 35600, 1733–1741, folio 150 recto; reference courtesy of Professor Norma Landau.

175. The typical London juror was probably a tradesman: Peter Linebaugh, *The London Hanged. Crime and Civil Society in the Eighteenth Century* (London: Allen Lane, 1991), p. 85; John M. Beattie, *Policing and Punishment in London 1660–1750. Urban Crime and the Limits of Terror* (Oxford: Oxford University Press, 2001), p. 268.

176. There were very few prosecutions for this particular: Nicholas Rogers, "Popular Protest in Early Hanoverian London," in *Rebellion, Popular Protest and the Social Order in Early Modern England*, ed. Paul Slack, *Past and Present Publications* (Cambridge: Cambridge University Press, 1984), p. 281; Joyce Ellis, "Urban Conflict and Popular Violence. The Guildhall Riots of 1740 in Newcastle upon Tyne," *International Review of Social History* 25, no. 3 (1980), p. 346; Robert B. Shoemaker, "The London "Mob" in the Early Eighteenth Century," *Journal of British Studies* 26, no. 3 (1987), pp. 277, 295–296; Edward P. Thompson, *Customs in Common* (London: The Merlin Press, 1991), p. 326.

176. Of the thirty-one informers known to have been indicted for perjury: Jessica F. Warner, Frank Ivis, and Andrée Demers, "A Predatory Social Structure: Informers in Westminster, 1737–1741," *Journal of Interdisciplinary History* 33, no. 4 (2000), p. 631.

178. "Prosecutions on the celebrated Gin-Act, which seem to have slumber'd": *The Country Journal: or, the Craftsman*, 15 March 1740, p. 2.

178. Eleven people had been convicted: *The London Evening-Post*, 23–25 September 1740, p. 2.

178. The commissioners were trying cases put on hold: *The London Evening-Post*, 16–18 October 1740, p. 2.

178. And by June 1741 the conviction of several more people: *The London Evening-Post*, 30 June–2 July 1741, p. 1.

CHAPTER EIGHT

PAGE

181. Bathurst epigraph: *The Gentleman's Magazine*, November 1743, p. 580.

181. "Who had Notice given them of the Affair": *The London Evening-Post*, 21–23 July 1743, p. 2.

181–182. "Favour he promis'd to give his Men as much Strong-Beer": *The London Evening-Post*, 7–10 May 1743, p. 2.

182. Two excisemen, disguised "in Sailor Jackets and Trousers": *The London Evening-Post*, 10–12 May 1743, p. 2.

183. The despised informers were among the first men: *The Gentleman's Magazine*, November 1743, p. 137.

183. Early in January, the Excise Office gave its input: Public Record Office, CUST, 48/13, 1733–1745, p. 398.

184. "A distilled spirituous water, made with no better an ingredient than oil": Pat Rogers, ed., *Johnson and Boswell in Scotland. A Journey to the Hebrides* (New Haven: Yale University Press, 1993), p. 113.

184–185. Johnson modified the orators' names in perfectly obvious ways: Arthur Stanley Turberville, *The House of Lords in the XVIIIth Century* (Greeenwood Press, Publishers: Wesport, Connecticut, 1970), pp. 515–517.

185. "A Tax upon Theft or Adultery": *The Gentleman's Magazine*, November 1743, p. 628.

186. "We know that they [strong liquors] produce in almost every": *The Gentleman's Magazine*, November 1743, p. 567.

186. Most had been handpicked by Walpole or Newcastle in an attempt: John Wilson Croker, ed., *Memoirs of the Reign of King George the Second, from his Accession to the Death of Queen Caroline. By John, Lord Hervey*, 3 vols., vol. 1 (London: John Murray, 1848), p. 5; John Harold Plumb, *Sir Robert Walpole*, 2 vols., vol. 1 (London: The Cresset Press, 1956), p. 69; Clyve Jones, "The House of Lords and the Growth of Parliamentary Stability," in *Britain in the First Age of Party 1680–1750: Essays Presented to Geoffrey Holmes*, ed. Clyve Jones (London: Hambledon Press, 1987), pp. 93–94.

186–187. Some, such as Francis Hare: Robert Louis Haig, *The Gazetteer 1735–1797. A Study in the Eighteenth-century English Newspaper* (Carbondale: Southern Illinois University Press, 1960), p. 5; H.T. Dickinson, "Walpole and his Critics," *History Today* 22, no. 6 (1972), p. 416.

187. "To give their opinions of the fatal consequences": *Journals of the House of Lords*, vol. 26 , p. 210; James E. Thorold Rogers, ed., *A Complete Collection of the Protests of the Lords*, vol. 2 (Oxford: Clarendon Press, 1875), p. 33.

187. Justices who "had not always been equally zealous": *The Gentleman's Magazine*, November 1743, p. 563.

187. "I myself suffer by some Indulgence": *Supplement to the Gentleman's Magazine*, December 1743, p. 674.

187–188. "Determined . . . not to be governed by this Law": *The Gentleman's Magazine*, November 1743, p. 634.

188. On 25 February the lords passed the bill eighty-two to fifty-five: *The Norwich Mercury*, 12–19 March 1743, p. 1.

188. The contract to print the new licenses was itself eagerly sought: Public Record Office, SP 36/60, 7 March 1742, folio 92 recto.

189. The framers of the new act had the good sense: Peter Mathias, *The Brewing Industry in England 1700–1830* (Cambridge: Cambridge University Press, 1959), p. 342; T.S. Ashton, *An Economic History of England: the 18th Century* (London: Methuen & Co., 1961), p. 115.

189. "Hang'd himself in his Chamber": *The London Evening-Post*, 4–7 June 1743, p. 2.

189–190. In the first round, twenty-two retailers were tried: *The London Evening-Post*, 17–19 May 1743, p. 2.

190. Less than one month later, in June, there were nearly a thousand cases: *The London Evening-Post*, 9–11 June 1743, p. 2.

190. By March of 1744 that number had fallen: *The Westminster Journal*, 17 March 1744, p. 4.

190. "Entirely out of Hopes of obtaining": *The London Evening-Post*, 29–31 March 1743, p. 2.

190. The justices in Southwark were the first to act: *The London Evening-Post*, 7–10 May 1743, p. 2.

190. They also convicted several more people in December: *The Westminster Journal*, 17 December 1743, p. 3.

190. The Privy Council intervened, asking Newcastle: London Metropolitan Archives, MR/LV/6/65, 31 March 1743.

190–191. It was not until the early nineteenth century that consumption would again: Josephine A. Spring and David H. Buss, "Three Centuries of Alcohol in the British Diet," *Nature* 270 (1977), p. 568.

191. This was the largest such decrease over the previous seven years: *The London Evening-Post*, 7–10 May 1743, p. 2.

191. In its halcyon days of the 1720s and '30s: Corporation of London Guildhall Library, Register of Freedom Admissions of the London Company of Distillers, 6215A, 1721–1956.

191. Publicans had purchased upwards of 200,000 annual licenses: *The Westminster Journal*, 7 January 1744, p. 3.

191. And a total of 481,400 between March of 1743 and June of 1747: Public Record Office, CUST 48/14, 1743–1752, p. 348.

191–192. "When the Cheapness of Licenses shall make it convenient for every Man": *The Gentleman's Magazine*, November 1743, p. 579.

192. Publicans "could not suffer any Enormities": *Journals of the House of Commons*, vol. 25 (London: 1803), p. 313.

192. Sales of gin continued to be soft: Corporation of London Guildhall Library, Journal of the Court of the London Company of Distillers, 6207/1A, 1730–1756, no pagination; *Journals of the House of Commons*, vol. 25 (London: 1803), pp. 312–313.

192. The commissioners of excise issued special licenses: Public Record Office, An Account of the Quantities of the Several Articles which Have Been Charged with Excise Duties in Each Year, and their Amounts of Duty According to the Respective Rates; from the Earliest Period the Same Can be Obtained from the Records in the Excise Office. Also Tables of the Rates of Duty Imposed on Each Article with their Variations from Time to Time, from the Commencement of Each Duty, no accession number, p. 233.

192. The largest number of these, 150, were issued to distillers: Public Record Office, CUST 48/14, 1743–1752, p. 354.

193. In October of 1748, the War of Austrian Succession: L. D. Schwarz, *London in the Age of Industrialisation. Entrepreneurs, Labour Force and Living Conditions, 1700–1850*, ed. Peter Laslett, et al., vol. 19, Cambridge Studies in Population, Economy and Society in Past Time (Cambridge: Cambridge University Press, 1992), p. 95.

193. With their return the public's attention naturally turned: John M. Beattie, *Crime and the Courts in England 1660–1800* (Princeton: Princeton University Press, 1986), p. 66; John Styles, "Crime in Eighteenth-Century England," *History Today* 38 (1988), p. 38; Nicholas Rogers, "Confronting the Crime Wave: the Debate over Social Reform and Regulation, 1749–1753," in *Stilling the Grumbling Hive. The Response to Social and Economic Problems in England, 1689–1750*, ed. Lee Davison, et al. (New York: St. Martin's Press, 1992), pp. 77–98.

193. These fears persisted into the early 1750s: John M. Beattie, *Crime and the Courts in England 1660–1800* (Princeton: Princeton University Press, 1986), p. 66; Lee Davison, "Experiments in the Social Regulation of Industry: Gin Legislation, 1729–1751," in *Stilling the Grumbling Hive. The Response to Social and Economic Problems in England, 1689–1750*, ed. Lee Davison, et al. (New York: St. Martin's Press, 1992), p. 43.

193. "The Author of all Sin: The DEVIL himself": The General Advertiser, 20 February 1751, p. 1; *The Norwich Mercury*, 16–23 February 1751, p. 3.

193. "This wicked GIN": *The London Evening-Post*, 12–14 March 1751, p. 1.

193. He had contributed articles to opposition newspapers: J.A. Downie, "Walpole, 'the Poet's Foe'," in *Britain in the Age of Walpole*, ed. Jeremy Black, Problems in Focus (London: Macmillan, 1984), p. 182; Michael Harris, *London Newspapers in the Age of Walpole. A Study of the Origins of the Modern English Press* (Toronto: Associated University Presses, 1987), p. 125.

194. "So many temporal Mischiefs": Henry Fielding, *An Enquiry into the Causes of the Late Increase of Robbers*, ed. Malvin R. Zirker (Middletown: Wesleyan University Press, 1988), pp. 84–85.

194. Fielding may even have been asked to comment: Horace Walpole, *Memoirs of King George II*, ed. John Brooke, vol. 1 (New Haven: Yale Unversity, 1985), p. 30.

194. "Calculated to reform some reigning Vices peculiar to the Lower Class": *The General Advertiser*, 13 February 1751, p. 3.

195. "The dreadful consequences of gin-drinking appeared": William Hogarth, *Anecdotes of William Hogarth, Written by himself*, ed. John Bowyer Nichols (London: Cornmarket Press, 1970), p. 64.

195. The boy's eyes are strongly suggestive of fetal alcohol syndrome: Alvin E. Rodin, "Infants and Gin Mania in 18th-century London," *Journal of the American Medical Association* 245, no. 12 (1981), p. 1239.

195. As are those of the infant on the right margin: Ronald Paulson, *Hogarth: his Life, Art, and Times*, 2 vols., vol. 2 (New Haven: Yale University Press, 1971), p. 101.

199. "All is joyous and thriving. Industry and jollity": William Hogarth, *Anecdotes of William Hogarth, Written by himself*, ed. John Bowyer Nichols (London: Cornmarket Press, 1970), p. 64.

199. "Wrote an account of the conversation to the Bishop of Worcestor": C.L.S. Linnell, ed., *The Diaries of Thomas Wilson* (London: The Camelot Press Ltd., 1964), p. 257.

199. Wilson, Hales, and Tucker all assisted in printing: Josiah Tucker, *An Impartial Enquiry into the Benefits and Damages Arising from the Present Very Great Use of Low-priced Spirituous Liquors* (London: Printed for T. Trye, 1751), pp. 4–5.

199. Of the lesser known players, Isaac Maddox was by far the most important: *The London Magazine*, March 1751, pp. 112–113.

200. He was a prominent bishop, in addition to being a patron: Ernest Caulfield, *The Infant Welfare Movement in the Eighteenth Century* (New York: Paul B. Hoeber Inc., 1931), p. 51–52.

200. He had also been active in the now moribund Societies for the Reformation of Manners: *The Norwich Mercury*, 15–22 January 1737, p. 2.

200. In 1743, he had adamantly opposed the gin act: James E. Thorold Rogers, ed., *A Complete Collection of the Protests of the Lords*, vol. 2 (Oxford: Clarendon Press, 1875), p. 32.

200. The sermon was in many ways a reprise of the speeches: *The Norwich Mercury*, 2–9 March 1751, p. 1.

201. The parish registers had been consulted: *The Gentleman's Magazine*, February 1732, p. 604.

201. Deaths were more routinely recorded that births: P.E. Razzell, "The Evaluation of Baptism as a Form of Birth Registration through Cross-matching Census and Parish Register Data," *Population Studies* 26, no. 1 (1972), pp. 121–146.

201. The births of foundlings were especially prone: Valerie Fildes, "Maternal Feelings Re-assessed: Child Abandonment and Neglect in London and Westminster, 1500–1800," in *Women as Mothers in Pre-industrial England. Essays in Memory of Dorothy McLaren*, ed. Valerie Fildes (London: Routledge, 1990), p. 144.

202. This particular population was substantial: H. J. Habakkuk, "English Population in the Eighteenth Century," *Economic History Review* 6, no. 2 (1953), p. 127.

202. "To prevent the pernicious Use of Spirituous Liquors": Corporation of London Records Office, Journals of the Common Council, 1745–1751, folio 323 verso; *The Norwich Mercury*, 9–16 February 1751, p. 1; William Maitland, *The History and Survey of London from its Foundation to the Present Time*, third ed., 2 vols., vol. 2 (London: Printed for T. Osborne, 1760), p. 686.

202. Other jurisdictions—including several local parishes: *Journals of the House of Commons*, vol. 26 (London: 1803); W.E. Minchinton, ed., *Politics and the Port of Bristol in the Eighteenth Century. The Petitions of the Society of Merchant Venturers 1698–1803*, vol. 23, Bristol Record Society's Publications (Bristol: Bristol Record Society, 1963), pp. 77–78; Norfolk Record Office, Folio Book of Proceedings of the Municipal Assembly, Case 16d 10, 1745–1773, folio 40 recto.

202. "BRITTON! If thou wou'dst": *Read's Weekly Journal*, 2 February 1751, p. 3.

203. *The General Advertiser* was perhaps the worst offender: Todd M. Endleman, *The Jews of Georgian England 1714–1830. Tradition and Change in a Liberal Society* (Philadelphia: The Jewish Publication Society of America, 1979); *The General Advertiser*, 20 February 1751, p. 1.

203–204. "To concur in any Measures which might conduce": *The London Evening-Post*, 12–14 March 1751, p. 1.

204. Toward the end of March its representatives prevailed: *The General Advertiser*, 20 February 1751, p. 1.

204. The Company's efforts in Parliament also came to naught: Corporation of London Guildhall Library, Journal of the Court of the London Company of Distillers, 6207/1A, 1730–1756.

204. "Court did not think fitt to Appoint": Corporation of London Guildhall Library, Court Minute Books of the London Company of Distillers, 6209/3, 1748–1758.

204. Helping him was Slingsby Bethell of Tower Hill: Romney Sedgwick, ed., *The History of Parliament. The House of Commons 1715–1745*, 2 vols., vol. 1 (New York: Oxford University Press, 1970), pp. 460–461.

205. Despite the enormous pressure that had been brought to bear: William Coxe, *Memoirs of the Administration of the Right Honourable Henry Pelham*, 2 vols., vol. 2 (London: Longman, Rees, Orme, Brown, and Green, 1829), pp. 181–182.

205. Early in June, when two last-minute amendments were added to the bill: *The London Morning Penny Post*, 17–19 June 1751, p. 2.

206. Once the fee stipulated in the Gin Act of 1751: Public Record Office, An Account of the Quantities of the Several Articles which Have Been Charged with Excise Duties in Each Year, and their Amounts of Duty According to the Respective Rates; from the Earliest Period the Same Can be Obtained from the Records in the Excise Office. Also Tables of the Rates of Duty Imposed on Each Article with their Variations from Time to Time, from the Commencement of Each Duty, no accession number, p. 233.

206. "Twenty-two Distillers, and upwards of seventy others ... made their Morning's Work worth upwards of £50": *The London Evening-Post*, 11–13 July 1751, p. 4.

206. A woman was "detected by the Turnkey": *The London Morning Penny Post*, 31 July–2 August 1751, p. 2.206. In August three more women were convicted by Bethell: *The London Morning Penny Post*, 19–21 August 1751, p. 2.

206. In September, a prominent distiller on Fleet Street: *The London Morning Penny Post*, 2–4 September 1751, p. 2.

207. Early in 1752 ... casks containing approximately: *The Gentleman's Magazine*, January 1752, p. 40.

207. "Several eminent Malt Distillers have come to a Resolution": *The Norwich Mercury*, 9–16 February 1751, p. 1.

208. Contemporaries naturally credited the Gin Act of 1751: M. Dorothy George, *London Life in the Eighteenth Century*, second ed. (New York: Harper Torchbooks, 1964), p. 38.

208. Jonas Hanway, who is best remembered for his failed attempts: James Stephen Taylor, "Philanthropy and Empire: Jonas Hanway and the Infant Poor of London," *Eighteenth-century Studies* 12, no. 3 (1979), pp. 285–305.

208. Claimed that thanks to "the Hand of Providence": Jonas Hanway, *A Candid Historical Account of the Hospital for the Reception of Exposed and Deserted Young Children* (1759), p. 10.

208. Hanway ... was writing in 1759, a year when real wages: E.H. Phelps Brown and Sheila V. Hopkins, "Seven Centuries of the Price of Consumables, Compared with Builders' Wage-rates," in *Essays in Economic History*, ed. E.M. Carus-Wilson (London: Edward Arnold (Publishers) Ltd., 1962), p. 195; L. D. Schwarz, "The Standard of Living in the Long Run: London, 1700–1860," *Economic History Review* 38, no. 1 (1985), pp. 39–40.

208. The calamitous drop in real wages: Jessica F. Warner et al., "Can Legislation Prevent Debauchery? Mother Gin and Public Health in Eighteenth-century England," *American Journal of Public Health* 91, no. 3 (2001), pp. 375–384.

CHAPTER NINE
PAGE

209. Fielding epigraph: Henry Fielding, *An Enquiry into the Causes of the Late Increase of Robbers*, ed. Malvin R. Zirker (Middletown: Wesleyan University Press, 1988), p. 90.

209. Rangel epigraph: *Cocaine babies: Hearing before the Select Committee on Narcotics Abuse and Control, House of Representatives, One Hundredth Congress, First Session, October 16, 1987*, 1988., p. 5.

210. "This has shattered the myth of motherhood as we know it": *Cocaine babies : Hearing before the Select Committee on Narcotics Abuse and Control, House of Representatives, One Hundredth Congress, First Session, October 16, 1987*, 1988., p. 13.

210. Citing "specialists in drug addiction": Michael deCourcy Hinds, "The Instincts of Parenthood Become Part of Crack's Toll," *The New York Times*, 17 March 1990, p. 8, col. 1.

210. Another reporter, citing yet another specialist: Susan Sward, "The 'Next Hit' Came before Baby. Cocaine Overwhelms the Maternal Instinct in Addicted Women," *San Francisco Chronicle*, 18 March 1988, p. B3, col. 4.

210. Many editorial boards came to their senses: Steven R. Belenko, *Crack and the Evolution of Anti-drug Policy*, ed. James Inciardi, vol. 42, Contributions in Criminology and Penology (Westport: Greenwood Press, 1993), p. 28.

210. "The image of bad women destroying their babies in the womb": "Truth Is a Casualty: 'Crack Babies,' Because of Hype and Hysteria, Are Unfairly Labeled," *San Jose Mercury News*, July 28 1991, p. 6C.

211. Some politicians, of course, simply lie.: Steven R. Belenko, *Crack and the Evolution of Anti-drug Policy*, ed. James Inciardi, vol. 42, Contributions in Criminology and Penology (Westport: Greenwood Press, 1993), p. 26; Craig Reinarman and Harry Gene Levine, "The Crack Attack: Politics and Media in the Crack Scare," in *Crack in America. Demon Drugs and Social Justice*, ed. Craig Reinarman and Harry Gene Levine (Berkeley: University of California Press, 1997), pp. 22–23.

212. By singling out drugs and the people who use them: Craig Reinarman and Harry Gene Levine, "The Crack Attack: Politics and Media in the Crack Scare," in *Crack in America. Demon Drugs and Social Justice*, ed. Craig Reinarman and Harry Gene Levine (Berkeley: University of California Press, 1997), p. 37.

212. "Communities that are slow and stingy with support may be quick": Ellen Goodman, "A Special Class of Criminals," *San Francisco Chronicle*, 8 February 1990, p. A21, col. 4.

213. Most of London's working poor led lines of unspeakable misery: L. D. Schwarz, "The Standard of Living in the Long Run: London, 1700–1860," *Economic History Review* 38, no. 1 (1985), pp. 24–41.

214. Although its use gave rise to periodic panics: Craig Reinarman, "Moral Entrepreneurs and Political Economy: Historical and Ethnographic Notes on the Construction of the Cocaine Menace," *Contemporary Crises* 3 (1979), pp. 225–254; David F. Musto, *The American Disease. Origins of Narcotic Control*, third ed. (Oxford: Oxford University Press, 1999).

214. The same … will also be true of synthetic or "designer" drugs: Philip Jenkins, *Synthetic Panics. The Symbolic Politics of Designer Drugs* (New York: New York University Press, 1999).

214. Smoking cocaine is certainly more efficient than snorting it: John P. Morgan and Lynn Zimmer, "The Social Pharmacology of Smokeable Cocaine. Not All it's Cracked up to Be," in *Crack in America. Demon Drugs and Social Justice*, ed. Craig Reinarman and Harry Gene Levine (Berkeley: University of California Press, 1997), pp. 131–170.

214. "As dangerous as cocaine powder is, it's nothing compared to its smokable forms": Calvin Chatlos, *Crack: what you Should Know about the Cocaine Epidemic*, ed. Lawrence D. Chilnick (New York: Perigree Books, 1987), p. 19.

214. "Crack … is highly addictive. Users have been known to become addicts": Joan L. Johnson, *America's War on Drugs* (New York: Franklin Watts, 1990), p. 23.

215. In Victorian England … mothers who worked: Virginia Berridge and Griffith Edwards, *Opium and the People: Opiate Use in Nineteenth-century England* (New Haven: Yale University Press, 1987), pp. 97–105.

215. "These mothers don't care about their babies": Douglas J. Besharov, "The Children of Crack. Will we Protect them?," *Public Welfare* 47, no. 4 (1989), p. 7.

215. "The focus on maternal behavior allows the government": Katha Pollitt, "'Fetal Rights.' A New Assault on Feminism," *The Nation*, March 26 1990, p. 410.

215–216. Very similar concerns animated the early American temperance movement: Joseph R.

Gusfield, *Symbolic Crusade. Status Politics and the American Temperance Movement* (Urbana: University of Illinois Press, 1963), pp. 4–7.

216. Opium . . . was originally associated with Chinese immigrants: John Helmer, *Drugs and Minority Oppression* (New York: The Seabury Press, 1975); David T. Courtwright, *Dark Paradise. Opiate Addiction in America before 1940* (Cambridge, Massachusetts: Harvard University Press, 1982); David F. Musto, *The American Disease. Origins of Narcotic Control*, third ed. (Oxford: Oxford University Press, 1999).

216. The socioeconomic status of smokers continues to decline: John P. Pierce et al., "Trends in Cigarette Smoking in the United States. Projections to the Year 2000," *Journal of the American Medical Association* 261, no. 1 (1989), p. 64; Gary A. Giovino et al., "Surveillance for Selected Tobacco-use Behaviors—United States, 1900–1994," *MMWR* 43, no. SS-3 (1994), p. 9; references courtesy of Dr. Joanna Cohen.

216. "Short-skirted, high-heeled, with cigarettes dangling from their lips": John Mortimer, "Rumpole and Remembrance of Things Past," in *Rumpole Rests his Case* (London: Viking, 2001), p. 27.

217. Informers, ironically, have also made a comeback: "Snitch," in *Frontline*, ed. Ofra Bikel (1999).

218. "Whole body orgasm": Craig Reinarman and Harry Gene Levine, "The Crack Attack: Politics and Media in the Crack Scare," in *Crack in America. Demon Drugs and Social Justice*, ed. Craig Reinarman and Harry Gene Levine (Berkeley: University of California Press, 1997), p. 45.

218. A rush that is "better than sex": Philip Jenkins, *Synthetic Panics. The Symbolic Politics of Designer Drugs* (New York: New York University Press, 1999), p. 40.

INDEX

abstinence from drink, 8, 9, 10

Allen, Roger, 170–71, 175–76

Amhurst, Nicholas, 9

aqua vitæ. *See* distilled spirits, early history

Barnard, Sir John, 100–101

Bath, 126

beer, 3, 9, 17, 33, 35, 37, 38, 188

Beer Street, 194–99, 213

    See also Hogarth, William

Bethell, Slingsby, 204, 206

"boy patriots," 107

    See also Whigs

brandy, 23, 24, 25, 28, 29, 32, 33, 75

brewers, 10

Bristol, 39, 123, 126–29, 141, 202

Bryan, Mary, xiii, xvii, 51, 151–53, 155

Caroline of Ansbach, xiii, xv, xvi, 95, 97, 108, 109, 114, 125, 133, 162, 198

Cave, Edward, 75, 184, 195

charivari. *See* rough music

Chesterfield, Lord, xiii, 185

Cheyne, George, 94

cigarettes, 216

City Elections Act, 87–89, 90, 100

Clark, Peter, xi, 225

cocaine, 209–14, 216, 218, 219

commissioners of excise. *See* excise, commissioners of

compound distillers, 27–28, 98–99, 100, 120, 221

    See also gin, additives; gin, industrial process

constables, 115, 165, 166–67

    lack of compensation, 5

    reluctance to enforce the gin acts, 5, 167–69, 171, 177, 191, 223

consumerism, x, 8, 22, 36–39, 71, 112–13

Court of Aldermen, 87–89, 90, 100, 113–14, 198, 202, 204

    See also London, City of

crack cocaine. *See* cocaine

Croft, Catherine, xv, 53, 153–54, 155, 165–66

Croft, Thomas, xv, 62, 154–55, 165–66

Defoe, Daniel, xiv, 25, 27, 28, 36, 37, 67–68, 93, 116

De Veil, Sir Thomas, 125, 135, 145, 148, 149–51, 168, 169–71, 194

Dickens, Charles, 76, 82

distilled spirits

    earliest excises on, 25, 32–33

    early history, 2, 22–25, 78, 213

    medicinal properties, 2, 23–24, 128, 131, 135–36, 188

    See also gin